Unforgetting God

Unforgetting God

Defeating Culture-Destroying Materialism
Through Christian Renewal

Barry Arrington

Inkwell PRESS

Description

Materialism is the idea that matter moved by mindless forces explains all of reality. This radically secular philosophy dominates the minds of Western cultural elites and is at the root of tribalism in our politics, lawlessness in our courts, chaos in our universities, and the crisis of meaning rampaging among young people. In his thirty-eight years of practicing law, Barry Arrington has seen the toxic impact of materialism firsthand. From representing victims of the Columbine school shooting to litigating challenges to unconstitutional laws before the US Supreme Court, he has seen how materialism destroys lives and hollows out once vibrant cultural institutions. In *Unforgetting God*, Arrington shines a light on the path out of the soul-numbing materialist wilderness we find ourselves in. He demonstrates that materialism is false, even absurd, and points the way to a loving God who has revealed himself in Jesus Christ, who is our best hope for personal salvation and cultural renewal.

Copyright Notice

©2025 by Barry Arrington. All Rights Reserved.

Library Cataloging Data

Unforgetting God by Barry Arrington
279 pages, 6 by 9 inches
Library of Congress Control Number: 2025937846
ISBN: 979-8-89946-000-5 (Hardcover), 979-8-89946-003-6 (Paperback), 979-8-89946-004-3 (Kindle)
BISAC: REL067030 RELIGION / Christian Theology / Apologetics
BISAC: PHI005000 PHILOSOPHY / Ethics & Moral Philosophy
BISAC: LAW111000 LAW / Judicial Power

Book Cover Design:

The image on the book cover was generated in part with ChatGPT, OpenAI's AI model.

Publisher Information

Inkwell Press
2321 Sir Barton Way
Suite 140-1032
Lexington, KY 40509
Inkwell.Net

Advance Praise for *Unforgetting God*

The philosophy of materialism—the doctrine that only material things exist—has advanced mainly by stealing prestige from science. Yet, among much else in his marvelous book, Barry Arrington shows that the more modern science learns about nature, the more science itself undercuts materialism. From the realization that nature had a beginning, to the immateriality of the quantum world, to the discovery that DNA contains coded information, the more science advances, the more it points to the essential role of mind.
—Michael J. Behe, Professor of Biological Sciences, Lehigh University, author of *Darwin's Black Box: The Biochemical Challenge to Evolution*

Barry Arrington brings a fresh perspective to the topic of materialism, the view that all of reality is merely an assembly of material particles controlled by mindless forces. As a seasoned litigator who has brought cases before the US Supreme Court, he shows how materialism has subverted legal theory by relativizing law and morality. But his critique of materialism doesn't stop there, showing how materialism subverts everything it touches. Critiques of materialism are typically made by scientists, philosophers, and theologians. His perspective as an attorney adds a particularly insightful dimension to the critique of materialism. Indeed, one wonders on reading this book whether attorneys acting in the courts will be the key to toppling materialism.
—William A. Dembski, author of *The Design Inference*

If you're grappling with the big questions of life, meaning, and faith, you need to check out *Unforgetting God* by Barry Arrington. The author does an incredible job of breaking down why the philosophy of materialism just doesn't hold up when you really look at all the evidence for God's existence, and he makes a compelling case that the Christian worldview is the only one that makes sense. It's an in-depth read that'll make you rethink what the world is saying—definitely worth your time!
—Dr. Jack Graham, Senior Pastor, Prestonwood Baptist Church

In his excellent book *Unforgetting God* Barry Arrington ably explains how materialist thinking has contributed to many of our social problems. Then

he provides the remedy, not only by providing cogent arguments against materialism, but also by demonstrating the truth of Christianity.
—Richard Weikart, Emeritus Professor of History, Cal State University, Stanislaus, author of *Death of Humanity: And the Case for Life*

With the precision of a surgeon, attorney Arrington powerfully affirms the truth of Christianity while dismantling the hollow promises of materialism. This is an urgent clarion call to thinking undecideds, urging them to reexamine the bedrock of truth before the materialist foundation crumbles beneath their feet.
—Robert J. Marks, II, Distinguished Professor of Electrical and Computer Engineering, Baylor University, author of *Non-Computable You: What You Do That Artificial Intelligence Never Will Never Do*

When the natural knowledge of God is suppressed and the creation put in God's place (Romans 1:18-21), men and women can force themselves to forget God and deny their status as creatures and their conscience (Romans 2:14-15). This is the worst possible memory loss, since forgetting God means to deny all that is fundamental to existence. When philosophical materialism attempts to explain anything—the existence or nature of the cosmos, the reality of moral value, beauty, the uniqueness of humans—it fails utterly, however loud it may yell otherwise. When philosophical materialism attempts to order society in godless ways, it releases the acids of dehumanization, totalitarianism, and the devaluation of human life. This clearly-written and well-documented book makes a cogent case against this irrational and God-denying worldview on the basis of the best arguments and evidence. I recommend it highly.
—Douglas Groothuis, Distinguished University Research Professor of Apologetics and Christian Worldview, Cornerstone University and Seminary, author of *Christian Apologetics*, 2nd ed. (InterVarsity)

After nearly forty years of practicing law, including writing briefs, pleading at the bar and cross-examining witnesses, Barry Arrington has learned the art of assessing evidence. In this book, he applies that art to the evidence for God's existence. He looks at the demands of logic, design in nature, what science can (and can't) tell us, the problem of evil, and—inevitably—contemporary efforts to evade the important questions. Readers who are

new to the controversies will find this book a valuable guide. Those who are familiar with them will find new insights."
—Denyse O'Leary, co-author with Michael Egnor of *The Immortal Mind: A Neurosurgeon's Case for the Existence of the Soul*

Barry Arrington is in the business of persuasion. In his book *Unforgetting God* Arrington lays out the case for a culture that attempts to suppress and then forget the God of the Bible. Arrington knows that reason and facts and evidence serve as the foundation for persuasive argument. But what happens when the individual abandons reason, redefines facts and simply refuses to allow the evidence to speak for itself? Arrington exposes the holes in naturalism or philosophical materialism and makes the case for historical biblical Christianity. The skeptic will be challenged. The cynic may remain in a state of incoherent cynicism. But it's only because he or she has abandoned reason, facts and evidence. What a wonderful and edifying read! Enjoy.
—Gino Geraci, Emeritus Pastor of Calvary South Denver, Salem Talk Show Host

With precision expected of a highly trained legal mind, Barry Arrington has penned a masterful apologetic, incisive and cogent at every turn. *Unforgetting God* points out the origins of materialism and its effects upon western civilization. I recommend this book without reservation. It will serve as a change agent for western civilization and as a cultural revival, by returning to truth and "Unforgetting God."
—Ernest J. Zarra III, Ph.D., author of 17 books, including *Understanding Radicalism: How it Affects What's Happening in Education and Its Impact on Students*

To Ed and Carol Arrington

If I were asked today to formulate as concisely as possible the main cause of the ruinous Revolution that swallowed up some 60 million of our people, I could not put it more accurately than to repeat: "Men have forgotten God; that's why all this has happened."

—Aleksandr Solzhenitsyn

Table of Contents

1	Introduction	1
2	Materialism 101	13
3	Where do "Rights" Come From?	25
4	Lawless Law	35
5	You're Gonna Have to Serve Somebody	51
6	The Case for Christianity	63
7	Objection!	97
8	Can We Fake it Till We Make it?	165
9	Give Love a Chance	173
	About the Author	177
	Acknowledgments	179
	Notes	181
	Bibliography	249
	Index	263

1. Introduction

The director of a prestigious chemistry lab arrives one morning to find one of his chemists feverishly working among several beakers filled with bubbling, foul-smelling liquids. The chemist's clothes are wrinkled, his hair is awry, and it looks like he hasn't slept in days. Alarmed, the director asks, "What on earth are you doing?" The wild-eyed chemist looks up from his work, and in a cackling, mad-scientist voice, he yells, "I'm on the verge of inventing an acid so corrosive that it will eat through all known substances!" The director calmly replies, "Oh yeah? What are you going to put it in?"

"Materialism" is the idea only matter and energy exist, moving and rearranging themselves by blind forces of attraction and repulsion through space and time.[1] If, as materialists believe, only such material stuff exists, it follows that an immaterial God does not exist. The late philosopher Daniel Dennett compared the materialism that came to dominate the minds of Western intellectuals[2] following the publication of Darwin's *Origin of Species* to a "universal acid" like the one our hapless chemist was trying to invent. Only, instead of eating through matter, this acid ate "through just about every traditional concept" in Western culture and left in its wake "a revolutionized world-view."[3]

This book is about the impact materialism has had on our culture, how it has hollowed out our institutions, left people adrift in a sea of meaninglessness, and corroded our sense of right and wrong to the point that it is nearly unrecognizable. It is also about shining a light on the path out of the soul-numbing materialist wilderness we find ourselves in. Along that path, we will discover that materialism is not only false; it is incoherent. Further along, we will find that there is a God and that he has revealed himself to us in the person of Jesus Christ, who is now, as he has always been, our best hope for personal salvation and cultural renewal.

We will start with Dennett, who was surely right about one thing. Darwin changed the world.[4] Materialism and materialist evolution were not new concepts in 1859 when *Origin of Species* was published.[5] Greek and Roman philosophers had debated these ideas more than two thousand years earlier,[6] but they never gained much traction before Darwin, whose genius lay in proposing a solution to what had always been seen as materialist evolution's fatal flaw—its reliance on sheer randomness as a creative force.[7] The ancient theory posited that "atoms"[8] randomly floated through the void and alternately bounced off each other or clumped together, and complex living organisms somehow emerged from the interaction of these randomly floating atoms. It is not hard to see why that idea never caught on. Anyone who has contemplated the staggering complexity and intricate organization of living organisms intuitively knows that "atoms randomly bumping together" is a non-starter as an explanation for how they came to be.

Darwin's revolutionary idea was that a non-random mechanism called natural selection scrutinizes barely perceptible variations in arrangements of atoms and rejects those that are bad and "preserv[es] and add[s] up all that are good,"[9] and over millions of years this mechanism gradually transformed the simple organisms that existed on the primordial earth into the complex living things we see around us today.[10] Darwin provided a seemingly plausible explanation for the undeniable appearance of design in living things without invoking a designer. It is no exaggeration to say that the history of thought among Western intellectuals in the last two centuries pivoted on that idea.[11]

Perhaps Richard Dawkins put it best when he said he could not imagine being an atheist at any time before 1859, because, prior to that time, it was impossible to explain the "organized complexity" of living things on materialist grounds.[12] "Darwin," Dawkins explained, "made it possible to be an intellectually fulfilled atheist."[13] No matter what one thinks about the merits of Darwin's theory of biological evolution,[14] there cannot be the slightest doubt about Darwin's critical role in taking the stopper off the bottle in which materialism had been contained for nearly two thousand years since the days of Lucretius.

Dennett was also right about the overwhelming cultural impact of Darwin's idea. Perhaps the most obvious traditional concept the "universal acid" ate through is the idea that our lives are meaningful because they are lived in a universe framed by a transcendent moral order grounded in the existence of God. In his book *River Out of Eden*, Dawkins explained how that belief is not tenable under the materialist worldview ushered in by Darwin:

> In a universe of blind physical forces and genetic replication, some people are going to get hurt, other people are going to get lucky, and you won't find any rhyme or reason in it, nor any justice. The universe we observe has precisely the properties we should expect if there is, at bottom, no design, no purpose, no evil and no good, nothing but blind, pitiless indifference.[15]

If it is true that God does not exist and the universe consists of nothing but blind physical forces acting on the fundamental particles, it has profound consequences for everything. Friedrich Nietzsche was one of the first to grasp the implications of this radical materialist outlook and what it portended for Western culture. In his famous "Parable of the Madman,"[16] Nietzsche tells of a man who ran into the marketplace crying "I seek God! I seek God!" only to be mocked and jeered by those who had abandoned their belief in God. In one of the most vivid and haunting passages in all of Western literature, Nietzsche continued:

> The madman jumped into their midst and pierced them with his eyes. "Whither is God?" he cried; "I will tell you. *We have killed*

him—you and I. All of us are his murderers. But how did we do this? How could we drink up the sea? Who gave us the sponge to wipe away the entire horizon? What were we doing when we unchained this earth from its sun? Whither is it moving now? Whither are we moving? Away from all suns? Are we not plunging continually? Backward, sideward, forward, in all directions? Is there still any up or down? Are we not straying, as through an infinite nothing? Do we not feel the breath of empty space? Has it not become colder? Is not night continually closing in on us?

Nietzsche understood that concepts that make sense only in the sustaining light of a transcendent moral order—human dignity, the universal rights of man, equality, justice, good and evil, to name but a few—disappear in the darkness of God's death. Materialism has cast humanity adrift in an "infinite nothing" from which we must gaze into—or struggle to look away from—the gaping maw of the abyss of an ultimately meaningless life followed by inevitable annihilation at death.[17]

To be sure, philosophers since Darwin and Nietzsche have labored valiantly to establish a basis for moral transcendence that does not rely on the existence of God. However, as atheist Yale Professor Arthur Leff reluctantly concluded in a highly influential article examining the history of these efforts, they have all failed.[18] Leff started by stating the problem. When expressing any moral standard—such as it is wrong to commit adultery—one must be able to answer the question "sez who?"[19] Answering that question requires an "evaluator" whose evaluations are beyond question. But to fulfill that role, the evaluator "must be the unjudged judge, the unruled legislator, the premise maker who rests on no premises, the uncreated creator of values."[20] "Now, what would you call such a thing if it existed?" Leff asks. "You would call it Him."[21]

A moral standard grounded in God's existence can easily pass the "sez who?" hurdle. But the problem for a materialist like Leff is that he does not believe God exists and there is nothing that is remotely equivalent to God that can take His place. "The so-called death of

God," Leff explains, "turns out not to have been just *His* funeral; it also seems to have effected the total elimination of any coherent, or even more-than-momentarily convincing, ethical or legal system dependent upon finally authoritative extrasystemic premises."[22] There is no way to demonstrate that one person's ethical choices are superior to another person's ethical choices unless the two choices are compared to a standard that transcends both of them. By definition, the materialist insists that such a standard cannot exist. It follows that every standard for judging between moral choices is completely *arbitrary*.[23] Leff concludes his article with a famous epilogue:

> All I can say is this: it looks as if we are all we have. Given what we know about ourselves and each other, this is an extraordinarily unappetizing prospect; looking around the world, it appears that if all men are brothers, the ruling model is Cain and Abel . . . As things now stand, everything is up for grabs.
>
> Nevertheless:
> Napalming babies is bad.
> Starving the poor is wicked.
> Buying and selling each other is depraved.
> Those who stood up to and died resisting Hitler, Stalin, Idi Amin, and Pol Pot—and General Custer too—have earned salvation.
> Those who acquiesced deserve to be damned.
> There is in the world such a thing as evil.
> [All together now:] Sez who?
> **God help us.**[24]

Leff's final plea to a God in whom he does not believe was probably meant to be ironic, but it came off as tragic. He understood that his logic applies equally to his own moral views. If God does not exist—and he does not believe that he does—then his own deepest moral intuitions, such as that it is bad to napalm babies, are as arbitrary and ungrounded as everyone else's.

None of this is to say that the world immediately descended into a nihilistic hellscape after the publication of *Origin of Species*.

The effect of the widespread embrace of materialism among Western intellectuals after Darwin was neither immediate nor linear. The West had a deep reservoir of belief in transcendence that it had filled over nearly two millennia, and that reservoir was not going to dry up overnight. Indeed, we are still drawing on it today. But the reservoir is not inexhaustible. Will Herberg coined the term "cut flower culture" to describe the gradual decline of a once-vibrant culture that has abandoned its founding principles. He wrote: "Cut flowers retain their original beauty and fragrance, but only so long as they retain the vitality that they have drawn from their now-severed roots; after that is exhausted, they wither and die. So with freedom, brotherhood, justice, and personal dignity—the values that form the moral foundation of our civilization. Without the life-giving power of the faith out of which they have sprung, they possess neither meaning nor vitality."[25] Hemingway wrote of a man who went bankrupt. When asked how it happened, he replied, "Two ways, gradually and then suddenly."[26] As anyone who watched the demise of the Soviet Union knows, cultures collapse in the same way. I wonder if the gradual phase of the collapse of the West is drawing to a close. Should we brace ourselves for the sudden part?

The crisis of meaning is a particularly alarming symptom of impending collapse. According to the CDC, suicide rates increased 36% between 2000 and 2022, a year in which an American died from suicide once every 11 minutes.[27] This should hardly surprise us. The French existentialist philosopher Albert Camus argued that in the face of the absurdity of a meaningless existence,[28] the only serious philosophical question is whether to commit suicide.[29] Camus compared our situation to the plight of Sisyphus, whom the gods doomed to spend every day for eternity rolling a boulder up a hill, only to have it roll back again each evening before he could reach the top. We are tempted to despair because materialism teaches us that, like Sisyphus's punishment, life is a pointless struggle in an absurd universe. Camus's proposed solution was to actually lean into that despair, embrace the pointless struggle, and even find fulfillment in it. Camus ends his book with: "The struggle itself toward the heights is enough to fill a man's heart. One must imagine Sisyphus happy."[30] Camus was an idiot. No one believes Sisyphus was happy. "Embrace the futility; be happy" is hardly a satisfactory answer to existential despair. The sheer arbitrariness of Camus's advice is deeply unsatisfying, but in his defense, no one else has proposed a better way to navigate through Nietzsche's "infinite nothing."[31]

Another of the traditional concepts the materialist acid has eaten through is the belief that we can live together in communities bound by deference to universal principles of justice and human rights. As we shall see, materialism teaches that such principles do not exist and power is the sole arbiter of all differences.[32] Thrasymachus was a sophist philosopher best known for his debate with Socrates in Plato's *Republic*. Like modern materialists, he believed that transcendent principles of justice do not exist, which is why he famously declared that justice "is nothing else than the advantage of the stronger."[33] When absolutely every human relationship plays out within a struggle for power, we must soon arrive at a state of *bellum omnium contra omnes*—"The war of all against all." In such a society, tribes of people with converging interests band together to fight the other tribes. Have you noticed lately that our politics seems like it is devolving into tribalism? Now you know why.

The point of this book is that it doesn't have to be this way. There is an alternative. Ironically, none other than Richard Dawkins pointed to that alternative in a recent exchange he had with newly-minted Christian Ayaan Hirsi Ali.[34] Dawkins said: "[T]he idea that the universe was actually created by a supernatural intelligence is a dramatic, important idea. *If it were true, it would completely change everything we know*. We'd be living in a totally different . . . universe."[35] Dawkins does not believe that God exists, but he recognizes that if we were to accept the idea that God does exist, our understanding of the universe would fundamentally change. We would no longer inhabit the materialist universe where, at bottom, there is nothing but blind, pitiless indifference. Instead of Nietzsche's cold infinite nothing, we would have a foundation for objective moral truth. And from that foundation, we could launch a counter-revolution against the materialism that has hollowed out almost every important institution of our society.

I anticipate that many readers' reaction to that last paragraph was something like, "Even if I were to agree that society would benefit from a belief in an objective morality grounded in the existence of God, I cannot force myself to believe that which I do not actually believe." True enough. But I am not asking you to do that. "Fideism" is a grit-your-teeth-and-believe-despite-the-evidence sort of belief. I am not asking anyone to retreat into an unreflective fideism. Indeed, I am calling for just the opposite – a revival of skepticism. For centuries, "skepticism" was associated with unbelievers such as the Enlightenment thinkers David Hume and Voltaire. This is because they were skeptical of the dominant cultural narrative, which in their time was Christianity. In our time, materialism is the dominant narrative, especially in the media and academia, which are the joint heralds of our culture's received wisdom. My purpose in writing this book is to urge everyone to re-examine the evidence for the existence of God with a *skeptical* perspective toward the secular received wisdom that has long dominated the discourse in our nation.

In other words, we need to change how we think about what it means to be skeptical. I once came across a website that claimed to be a sanctuary for skeptics, where no idea was considered beyond questioning, and all conclusions were to be held tentatively. It was amusing. The site was chock-a-block with article after article touting one materialist narrative after another. None of the articles would have caused the slightest stir in the typical college faculty lounge. The denizens of the site were indeed skeptical of the claims of theists, but they clung to the shibboleths of materialist orthodoxy with a brass-bound intransigence that would have made a medieval monk blush. I thought to myself that maybe they should rebrand as "skeptical of everything except the pronouncements of the hegemonic cultural orthodoxy." The new branding would be a mouthful, but it would have the benefit of honesty.

The "skeptics" at the website did not seem to have gotten the memo. Materialism has taken over the world. The overwhelming majority of the intellectual elite in our country are thoroughgoing materialists. They have been taught that materialism is obviously true, and they seem to have lost the capacity to question it. At the heights of our culture, materialism is no more up for debate than the heliocentric theory of the solar system. Our universities, our legal institutions, the media, professional associations, and just about every other institution in our country are now dominated by people who take materialism for granted. For them, it is hardly even a philosophical theory; it is a settled fact known for certain by all intelligent people.

The "skeptical" website was like the news stories one frequently sees about the latest Hollywood celebrity who has taken some cultural or political stance that is sure to *épater les bourgeois*.[36] Invariably, the reporter heaps praise on the celebrity for being unafraid of the consequences of their bold take on a controversial issue. Unafraid of what? I wonder, the adulation of practically everyone they encounter in their daily lives? "Transgressive" celebrities are boring. They are boring because they are not transgressive at all; they are utterly conventional. They have not gotten the memo either – the counterculture has become the culture.

Do you know what is interesting? Occasionally, one sees a story about a celebrity who has taken a different path from the one trodden by the herd of independent minds.[37] Those celebrities really are brave because there is a price to be paid for bucking the narrative. Just ask Gina Carano.[38] We need more Gina Caranos, brave souls who are unwilling to bend the knee to the conventional narrative because it is the path of least resistance. Carano is a true skeptic in the noble sense of the word.

As I mentioned, in Hume's and Voltaire's day, Christendom was the cultural hegemon, and it took true courage to stand up and say,

"Count me out of the dominant cultural idea and here's why."[39] Now, just the opposite is true. Today, claiming the mantle of "skeptic," because one is a materialist is almost ironic. It's like going to a Taylor Swift concert and claiming you "courageously" admitted to your fellow concert-goers that you enjoy her music.

I am calling for a renewal of an attitude of genuine skepticism toward the cultural hegemon of materialism. Again, I am not asking anyone to retreat into fideism. That is both irrational and unsustainable in the long run. I am not asking anyone to endure and believe despite all the evidence to the contrary. I am asking for the opposite. The point of this book is to encourage people to examine the evidence again, especially in light of the scholarship summarized in chapter six that demonstrates that accepting the existence of God and the truth of Jesus Christ's message of love, peace, and redemption are the overwhelmingly more rational positions to hold.

In the pages that follow, I will examine the claims of materialist philosophy and demonstrate why those claims are incoherent. In chapters three and four, I will discuss the corrosive effects materialism has had on our politics and our legal institutions. In chapter five, I address the destructive impact materialism has had on Western culture and why a course correction is necessary if we hope for the survival of our civilization. Chapter six is the heart of the book, where I provide a summary of the evidence for God's existence and the historical evidence for the resurrection of Jesus Christ.

It was not that long ago that many atheists claimed that "science" had somehow "proven" that God does not exist. One rarely hears that nowadays, and then only from village atheist know-nothings. The New Atheist movement has collapsed,[40] and atheist rhetoric has become more circumspect. This is due, no doubt, to recent scholarship in cosmology, physics, philosophy, biology, psychology, and other fields that has advanced the intellectual case for theism and made smug atheistic certitude passé. In chapter eight, I will respond to many of the objections to theism in general and Christianity in particular that I have encountered over the years.

As late as the 1980s, when materialism's iron grip on the minds of intellectuals was at its zenith, it would have probably been pointless for me to write a book like this. To be sure, many people continued to believe in God, but that belief was under assault from a militant and ascendant materialist elite that accused believers of clinging to superstitious myths. Times have changed, and we live in an exciting intellectual age for theists in general and Christians in particular. The materialist edifice has been crumbling for some time now. Nevertheless, while materialism is no longer intellectually ascendant, it remains culturally dominant, and the cultural course materialists have set us on is fraught with danger. Destruction and chaos lie at the end of our current path. But there is another way. Indeed, from the beginning, it has been called "the Way."[41] Our Nation has strayed from that true and sure path. I hope this book helps us find our footing again.

2. Materialism 101

Everyone old enough to remember the Kennedy assassination will probably be able to tell you where they were and what they were doing when the news broke. Some events are so shocking that the moment we hear about them is etched into our consciousness like a photograph. Psychologists call such memories "flashbulb memories." I have a flashbulb memory of the moment I heard about the Columbine shootings. It was the early afternoon of April 20, 1999. I had a client in the telecommunications business, and I had just arrived at their offices. They had a bank of televisions in their reception area, which they kept tuned to various stations. When I walked through the door, I noticed all the stations had broken away from their regular programming to cover a breaking news event. Police cars with flashing lights were rushing toward a large school building, and the text on one of the screens said dozens of students had been shot at a Littleton high school. I watched the news coverage in stunned silence. I would have been even more shocked if I had known that I would soon be wading through the swirling maelstrom of one of the killer's minds.

A few months after the shootings, the parents of some of the students who were killed that day contacted my firm. They asked us to represent them in connection with a constitutional challenge to the school district's decision to exclude them from a community art project at the school.[1] Over the next several years, I represented these parents in this and other legal matters concerning the shootings. During that time, I spent hundreds of hours investigating the incident. I sifted through thousands of pages of documents and reviewed many hours of audio and video recordings that Harris and Klebold left behind, including the notorious "basement tapes."[2] Finally, I spent a week in a federal courthouse taking the sworn depositions of the killers' parents.[3] Of all the materials I examined, one video stands out. It was a video of Harris alone in his car at night as he drove up and down random streets while ranting at the camera. The frame was close-up, and I will always remember the chilling image of the tortured, demented eyes of a vicious killer preparing to go on his infamous rampage.

I learned a great many things during that investigation, many of which conflict with myths that emerged after the shootings. One enduring myth is that Eric Harris[4] was a hapless geek who mindlessly lashed out at "jocks" in retaliation for the bullying he experienced at school. This is not true.[5] Harris was a very intelligent young man who spent considerable time reflecting on and writing about his motivations. Those motivations had little to do with seeking revenge for bullying. I believe the myth of retaliation originated because, psychologically, it is easier to dismiss the killers as ruthless savages driven by uncontrollable rage. It's much harder to accept that two suburban teenagers who lived conventional lives in a conventional middle-class neighborhood could spend nearly a year calmly planning the mass murder of hundreds of people[6] who had done them no harm. But that is what happened.

Why did it happen? There isn't a simple, straightforward answer to that question. However, one thing is sure: Harris was not a stupid beast lashing out in insensate rage. He was a thinker and a meticulous planner. He had even taken a class in philosophy, and he took the philosophical ideas he learned very seriously indeed. He often alluded to those ideas in his journals and recordings. That's how we know that Harris affirmatively believed those philosophical ideas justified his actions. Unfortunately for those he murdered and maimed, those ideas were a toxic miasma of Charles Darwin funneled through Friedrich Nietzsche.[7]

Ideas have consequences. In this case, those consequences were deadly. Dr. Peter Langman spent years studying many of the same sources I reviewed in my investigation, and he has written a summary of many of the ideas jumbled together in Harris's writings.[8] Langman's article assembles many quotations from Harris that reveal his mindset. If there is one quotation that sums up Harris's views, it is probably this one: "F**k money, f**k justice, f**k morals, f**k civilized, f**k rules, f**k laws ... DIE manmade words ... people think they apply to everything when they don't/can't. There's no such thing as True Good or True evil, it's all relative to the observer. It's just all nature, chemistry, and math."[9] Harris was a deeply committed materialist who believed that "morality" is just a word; there is no such thing as good or evil, and everything ultimately reduces to chemistry and math.

My friend Gino Geraci was the pastor of Calvary Chapel of South Denver, which was only two blocks from Columbine High School. Gino was a chaplain for the Arapahoe County Sheriff's Department, and he immediately rushed to the scene that terrible day to minister to survivors and first responders.[10] While he was there, Gino came across the school district superintendent standing with tears streaming down his face. He turned to Gino and asked him how such a thing could happen. Gino responded with a harsh reproof: "You have taught our children that they come from nowhere, and that is where they're going, and that life is a point of pain in a meaningless existence. And they believed you." Gino did not know Eric Harris and could not have known that he was speaking the literal truth. He had no idea that Harris had drunk deeply from the well of materialist philosophy at Columbine High School. But he understood the secular education establishment very well, and it was no great leap for him to deduce what the killers had been taught. Materialism is corrosive to the spirit, and, for some, it can lead to a despondent nihilism that erupts in violence.

Harris understood all too well that materialism is the philosophy of ultimate meaninglessness. It is not difficult to see why this is the case. If materialists had a creed, it would go something like this:

> In the beginning were the particles, and the particles were in motion, and in the entire universe there is, and never has been, and never will be anything other than particles in motion.[11]

Materialism is the anti-god, and Carl Sagan is its prophet. Like a pious Muslim reciting the Shahada,[12] Sagan frequently solemnly intoned, "The cosmos is all that is or was or ever will be."[13] While Sagan was a scientist, the first and most obvious thing to understand about his mantra is that it is not a conclusion of science. No scientist has ever stood outside of the cosmos and performed a measurement to determine whether there is anything other than the cosmos. Sean M. Carroll, a professor in the Department of Physics and Astronomy at Johns Hopkins University, is one of the world's leading scientists, and he is quite candid about this. Carroll is an atheist, and he concedes that every attempt to explain why the universe exists on materialist grounds ends in declaring it to be an inexplicable "brute fact." The universe just is and we cannot "demand . . . that there be something we humans would recognize as a satisfactory reason for its existence."[14] Science is the study of nature. It cannot tell us why nature exists in the first place or if there is anything other than nature. Those are not scientific questions. Sagan was a profoundly committed materialist, but even he knew that materialism could not be proven scientifically.[15]

If Sagan's mantra is not a conclusion of science, then what is it? If one defines a "religious belief" as a belief held as a matter of faith on account of one's metaphysical commitments, then Sagan's mantra is a religious belief. Let's assume for a moment that Sagan's materialist beliefs were correct—in the entire universe, nothing exists but particles in motion through space-time. Where does that leave us? Scientists say the universe once existed in an unimaginably hot and dense state that physicists describe as a mathematical "singularity."[16]

At the "Big Bang," the universe began expanding. Gravity pulled lighter elements, mostly hydrogen and helium, together to form stars, and heavier elements were fused in the nuclear furnaces that ignited at the center of those stars. Eventually, over billions of years, some of those stars burned out, leaving the heavier elements behind. Planets eventually coalesced from those heavier elements, and eons later, on one of those planets, a simple single-celled living organism somehow arose spontaneously from non-living matter. The descendants of that first simple cell evolved into more complex life forms until, millions of years later, a species of intelligent hairless apes emerged to dominate the planet.

Those clever hairless apes call themselves "humans." Many of those humans believe they have an immaterial spirit, but the materialist insists they are wrong. Humans consist only of the chemical elements that make up their bodies, elements that were fused in the nuclear furnaces of long-dead stars. Sagan wrote: "All of the rocky and metallic material we stand on, the iron in our blood, the calcium in our teeth, the carbon in our genes were produced billions of years ago in the interior of a red giant star."[17] We are made of an amalgamation of "starstuff"[18] and nothing else. We have no immaterial spirit.

What about consciousness—the state of being self-aware—and free will? Surely, even a materialist will concede that these attributes set humans apart from mere particles in motion? Not so, says the materialist. If particles in motion are all that exists, it follows that "mental" is not a separate category from "physical." This means that when a person perceives his own consciousness, what he perceives can be explained solely by the electrochemical processes of his physical brain. Everything about us, including our sense of having an inner self and free will, is caused by those purely physical processes. Particles are not self-aware. Nor do they choose.

Materialists do not deny that everyone *feels* as if they are conscious. Famous materialist psychologist and philosopher Bruce Hood asserts, "Most of us have an experience of a self. I certainly have one, and I do not doubt that others do as well—an autonomous individual with a coherent identity and sense of free will. But that experience is an illusion."[19] Hood's statement is the ultimate counterintuitive conclusion. But, to his credit, Hood does not run from the conclusions compelled by his materialist premises. He admits that he feels self-aware like everyone else but insists that feeling is a trick played on him by the burnt-out starstuff that makes up his physical body.

What about morality? Surely, that sets us apart from the rocks? No, it does not. The next conclusion that follows inevitably from materialist premises is that objective morality cannot exist. Have you ever met an immoral rock? A rock is an amalgamation of burnt-out starstuff, and your body is an amalgamation of a different kind of burnt-out starstuff. A rock and a human body are the same in that they are nothing but starstuff. And burnt-out starstuff is neither good nor bad. It just is. As we saw earlier, Richard Dawkins assures us that in a universe of blind physical forces, "there is, at bottom, no design, no purpose, no evil, no good, nothing but pitiless indifference."[20]

But every sane person feels strongly that some things are "right" and some things are "wrong." Again, materialists do not deny that strong moral feelings exist. Certainly, we feel strong urges to do certain things (which we call good) and not to do other things (which we call evil). But those urges are also entirely reducible to the electrochemical processes of our physical brains. The urges that we call morality are an evolutionary holdover like our appendix.[21] Materialism says we have an appendix because, at some point in evolutionary history, it gave our ancestors an advantage in the Darwinian struggle for relative reproductive success. And the materialist says we have strong feelings of revulsion about the Holocaust for the same reason. Materialist professor Michael Ruse put the matter this way.

> The position of the modern evolutionist, therefore, is that humans have an awareness of morality—a sense of right and wrong and a feeling of obligation to be thus governed—because such an awareness is of biological worth. *Morality is a biological adaptation no less than are hands and feet and teeth.*[22]

At this point, you might think I am exaggerating what materialism teaches. I assure you I am not. The late arch-materialist Cornell Professor William Provine summed up the materialist worldview when he wrote: "Humans are complex organic machines that die completely with no survival of soul . . . [Their choices] are determined by the interaction of heredity and environment and are not the result of free will. No inherent moral or ethical laws exist, nor are there absolute guiding principles for human society. The universe cares nothing for us and we have no ultimate meaning in life."[23]

All very theoretical and heady stuff for academics like Provine to bandy about, you might say, but no one with any practical influence in our society holds such views. Unfortunately, that is not the case. These views are mainstream among our intellectual elite. As Exhibit A for this proposition, I submit Judge Richard Posner. Posner could be the poster child of our intellectual elite. He graduated from Yale University *summa cum laude* and from Harvard Law School *magna cum laude* (indeed, first in his class), after which he went on to a clerkship at the Supreme Court, followed by a distinguished career as an academic in the 1970s. President Reagan appointed Posner to the Seventh Circuit Court of Appeals in 1981 (an appellate court one level below the Supreme Court), where he served as Chief Judge from 1993 to 2000. Posner retired as a federal judge in 2017. Posner, who has written dozens of books and hundreds of academic articles, is, without the slightest doubt, one of the most highly influential intellectuals in the United States in the last 50 years. Indeed, according to a list compiled by the librarian of Yale Law School, Posner is the most cited legal scholar *of all time* by a wide margin.[24]

This is disturbing because, for all of his impressive academic credentials and influence, Posner's moral views, which he summarized in an article in *The Harvard Law Review*[25] are horrifying. Professor Samuel Calhoun wrote an excellent summary of the moral nihilism Posner expressed in that article:

Posner's chief point is "that the criteria for pronouncing a moral claim valid are local, that is, are relative to the moral code of the particular culture in which the claim is advanced, so that we cannot call another culture 'immoral' unless we add 'by our lights.'" Posner does not flinch from the full consequences of this view. No practice whatever—not adultery, treason, infanticide, Nazi and Cambodian genocide, human sacrifice, female genital mutilation, suttee, slavery, torturing babies for fun, head-shrinking, cannibalism, or hurling virgins into volcanoes to stimulate crop growth—can be shown to be truly wrong. Posner admits that his position makes him "a moral relativist," but says that he does not "embrace . . . the 'vulgar relativism' that teaches . . . that we have a moral duty to tolerate cultures that have moral views different from ours." He would be quite willing to stamp out certain practices prevalent in other cultures, but only because he found them to be "disgusting," not because they could be said to be "really" morally unsound.[26]

Like Arthur Leff, Posner agrees "that one needs a lawgiver if there are to be moral universals" and "that no human lawgiver could lay down universal moral duties"; therefore, "the only tenable ground for believing in a universal moral law is religious."[27] Posner rejects the idea that such a lawgiver exists, which is why he is a moral nihilist who insists that *power* is the only arbiter of moral conflicts. This is what he means when he says he would be willing to "stamp out" moral practices that he personally feels are "disgusting."

It is hard for many people to accept just how pervasive moral nihilism is among our intellectual elite. In a recent article in *The New Yorker* magazine,[28] Professor Manvir Singh provided a service by exploring his journey through that culture of nihilism. Singh, who is the director of the Anthropology Lab at the University of California, Davis, has a Ph.D. in evolutionary biology from Harvard. He described his journey out of religion into materialism and his struggle to erect a workable moral framework in light of the death of God heralded by Nietzsche. Singh takes for granted the universal consensus of his tribe (secular intellectual elites) that objective moral truth does not exist and that what we call morality is an evolutionary adaptation. He writes, "moral tenets—such as the rightness of loyalty or the wrongness of murder—do not exist unless natural selection produces organisms that value them." All morality is subjective, which means that the moral statement "killing is bad" means nothing but "I don't like killing."

Singh acknowledges that this is deeply disturbing at an emotional level, and he asks, "How does one exist in a post-moral world? What do we do when the desire to be good is exposed as a self-serving performance and moral beliefs are recast as merely brain stuff?" His solution is to adopt the "moral fictionalism" advocated by Richard Joyce. Moral fictionalism suggests that a person should speak as if morality exists because such language makes one likable despite referring to nothing real. Singh says he still accepts that he is "a selfish organism produced by a cosmic mega-force, drifting around in a bedlam of energy and matter and, in most respects, not so very different from the beetles" he scrutinized in his undergraduate studies. He says that traces of unease linger, but he tries to do right by people. He does this not because the word "right" has any objective meaning but because it allows him to feel like his life has meaning even though he would be the first to tell you it does not.

Some years ago, I was having a discussion with an atheist college student. I tried to move him with an appeal to objective morality. I said if there is no God, there is no objective basis for morality. That means that you cannot really say that killing six million innocent Jews in the Holocaust was wrong in any objective sense of that word. The most you could say is that you strongly disagree with the Holocaust and find it personally repulsive. I was shocked when he replied, "Yeah, I guess that's right." In retrospect, it is surprising that I was surprised. The young man was in college, which means he was wading through a moral sewer. How could the stink not get on him? Posner wrote that the Nuremberg trials could not prove the Nazis had been objectively immoral; he insists they were immoral only "according to our lights, not theirs."[29] The young man was following in Posner's intellectual footsteps.

Again, ideas have consequences. There cannot be the slightest doubt that Professor Provine's and Judge Posner's moral nihilism is correct—*if their materialist premises are true.* In other words, if their premises are true, their conclusions surely follow as a matter of indisputable logic. For the sake of argument, let us assume that they have given us a true account of reality.[30] There is no good; there is no evil. Our lives are ultimately meaningless. What if a person acted based on a clear-eyed and unsentimental understanding of those principles? If that person had the courage not to be overwhelmed by the utter meaninglessness of his existence, he would be transformed. He would be bold, self-confident, assertive, uninhibited, and unrestrained. He would consider empathy to be nothing but weak-kneed sentimentality. To him, others would not be ends; they would be objects to be exploited for his gratification. He would not flinch at being called cruel because he would know that the word "cruel" is a meaningless expression of sentimentality.[31] In short, he would be what we call a psychopath, but Nietzsche would call him an Übermensch.[32] Nietzsche believed the Übermensch would evolve from man just as man had evolved from the apes. In *Thus Spake Zarathustra* he wrote:

> *I teach you the [Übermensch].* Man is something that is to be surpassed . . . Man is a rope stretched between the animal and the {Übermensch]—a rope over an abyss. . . . What is great in man is that he is a bridge and not a goal.[33]

The Übermensch has evolved beyond the morality of the petty people, which he holds in contempt because it seeks to inhibit the unfettered expression of his will. Zarathustra goes on:

> He who seeth the abyss, but with eagle's eyes,—he who with eagle's talons *graspeth* the abyss: he hath courage. . . . "Man must become better and evil"—so do *I* teach. The evilest is necessary for the [Übermensch's] best. It may have been well for the preacher of the

petty people to suffer and be burdened by men's sin. I, however, rejoice in great sin as my great *consolation*.[34]

With indomitable courage, the Übermensch reflects upon the abyss—the vast, indifferent, and meaningless universe—and does not lose heart. He has evolved beyond man and is therefore able to see past the empty categories of "good" and "evil" held so dear by the petty people. He becomes evil and, therefore, better because "better" means the successful assertion of his will to power.

Eric Harris loved Nietzsche,[35] and Nietzsche's invocation of evolution was not lost on him. It was no coincidence that Harris's choice of attire for the massacre was a shirt with the words "natural selection" emblazoned across the front. Harris literally believed he had evolved into a Nietzschean Übermensch. He wrote: "How dare you think that I and you are part of the same species when we are sooooooo different. You aren't human. You are a robot."[36] Elsewhere he wrote, "I feel like God and I wish I was, having everyone being OFFICIALLY lower than me."[37]

David Brooks summed up Harris's motivations:

> It's clear from excerpts of Harris's journals that he saw himself as a sort of Nietzschean Superman—someone so far above the herd of ant-like mortals he does not even have to consider their feelings. He rises above good and evil, above the contemptible slave morality of normal people. He can realize his true, heroic self, and establish his eternal glory, only through some gigantic act of will.[38]

This brings us back to the question I asked above. What if Provine's and Posner's premises were correct, and a person was able to act based on a clear-eyed and unsentimental understanding of the ethical nihilism counseled by materialism? We are repulsed by Harris, and we use words like "evil" to describe him. But if materialism is true, are we not engaging in mere sentimentality when we say Harris was evil? If materialism is true, human beings are nothing but "sentient meat," to quote Detective Cohle[39] from "True Detective." On what basis can we assert that one bag of sentient meat has any obligation to allow another bag of sentient meat to live? Harris believed he was a lion and his classmates had no more rights than gazelles. If materialism is true, was he wrong?

I am not suggesting that all materialists are killers like Eric Harris; that is obviously not the case. There are millions of materialists, and thankfully, very few of them become psychopathic mass murderers. I am asserting—insisting, actually —that materialists' ethical premises prevent them from saying that what Harris did was *objectively* evil, and that has consequences for all of us. Harris was an extremist who acted on his materialist principles in an extreme way. What about people who hold the same ethical ideas as Harris but act on those ideas in subtler ways? What, for example, happens when belief in philosophical materialism becomes nearly ubiquitous among Western intellectual elites in law, media, education, and politics? What happens when in large segments of our people, the natural human longing to serve a greater good becomes untethered to a belief in the existence of objective good? In the following chapters, we will see how materialist philosophy is a cultural cancer that has metastasized to the point where it has become an existential threat to everything that is good in Western civilization.

3. Where do "Rights" Come From?

In February 2024, *Politico* reporter Heidi Przybyla appeared on *MSNBC* to sound a warning klaxon about "Christian nationalists," whom she described as extremist conservative Christians. Przybyla explained that, unlike normal Christians, Christian nationalists "believe that our rights as Americans, as all human beings, don't come from any earthly authority. They don't come from Congress; they don't come from the Supreme Court. They come from God."[1] Her comments sparked considerable controversy, with many pointing out that the Declaration of Independence expresses the same view of the source of human rights that she implied is held only by fringe religious extremists.[2]

Przybyla[3] inadvertently raised a vitally important question: Where do our rights come from? There are two competing theories. The first theory asserts that a person has a right to a thing if it would be unjust to deprive him of it. An act is unjust if it deviates from a moral standard. Thus, to assert that a person has a right not to be discriminated against on the basis of his race is simply another way of saying that government-sanctioned racial discrimination is morally wrong. This is often referred to as the "natural law" theory of rights. Martin Luther King, Jr., appealed to this theory when he explained his civil disobedience to segregation laws in his Letter from Birmingham Jail:

> One may well ask: "How can you advocate breaking some laws and obeying others?" The answer lies in the fact that there are two types of laws: just and unjust. I would be the first to advocate obeying just laws. One has not only a legal but a moral responsibility to obey just laws. Conversely, one has a moral responsibility to disobey unjust laws. I would agree with St. Augustine that "an unjust law is no law at all." Now, what is the difference between the two? How does one determine whether a law is just or unjust? A just law is a man made code that squares with the moral law or the law of God. An unjust law is a code that is out of harmony with the moral law. To put it in the terms of St. Thomas Aquinas: An unjust law is a human law that is not rooted in eternal law and natural law.[4]

As Dr. King's appeal to Augustine and Aquinas implies, natural law theory is inherently theistic. Every person has a right to equal protection of the laws without regard to his race because racial discrimination is unjust. It is unjust because it violates the transcendent moral principle which asserts that racial discrimination is evil. This principle exists independently of whether a specific government acknowledges or enforces it, or, as was the case in the Jim Crow South, enacts laws that contradict it.

The second theory of rights asserts that a person has a right to a thing only if taking the thing from him violates a "positive law" enacted by the government.[5] The phrase "positive law" comes from the Latin word *positum*, which means "established." Thus, the phrase means law established by human authority.[6] This is the theory to which Przybyla appealed when she appeared on *MSNBC*. Materialists, who deny the existence of transcendent moral principles, must be legal positivists by definition. Under positive law theory, rights are established by the government, which implies that the government can also take them away.

Under the natural law theory of rights, Yitzhak has a right to life because it would be unjust—morally wrong—to murder him. The positive law theory of rights can make no such pronouncement. As we have seen, if materialism is true, any absolute moral claim is wrecked on the shoals of Authur Leff's "sez who?" Under materialism, there is no objective standard to judge between the moral claim "it is wrong to kill Yitzhak" and the moral claim "it is good to kill Yitzhak." This is what Judge Posner means when he insists that "no moral code can be criticized by appealing to norms that are valid across cultures."[7] Yitzhak has a right to life? Sez who? Who are you to judge another culture that thinks otherwise? "[W]e cannot call another culture 'immoral' unless we add 'by our lights.'"[8] The Final Solution[9] was perfectly legal under the positive law of Germany. Therefore, Yitzhak did not have a right to life, and if Hitler had succeeded "our moral beliefs would probably be different."[10]

Posner assures us that if one's visceral[11] response to another culture's practice is sufficiently intense, one can try to stamp it out but not because it is in any objective sense wrong. He writes, for instance, "Had I been a British colonial official (but with my present values) in nineteenth-century India, I would have outlawed suttee,[12] but because I found it disgusting, not because I found it immoral."[13] It is difficult to imagine a clearer expression of Thrasymachus's dictum[14]—justice is nothing else than the advantage of the stronger.[15]

One suspects that Przybyla did not have such nihilism in mind when she implied that "earthly authority" is the source of our rights, and her remarks were controversial because, as noted, they are directly contrary to the ideas expressed by the founders in the Declaration, which is a decidedly natural law document. In the Declaration, the founders appealed to "the Laws of Nature and of Nature's God," and they made the most famous assertion of natural law in the history of the world:

> We hold these truths to be self-evident, that all men are created equal, that they are endowed by their Creator with certain unalienable Rights, that among these are Life, Liberty and the pursuit of Happiness.

The Declaration derives its logical force from the fundamentally Judeo-Christian idea of the equality of all persons as bearers of God's image (Latin, *imago Dei*). For much of our nation's history, it was almost universally recognized that the American form of government rests on the two self-evident transcendent truths announced in the preamble to the Declaration: (1) All men are created equal; and (2) The Creator has endowed all men with certain rights. Nearly 250 years later, Dennett's universal acid has chewed through that consensus. The overwhelming majority of legal scholars are at least functional materialists. To the denizens of the legal academy and to much of the rest of the legal profession, the Declaration's propositions are not self-evidently true. Indeed, materialists insist they are self-evidently false. If the universe is a closed system of natural causes, there is no room for a creator who creates men with equal moral status and endows them with rights.

Atheist Yuval Noah Harari was remarkably candid about this in his international bestseller *Sapiens: A Brief History of Humankind*. He noted that the American founders imagined a reality governed by universal and immutable principles of justice. "Yet the only place where such universal principles exist is in the fertile imagination of Sapiens, and in the myths they invent and tell one another. These principles have no objective validity."[16] In a particularly brutal passage, Harari continued:

> According to the science of biology, people were not 'created'. They have evolved. And they certainly did not evolve to be 'equal'. The idea of equality is inextricably intertwined with the idea of creation. The Americans got the idea of equality from Christianity, which argues that every person has a divinely created soul, and that all souls are equal before God. However, if we do not believe in the Christian myths about God, creation and souls, what does it mean that all people are 'equal'? Evolution is based on difference, not on equality. Every person carries a somewhat different genetic code, and is exposed from birth to different environmental influences. This leads to the development of different qualities that carry with them different chances of survival. 'Created equal' should therefore be translated into 'evolved differently'. Just as people were never

created, neither, according to the science of biology, is there a 'Creator' who 'endows' them with anything. There is only a blind evolutionary process, devoid of any purpose, leading to the birth of individuals.[17]

According to materialists, human equality and universal rights are as mythological as the Christian superstition upon which they are based. This is not to say that materialists deny the concept of "rights" as such. But it is important to keep in mind that materialists often use the same words the rest of us use while meaning vastly different things. For example, when I say, "the Holocaust was evil," I mean that the Holocaust transgressed the transcendent, unchangeable, objective moral law woven by God into the very warp and woof of the universe. When a materialist says, "the Holocaust was evil," he means that evolution has programmed him to have strong feelings of revulsion towards the Holocaust. Judge Posner assures us that a person's subjective revulsion to Holocausts is in no way superior to a Nazi's subjective preference for Holocausts. Holocausts may not be your cup of tea, but there is no standard by which to say your tea preferences are superior to a national socialist's.

If universal human rights grounded in a transcendent, objective morality do not exist, Posner is surely correct. We can crush our opponents if their actions disgust us, but there is no basis to say those actions are, in any objective sense, immoral. In other words, power is the arbiter of all differences. This is why a materialist can assert contradictory positions regarding rights without a hint of irony. For example, not so long ago, materialists were the great champions of the right to freedom of expression. Now, they try to stifle dissenting speech. For a materialist, this is not a contradiction. Before they gained cultural hegemony, they championed freedom. Now that they have power, they crush their opponents. "When I am weaker than you, I ask you for freedom because that is according to your principles; when I am stronger than you, I take away your freedom because that is according to my principles."[18] Materialists never regarded freedom of expression as a universal principle to be upheld for its own sake. It is a tool to be used in the power game, and when that tool has served its purpose, it is put on the shelf like a wrench after the bolt is tightened. All that matters is to have and wield power.

In the 1920's and '30s, extreme rightwing Nazi Brownshirts attended their opponents' gatherings, shouted them down, and tried to stifle all dissent. In the 2020s, extreme leftwing agitators attend their opponents' gatherings, shout them down, and try to stifle all dissent. The materialist lust for power at the expense of human rights cuts across ideological divides.[19]

What happens when the rulers of a society embrace the full-throated moral nihilism that is an ineluctable logical entailment of materialism? The twentieth century was a blood-drenched examination of that question. The materialist totalitarian governments of Mao,[20] Stalin,[21] and Hitler[22] slaughtered over 100 million people and consigned tens of millions more to the camps, where their bodies were broken and their spirits crushed. To cite just one example among many, Stalin believed the road to his collectivist utopia needed to be paved with the corpses of the kulaks.[23] So, he ordered the implementation of a policy "eliminating the kulaks as a class."[24] Millions died.

How can any sane person command the liquidation of millions of human beings with such breathtaking insouciance? The answer is simple; Stalin took his materialism seriously. Like Yuval Noah Harari, he believed that universal principles of justice and equality do not exist, human rights do not exist, liberty does not exist, and an obligation to respect human dignity does not exist. All of these things are social constructs resulting from entirely contingent physical processes. It should not be surprising that a dictator with absolute power who believed this would not blanch at ordering the death of millions. This is why the aphorism "You can't make an omelet without breaking eggs," is widely attributed to Stalin.[25] In Stalin's materialist worldview, a human and an egg are essentially the same. They are both mere things; thus, breaking the former is no more morally consequential than breaking the latter. Stalin understood all too well the materialist insight into the utter meaninglessness of life, pain, and suffering articulated by Richard Dawkins when he said a wasp's approach to its prey "sounds savagely cruel but . . . nature is not cruel, only pitilessly indifferent. This is one of the hardest lessons for humans to learn. We cannot admit that things might be neither good nor evil, neither cruel nor kind, but simply callous—indifferent to all suffering, lacking all purpose."[26]

I can imagine the howls of indignation the last sentence will provoke in some of my readers. Unfair! Apples and oranges! Stalin killed people. Dawkins was referring to animal suffering. Yes, he was—and that is the point. For decades Dawkins has championed a totalizing materialism that insists there is no ontological daylight between humans and animals, or, as he would say, "humans and other animals." That is, in fact, what he did say in a recent exchange with Konstantin Kisin on the Triggernometry podcast. Kisin asked Dawkins if animals have consciousness, to which Dawkins replied, "we are animals."[27]

I am not suggesting that Dawkins would not be horrified by Stalin's order to liquidate the kulaks. I am certain he believes Stalin was evil. I am also certain he would not be able to reconcile that belief with his often-asserted opinion that evil, in any objective sense, does not exist. Dawkins himself recognizes the incoherence of his views. In that same podcast, the following exchange occurred:[28]

> Kisin: People are taught to think about the world in that way [i.e. that free will does not exist and everything is determined by material forces] and the logical conclusion of their beliefs is that. And yet we don't seem to actually live in that world, psychologically.
>
> Dawkins: No, no, you are quite right, we don't. We may philosophically believe that we are deterministic but yet we behave as though, our whole psychology is geared to the assumption that we're not, and that we and other people are free.

> Kisin: And what do you make of that? Because that's quite a contradiction . . .
>
> Dawkins: I will not answer [that question] and nor will anybody else in a satisfactory way. It's a philosophically difficult problem. . .
>
> Kisin:[29] What I'm saying is, we all live our lives in adherence to a belief that, based on our belief system, is false. Isn't that quite telling?
>
> Dawkins: It is interesting. It's an interesting point. And I find it telling and worrying but it doesn't stop me having a scientific worldview of the rest of the world. . . .

If Dawkins must choose between his materialism (which he calls a "scientific worldview" as if some of the greatest scientists of all time were not theists) and a logically coherent morality, he will choose materialism. Why? Recall our discussion of "fideism," the sort of grit-your-teeth-and-believe belief that is often attributed to religious people. Dawkins proves that atheists can succumb to fideism as well. Kisin presents Dawkins with evidence that is contrary to materialism—no sane person lives their life as if materialism is true; everyone believes they (and other people) are free moral agents and acts accordingly. Dawkins agrees and says it is a "difficult problem" and "worrying," but then blithely dismisses it without even attempting to come to grips with it. Dawkins's faith is strong, so strong in fact that he has said that he would prefer a materialist explanation to life on earth *even if there were no actual evidence in favor of it.*[30]

Nearly 80 years ago in his book, *The Abolition of Man*, C.S. Lewis anticipated the corrosive effect materialism would have on politics in the West. He envisioned a time when materialists (whom he called "Conditioners") would simultaneously recognize no abstract limits on their power and no basis other than their own subjective whims for exercising that power. He wrote, "For the power of Man to make himself what he pleases means, as we have seen, the power of some men to make other men what *they* please.[31] But what motivates the Conditioners? Lewis answered, "The Conditioners . . . must come to be motivated simply by their own pleasure . . . those who stand outside all judgments of value cannot have any ground for preferring one of their own impulses to another except the emotional strength of that impulse."[32]

We are faced with a stark choice. Either the universal moral principles announced in the Declaration are true or they are false. In the long run, we can have freedom under law only if we insist on choosing "true." If the Declaration's principles are false, there is no abstract restraint on the pursuit of raw power. If there is no abstract restraint on the pursuit of power, our politics will continue to degenerate into tribes warring against each other until only the strongest tribe remains. Lewis put it this way:

> Either we are rational spirit obliged for ever to obey the absolute values of the Tao [Lewis's word for the transcendent objective moral code], or else we are mere nature to be kneaded and cut into new shapes for the pleasures of masters who must, by hypothesis, have no motive but their own 'natural' impulses. Only the Tao provides a common human law of action which can over-arch rulers and ruled alike. *A dogmatic belief in objective value is necessary to the very idea of a rule which is not tyranny or an obedience which is not slavery.*[33]

Among all the beliefs, habits, and traditions the universal acid has dissolved, one of its most baleful effects has been eroding our understanding of the foundation of our rights. Before the acid was poured out, we rested assured in the belief that God endowed us with rights and that the government's primary responsibility is to protect those rights. While this is still widely believed by many, the overwhelming majority of our so-called elites—people like Heidi Przybyla—reject the idea as a quaint superstition at best and a dangerous idea held by dangerous religious fanatics at worst. What do they propose as a substitute foundation for our rights? Absolutely nothing. For the materialist, "rights" talk is just so much babbling by clever hairless apes that ultimately has no basis in any valid conception of the real world in which we live. For the materialist, only power and his will to exercise it are real.

4. Lawless Law

In early 2020, the COVID-19 pandemic was tightening its grip on the world, and a palpable sense of panic filled the air. Five years later, it's easy to forget how shocking those initial weeks were and the extraordinary measures that governments at all levels implemented in response to the crisis. Some of those measures were unconstitutional, and before the end of that *annus horribilis*, I would be litigating one of them all the way to the United States Supreme Court.

The story begins in mid-March. I was picking up a few items at Walgreens when my cell phone rang. It was my friend Gino Geraci, pastor of Calvary Chapel of South Denver, a large suburban church with an average weekly attendance of about 1,500.[1] Gino was upset because the State of Colorado had just issued an order limiting public gatherings—including gatherings in churches—to a maximum of ten people. Gino's feelings were understandable; the order effectively shut the doors to his church, and he wanted to know whether the order violated the First Amendment's guarantee of freedom of religion. I have been a litigator for decades, and my response to a client's report of an egregious wrong has often been, "Cry 'Havoc!' and let slip the dogs of war."[2] This time, I made an exception. I surprised even myself when I advised Gino to stand pat. I said Colorado Governor Jared Polis was in an impossible situation. People were panicking in response to a once-in-a-century health crisis of still unknown magnitude. I suggested that we give him the benefit of the doubt, keep our powder dry, and reevaluate in a couple of weeks. Gino reluctantly agreed. In April, Gino and I spoke again, and I gave him the same advice for the same reason.

In May, everything changed. Colorado issued a new public health order that maintained its ban on public gatherings of more than ten people, but this time, it added an exception to the ban for what it called "necessary activities." Necessary activities included grocery stores, marijuana dispensaries, liquor stores, and big box stores. Conspicuously, however, the State did not deem attending church services to be a "necessary activity."[3] Want to get your buzz on? Fine. Want to obey a scriptural command that Christians everywhere have been following for literally thousands of years?[4] No way. It was time to file a constitutional challenge.

I filed the challenge on behalf of High Plains Harvest Church, a tiny church in a small town in Northern Colorado. The day before I filed the case, I asked the pastor to drive to the nearest big box store and take photographs. He went to a Lowe's in Greeley, and when he got there, the parking lot was so crowded that he had to circle a few times to find a place to park. He reported back, and I filed the case. Here is the opening paragraph.

> Today in Colorado it is perfectly legal for hundreds of shoppers to pack themselves cheek by jowl into a Lowes. But if 50 people meet to worship God in a small rural church, they do so at the risk of being fined and imprisoned. Plaintiffs feel as though they have stepped through the looking glass into a world where the right to shop for gardening supplies and home improvement materials is protected by the Constitution, while meeting as a body to worship God corporately has been relegated to the category of unnecessary or even superfluous. Plaintiffs call upon the Court to come to their aid, vindicate their religious liberties under the First Amendment to the United States Constitution, and remedy the surreal state of affairs in which they inexplicably find themselves.

I was confident we would receive swift action from the federal court, and I was correct, but not in the way I anticipated. The court quickly denied the church's request to hold the Colorado health order unconstitutional and refused to enjoin it. I promptly appealed to the Tenth Circuit Court of Appeals, which swiftly upheld the district court's decision.

I was frustrated and depressed and losing hope. The next step in the appellate process involved requesting emergency relief from the Supreme Court, but the church's chances looked bleak. In the summer of 2020, the Supreme Court ruled on two COVID-related cases involving churches in similar circumstances.[5] It denied relief to both churches. Both of those cases were 5–4 decisions, with Chief Justice Roberts joining the liberal justices (Ginsburg, Breyer, Sotomayor, and Kagen) in voting to deny relief and the conservative justices (Thomas, Alito, Gorsuch and Kavanaugh) dissenting. Justice Gorsuch's dissent in the *Calvary Chapel Dayton Valley* case was especially trenchant. In that case, Nevada opened the casinos but kept the churches closed. Justice Gorsuch expressed his extreme frustration in his dissent when he wrote that, "there is no world in which the Constitution permits Nevada to favor Caesars Palace over Calvary Chapel."[6]

Shortly after *Calvary Chapel Dayton Valley* was decided, Ruth Bader Ginsburg died. That changed everything.[7] President Trump nominated Amy Coney Barrett to replace Ginsburg, and her nomination was quickly confirmed. In one of the first cases in which she participated, Barrett supplied the fifth vote to overturn the Court's First Amendment COVID madness. In *Roman Catholic Diocese of Brooklyn v. Cuomo*,[8] the Court held that New York's discrimination against churches in their COVID regulations violated the First Amendment and must be enjoined. Three weeks later, in a 6–3 decision, the Court granted relief to my client as well.[9]

How did we get to a point where five justices of the United States Supreme Court would vote to allow a state to shutter a church while simultaneously allowing nearby casinos to remain open? In *Calvary Chapel Dayton Valley*, it was glaringly obvious that Nevada's regulations violated the church members' rights under the First Amendment's Free Exercise Clause. That did not matter to the five justices in the majority. They valued commerce over religious worship even though the latter is protected by the Constitution and the former is not. The case makes sense only in a legal culture where judges feel free to elevate their policy preferences over the plain text of the Constitution. In this chapter, I will trace the history of how American law came to be dominated by that culture.

Prior to the Revolution, the colonists did not think of themselves primarily as "Americans." They thought of themselves as Englishmen living in America, and English common law was the law of the colonies. After the Revolution, English common law carried over as the law of the states of the new nation,[10] and William Blackstone's *Commentaries* were the preeminent authority on that law.[11] It is difficult to exaggerate Blackstone's influence on early American law. John Marshall, considered by many to be the greatest Chief Justice in our nation's history, read the *Commentaries* four times by the time he turned twenty-seven.[12] As one historian wrote, "In the first century of American independence, the *Commentaries* were not merely an approach to the study of law; for most lawyers they constituted all there was of the law."[13] To this day, the Supreme Court cites Blackstone when it is seeking to understand the state of the law in the early republic.[14]

For Blackstone, all legal matters implicating a moral question must be resolved by reference to natural law principles that God infused into the fabric of the universe at creation.[15] He wrote: "[When God] created man, and endued him with freewill to conduct himself in all parts of life, he laid down certain immutable laws of human nature, whereby that freewill is in some degree regulated and restrained, and gave him also the faculty of reason to discover the purport of those laws."[16] The Declaration of Independence speaks of the "Laws of . . . Nature's God." These are the immutable moral principles laid down by God of which Blackstone spoke.[17]

For both Blackstone and Thomas Jefferson, the essence of the natural law was that "man should pursue his own happiness."[18] The word "happiness" in this context is confusing to the modern ear. It does not mean "bliss" or "a feeling of pleasure." Rather, Blackstone and Jefferson were invoking the Greek concept of *"eudaimonia,"* which means the human flourishing that results from the pursuit of a rightly ordered life.[19] As Professor Robert George has summarized, natural law identifies "principles of right action—moral principles—specifying the first and most general principle of morality, namely, that one should choose and act in ways that are compatible with a will towards integral human fulfillment."[20]

A key idea in natural law theory is that men do not create natural law. Rather, the precepts of natural law have a freestanding existence and are discovered through human reason. This idea informed the founders' view of law when they signed the Declaration of Independence. It continued to predominate when Abraham Lincoln delivered the Gettysburg Address. Indeed, Blackstone's *Commentaries* were the first law books Lincoln purchased,[21] and they had a profound impact on him.[22] A young man asked Lincoln the best way to obtain a thorough knowledge of the law. On September 25, 1860—42 days before he was elected president—Lincoln sent the man a letter advising him to start his law studies by reading Blackstone's *Commentaries* all the way through at least twice.[23]

After he was elected, Lincoln stopped in Philadelphia on his way to Washington for his inauguration. He gave a speech at Independence Hall, and regarding the natural law concepts embraced by the founders in that very building, he said: "I have never had a feeling politically that did not spring from the sentiments embodied in the Declaration of Independence."[24] In a foreshadowing of events to come, Lincoln said that he would "rather be assassinated on this spot than surrender" the natural law principle of equal liberty for all people embodied in the Declaration.[25]

The natural law conception of the law as *discovered* rather than *created* prevailed for well over 100 years after the founding, only to collapse completely by the end of the nineteenth century, largely due to the enormous impact of a single man, Oliver Wendell Holmes, Jr. In 1897, the *Harvard Law Review* published an article by Holmes entitled "The Path of the Law,"[26] which for good reason has been called "the single most important essay ever written by an American on the law."[27] The essay was monumentally important because it was the door through which metaphysical materialism entered and ultimately came to dominate American law. As we shall see, Holmes was a committed materialist and a moral nihilist. As he candidly acknowledged, he came "devilish near to believing that might makes right,"[28] which is why he has aptly been called "the American Nietzsche."[29]

As the conduit through which the universal acid was poured onto American law,[30] Holmes was the most influential figure in American jurisprudence in the last 150 years. Therefore, we will pause to examine his influences and philosophy. As a young man, Holmes was conventionally religious and concerned with great questions of right and wrong and the relations of man to God.[31] In college, he was a strong supporter of the abolitionist cause, so much so that he left school early to join the Union Army in 1861. Holmes's experiences during the war, in which he was wounded in the battles of Ball's Bluff, Antietam, and Chancellorsville, radically changed his outlook.[32] The war transformed Holmes from an idealistic moral crusader into a bitter pessimist who viewed all of life as an amoral Darwinian struggle.

Contrary to popular belief, Darwin did not coin the phrase "survival of the fittest." The phrase was coined by Darwin's disciple Herbert Spencer.[33] Holmes said of Spencer's work: "I doubt if any writer of English except Darwin has done so much to affect our whole way of thinking about the universe."[34] Certainly, Spencer and Darwin had a profound impact on Holmes. In an article published in 1873, Holmes applied Spencer's phrase when summarizing his philosophy of law:

> The struggle for life, undoubtedly, is constantly putting the interests of men at variance with those of the lower animals. And the struggle does not stop in the ascending scale with the monkeys, but is equally

the law of human existence. . . . [W]hatever body may possess the supreme power for the moment is certain to have interests inconsistent with others which have competed unsuccessfully. *The more powerful interests must be more or less reflected in legislation; which, like every other device of man or beast, must tend in the long run to aid the survival of the fittest.*[35]

Holmes did not shrink from the moral nihilism that followed logically from his metaphysical commitments. His biographer, Grant Gilmore, wrote that Holmes "was savage, harsh, and cruel, a bitter and lifelong pessimist who saw in the course of human life nothing but a continuing struggle in which the rich and powerful impose their will on the poor and weak."[36] Holmes's materialism was absolute. In a letter to a friend, he wrote, "I see no reason for attributing to a man a significance different in kind from that which belongs to a baboon or to a grain of sand."[37] To another friend he wrote, "[M]y bet is that we have not the kind of cosmic importance that the parsons and philosophers teach. I doubt if a shudder would go through the spheres if the whole ant heap were kerosened."[38] Following Darwin, Holmes saw no discontinuity between humans and the lower animals: "I regard [man] as I do the other species . . . having for his main business to live and propagate, and for his main interest food and sex."[39]

Like all dogmatic materialists, Holmes believed that truth and morality are completely subjective:

[O]ne's own moral and aesthetic preferences . . . [are] more or less arbitrary, although none the less dogmatic on that account. Do you like sugar in your coffee or don't you?[40]

As I probably have said many times before, all I mean by truth is what I can't help believing—I don't know why I should assume except for practical purposes of conduct that [my "can't help"] has more cosmic worth than any others—I can't help preferring port to ditch-water, but I see no ground for supposing that the cosmos shares my weakness.[41]

With Nietzsche,[42] Holmes believed that all human relations are based on power and nothing else:

> You respect the rights of man—I don't, except those things a given crowd will fight for.[43]
>
> [A]ll law means I will kill you if necessary to make you conform to my requirements.[44]
>
> [W]hen men differ in taste as to the kind of world they want the only thing to do is to go to work killing.[45]
>
> I don't see why we mightn't as well invert the Christian saying and hate the sinner but not the sin. Hate. . . imports no judgment. Disgust is ultimate and therefore as irrational as reason itself—a dogmatic datum. The world has produced the rattlesnake as well as me; but I kill it if I get a chance, as also mosquitos, cockroaches, murderers, and flies. My only judgment is that they are incongruous with the world I want; the kind of world we all try to make according to our power.[46]
>
> Pleasures are ultimates and in cases of difference between oneself and another there is nothing to do except in unimportant matters to think ill of him and in important ones to kill him.[47]

Holmes disdained abstract moral theories, which he called "isms" (as in pacif*ism*). In a letter to Harold Laski he said, "All 'isms' seem to me silly—but this hyper aethereal respect for human life seems perhaps the silliest of all."[48] Holmes's callous attitude toward human life fit hand in glove with his passion for eugenics, a passion so brutal that he favored killing babies who did not measure up to his standards for an improved human race. In a law review article republished in the 1920 edition of his *Collected Legal Papers*, Homes wrote:

> I believe that the wholesale social regeneration which so many now seem to expect, if it can be helped by conscious, co-ordinated human effort, cannot be affected appreciably by tinkering with the

institution of property, *but only by taking in hand life and trying to build a race. That would be my starting point for an ideal for the law.*[49]

Professor Francis Philbrick reviewed the Collected Legal Papers and apparently did not believe Holmes was to be taken literally in this passage. But in a letter to Felix Frankfurter, Holmes expressed irritation with Professor Philbrick and doubled down:

> [Philbrick] says, "whatever that may mean" when I say that I don't think you can do much by tinkering with property without taking in hand life. I meant what I suppose he would think horrible—restricting propagation by the undesirables and putting to death infants that didn't pass the examination, etc. etc.[50]

A few years later, the State of Virginia ordered the sterilization of Carrie Buck, whom it deemed "feeble-minded." Unsurprisingly, Holmes approved of Virginia's eugenics project, and in his most infamous opinion, he wrote:

> It is better for all the world, if instead of waiting to execute degenerate offspring for crime, or to let them starve for their imbecility, society can prevent those who are manifestly unfit from continuing their kind. . . . Three generations of imbeciles are enough.[51]

Ten days after he delivered this opinion, Holmes wrote to Laski about the case. Echoing his earlier article, he said, "I wrote and delivered a decision upholding the constitutionality of a state law for sterilizing imbeciles the other day—and felt that I was getting near to the first principle of real reform."[52] In the years following *Buck v. Bell*, forced sterilizations exploded as the eugenics craze reached its apex. By 1940, thirty states had enacted sterilization statutes, and over 18,500 people were forcibly sterilized before the craze fizzled out.[53]

In law school, I was taught to venerate Holmes above all other Supreme Court justices. He was the great liberator of the law from the superstition of natural law and the rigidity of legal formalism.[54]

In "The Path of the Law," Holmes rejected the connection between morality and law. He wrote:

> For my own part, I often doubt whether it would not be a gain if every word of moral significance could be banished from the law altogether, and other words adopted which should convey legal ideas uncolored by anything outside the law. We should lose the fossil records of a good deal of history and the majesty got from ethical associations, but by ridding ourselves of an unnecessary confusion we should gain very much in the clearness of our thought.[55]

The "unnecessary confusion" to which Holmes was referring is the confusion that comes from thinking that "morality" means anything. As a committed materialist, Holmes believed that morality is purely subjective. He said as much in his article: "No one will deny that wrong statutes can be and are enforced, and we should not all agree as to which were the wrong ones."[56] Force is the only thing that is real, in his view, which is why he argued that law should always be viewed from the perspective of the "bad man" who cares nothing for moral rules:

> You can see very plainly that a bad man has as much reason as a good one for wishing to avoid an encounter with the public force, and therefore you can see the practical importance of the distinction between morality and law. A man who cares nothing for an ethical rule which is believed and practised by his neighbors is likely nevertheless to care a good deal to avoid being made to pay money, and will want to keep out of jail if he can.[57]

A good man honors the promise he makes in a contract because he believes it is his moral obligation to do so. However, for Holmes, the duty to keep a contract "means a prediction that you must pay damages if you do not keep it—and nothing else."[58] When I got to law school 88 years later, Holmes's amoral view of contracts had morphed into "efficient breach" theory, which holds that breaking a contractual promise is an affirmatively desirable thing if doing so is economically "efficient."

Before Holmes, legal principles were inseparably linked with moral principles. Holmes poured the universal acid on that link and dissolved it completely. Nowhere is this more evident than in the rise of the so-called "living constitution"—the view that the meaning of the Constitution is not fixed but instead "evolves" to keep up with the needs of society.[59] The idea of a "living constitution" has always seemed absurd to me. The founders did not use an enchanted pen to write the Constitution with magical shape-shifting words. They used an ordinary pen to write ordinary words, and the people who voted to ratify the Constitution understood those words to have a particular meaning. The whole point of a legal document—whether a constitution, a statute, or even a simple contract—is to capture the parties' intention in writing at a particular time. No one would sign a contract if they were told the words in the document might mean something radically different tomorrow than they mean today. Yet living constitution advocates say the American people did something very much like that when they ratified the Constitution. But if a judge can say the Constitution has "evolved" to mean anything he wants it to mean, are we not being ruled by that judge instead of the Constitution he pretends to be interpreting?

The idea that the words in the Constitution do not have a fixed meaning reminds me of Alice's conversation with Humpty Dumpty in *Through the Looking Glass*.[60] Alice says she likes birthday presents, but Humpty Dumpty argues that un-birthday presents are better because a person has more un-birthdays than birthdays. Humpty tops his argument off by exclaiming, "There's glory for you!" Alice has no idea what to make of that and replies:

"I don't know what you mean by 'glory.'"

Humpty Dumpty smiled contemptuously. "Of course you don't—till I tell you. I meant 'there's a nice knock-down argument for you!'"

"But 'glory' doesn't mean 'a nice knock-down argument,'" Alice objected.

> "When *I* use a word," Humpty Dumpty said in rather a scornful tone, "it means just what I choose it to mean—neither more nor less."
>
> "The question is," said Alice, "whether you *can* make words mean so many different things."
>
> "The question is," said Humpty Dumpty, "which is to be master—that's all."

Living constitution[61] judges are the Humpty Dumptys of the legal world. They ask themselves, which is to be master, the text of the Constitution or the judge interpreting it? *Grutter v. Bollinger*[62] is one of many cases illustrating this. In *Grutter*, applicants to a school were discriminated against based on their race, and they sued to overturn the school's racially discriminatory admissions policy. Any reasonably intelligent eighth grader can read the Equal Protection Clause of the Fourteenth Amendment and understand that it plainly prohibits racial discrimination. And even the most cursory examination of the clause's history reveals that prohibiting racial discrimination was its overriding purpose. Nevertheless, in *Grutter*, Justice O'Connor, writing for the majority, upheld the challenged racially discriminatory admissions policy. Stripped of its pretensions, *Grutter* stands for the proposition that racial discrimination is prohibited by the Equal Protection clause unless the discrimination is of a type fashionable among coastal elites.[63] When Justice O'Connor used a word, it meant just what she chose for it to mean—neither more nor less. In *Grutter*, she chose "equal protection" to mean "racial discrimination permitted." There's glory for you.

Racial discrimination is prohibited in the United States only if the government fails to convince five members of the Supreme Court it is a good idea. Am I too cynical? If I am, so was my constitutional law professor, who told us that all we needed to know about constitutional law was how to count to five. Indeed, the "count to five" rule is the only rule of constitutional law for Humpty Dumpty justices, and some of them admit this openly. Justice William Brennan once told

Nat Hentoff that he summarized constitutional law for his new clerks by wiggling five fingers and saying, "Five votes can do anything around here."[64]

The Constitution is a compact between the American people and their government, and a scene from *The Empire Strikes Back* is an apt analogy to Justice Brennan's "count to five" rule. Lando Calrissian agrees with Darth Vader to betray Han Solo in exchange for Vader's commitment to leave Leia and Chewbacca in Cloud City when he departs. Lando upholds his end of the bargain, but Vader takes Leia and Chewbacca anyway. As Vader is leaving, Lando protests that was not their deal. Vader turns and replies: "I am altering the deal. Pray I don't alter it any further."

Justice Brennan and his living constitution colleagues are able to get away with this because federal judges are given life tenure to insulate them from accountability to the people. If it were otherwise, the Supreme Court could not protect constitutional minorities[65] from majorities because it could not even protect itself from those same majorities. For example, *West Virginia Board of Education v. Barnett*[66] involved a law that required citizens to pledge allegiance to orthodox political views.[67] The Supreme Court struck the law down because it violated the First Amendment's guarantee of free speech. The government may not compel speech that violates a citizen's conscience.[68] But, if judges were accountable to the people in elections, the majorities who passed the unconstitutional law could also throw out the judges who struck it down.[69]

A problem with this system is immediately apparent. It is an ancient problem that Juvenal famously captured nearly two thousand years ago with the phrase *Quis custodiet ipsos custodes*—Who will guard the guardians themselves?[70] What is the answer to Juvenal's question? Who guards us from the guardians of our constitutional liberties? Robert Bork supplied the answer:

> [T]here is a historical Constitution that was understood by those who enacted it to have a meaning of its own. That intended meaning

has an existence independent of anything judges may say. It is that meaning the judges ought to utter. If law is more than naked power, it is that meaning the Justices had a *moral* duty to pronounce.[71]

The answer is that judges have a *moral* duty to guard themselves. This answer is far from satisfying. It is another way of saying, "No one guards the guardians; we are at their mercy." Every judge takes an oath to uphold the Constitution,[72] and the only thing that protects us when a judge is exercising his awesome power to defy democratically elected majorities is that judge's allegiance to his oath.[73] Every time a judge succumbs to the temptation to impose his political views on the American people under the guise of interpreting the Constitution, he has broken that oath. Whether to resist that temptation is ultimately a moral choice each judge makes in every case.[74]

Thus, the judicial usurpation of power that is the essence of the living constitution project is fundamentally a moral issue. That is why the damage done to American law by the universal acid has been so catastrophic. For a materialistic judge, the Constitution is just a piece of paper with scratchings made on it by clever, hairless apes.[75] Words on paper mean nothing to materialists, as the constitution of the Soviet Union illustrates perfectly. The Soviet constitution was, in theory, much better than the American constitution. But in the face of a relentlessly materialist governing structure, those guarantees were meaningless. In testimony before the Senate Judiciary Committee, Justice Scalia said:

> The bill of rights of the former evil empire, the Union of Soviet Socialist Republics, was much better than ours. I mean that literally. It was much better. We guarantee freedom of speech and of the press. Big deal. They guaranteed freedom of speech, of the press, of street demonstrations and protests, and anyone who is caught trying to suppress criticism of the government will be called to account. Whoa, that is wonderful stuff. Of course, they were just words on paper, what our Framers would have called "a parchment guarantee."[76]

The difference between a living constitution judge and a communist dictator is one of degree. The judge balances the hairless apes' scratchings against his own will to power. Should he allow those scratchings to prevent him from imposing his policy preferences on the nation? The scratchings never stand a chance. It does no good to remind him that he has a moral duty to a free people to uphold the democratic integrity of law. Holmes taught him that morality is not real. Only power is real, and so long as he can convince four of his colleagues to go along with him, he has the power. William Brennan recognized only one limit to his power: what he could convince four of his colleagues to go along with.

Unsurprisingly, Judge Posner regards Holmes as "the most illustrious figure in the history of American law."[77] And when he retired from the bench and no longer felt the need to keep his naked will to power under wraps, Posner revealed all in an "exit interview" with the *New York Times*:

> "I pay very little attention to legal rules, statutes, constitutional provisions," Judge Posner said. "A case is just a dispute. The first thing you do is ask yourself—forget about the law—what is a sensible resolution of this dispute?" The next thing, he said, was to see if a recent Supreme Court precedent or some other legal obstacle stood in the way of ruling in favor of that sensible resolution. "And the answer is that's actually rarely the case," he said. "When you have a Supreme Court case or something similar, they're often extremely easy to get around."[78]

Posner asks himself, "What is a sensible resolution of this dispute?" Sensible to whom? To Richard Posner, of course. Posner's resolution would certainly not seem sensible to the justices who wrote the Supreme Court case that he had "to get around." That is of no consequence to Posner. He has the power.[79]

More than two centuries after the Constitution went into effect, it is easy to lose sight of the fact that in 1789 the idea of governing a nation through a binding written constitution was revolutionary. In *Marbury v. Madison*, the great Chief Justice John Marshall referred to the constitution as our "greatest improvement on political institutions,"[80] and the theory of judicial review that he announced in that case was entirely premised on the fact that the Constitution is a *text* that binds both Congress and the judges who review the laws enacted by Congress. He wrote that when a law enacted by Congress conflicts with the constitutional text, a judge reviewing the law has a duty to give precedence to the latter and declare the law invalid.

The fact that the Constitution is a written text, and that text binds a judge, is the *sole* justification for that judge's power to declare a challenged law unconstitutional. It follows that for judicial review to be legitimate, judges must consider themselves bound by that text. The text both justifies and constrains judicial review. Of course, Justice Marshall's elegant theory of judicial review is completely nullified when judges throw off that constraint. Such judges—judges like Richard Posner—want to retain judicial review while simultaneously jettisoning the sole justification for it. For judges like Posner, law is about the exercise of "raw judicial power."[81] This is an affront to a free people.

5. You're Gonna Have to Serve Somebody

You're gonna have to serve somebody
Well, it may be the devil or it may be the Lord
But you're gonna have to serve somebody[1]

Several years ago, while traveling on a humanitarian mission to North Korea,[2] I had a brief but memorable exchange with a North Korean border guard. It was a hot summer day. The border station had no air conditioning, but several fans were blowing. I noticed something peculiar about one of the fans. It was pointed at a wall adorned with a larger-than-life painting of Kim Il Sung and Kim Jong Il.[3] Through our translator, I asked one of the border guards why they had a fan blowing air on the wall. He replied, "We must keep Great Leader and Dear Leader cool."[4] North Korea is probably the most militantly atheist country in the history of the world. People have been executed there for distributing Bibles.[5] Yet, like a Byzantine monk genuflecting before an icon of the Virgin Mary, this man was venerating an image of his semi-deified leaders.

There is a saying widely attributed to G.K. Chesterton: "When men stop believing in God, they don't believe in nothing; they believe in anything."[6] Bob Dylan was onto something. People have a deep longing to serve something greater than themselves, and if that something is not God, they will find a substitute. Richard Dawkins provides an example of Dylan's maxim in operation. Dawkins does not deny that the longing to serve a greater good exists, though he would undoubtedly argue that the object of the longing is an illusion, and when we feel it, we are merely dancing to the tune called by our DNA.[7] Still, isn't it ironic that a man who claims that in the universe there is "no evil and no good" is one of the world's most prolific, scolding moralists, constantly berating those who do not conform to his conception of how they should behave?[8] Dawkins has a vision for the greater good of mankind, and he has devoted his life to serving that vision.

Dawkins is also a great example of why the impulse to serve a greater good devolves into irrationality when it is unmoored from objective truth. In 1996, the American Humanist Association bestowed its "Humanist of the Year" award on Dawkins. In 2021, the AHA[9] revoked the award after he suggested that a "trans woman" (i.e., a man suffering from gender dysphoria who declares he is a woman) is not actually a woman. The leaders of the secular religion that canonized Dawkins revoked his sainthood, declared his message to be anathema, and excommunicated him as a penalty for his sins.[10]

Humanism, like all of the other "isms" is religious in nature. It is a God substitute. This is true even of militantly atheistic "isms" such as Marxism. Russian intellectual Nicolas Berdyaev wrote that Marxism is a messianic doctrine of deliverance into a future perfect society in which man will no longer depend on economics.[11] It even has a chosen people, the proletariat.[12] In our day, climate activism comes with all of the trappings of religion: a priestly class (climate experts), sin (capitalism), penances (recycling, driving an electric car), indulgences (carbon credits), and infidels (so-called "deniers" who must be discredited, shamed, and silenced).[13]

All secular religion substitutes have a common fatal flaw, which John Daniel Davidson identified in his masterful *Pagan America*. Western civilization was built on a foundation of Christian ethics, and all secular "isms" are parasitical on that ethical vision. As such, they rely on a source of vitality that does not originate from them and that they cannot replenish.[14] Davidson predicts that in the absence of Christian faith, we will revert to an older form of civilization, one in which power alone matters and the weak and the vulnerable count for nothing.[15] Ethical standards taken for granted for so long in the West, such as human rights, equality, care for the poor, mercy for the condemned, refuge for the persecuted, and charity for the marginalized and downtrodden are "unmistakably Christian ideas that rely on specifically Christian doctrines, without which they are unintelligible."[16] As we saw in chapter three, atheist Yuval Noah Harari agrees that the universal human rights we take for granted in the West derive their force from Christian doctrine and are incomprehensible under a secular materialist worldview.[17] Davidson asks a profound question. What happens when the Christian foundation upon which our society is built is undermined?

> Once the faith on which Western ideals rely fades away, the ideals themselves will dissipate as well. There is no neutral, secular, universal moral code that prohibits the strong from oppressing the weak, prevents the casual use of vulnerable people as sex objects by the powerful, or halts the administrative state's entropic descent into tyranny. Only Christian morality can stop these things. The Christian faith is the only thing that has ever stopped them, anywhere in the world, among any people. Without Christianity, the West will become something else, quite different than what it has been for the past sixteen centuries and quite unrecognizable compared to what it was even a few decades ago. This transformation will not take centuries or generations. It is happening now, all around us, and it is gaining momentum as Christianity falls into desuetude across the West.[18]

Secular ethical systems all fail because, by definition, their conception of morality must always be determined by subjective preferences, not objective reality. Secular ethical theorists try to dress this up with talk of "maximizing the satisfaction of preferences" or promoting the greatest happiness for the greatest number. But, as Edward Feser points out, the systems can never provide a non-arbitrary reason why anyone should care about the happiness or preference satisfaction of the greatest number—as opposed to his own or his tribe's.[19] "'Morality' becomes at best an assertion of the prevailing (and in principle ever-shifting) sensibilities of the majority, or at least of those with the loudest mouths. It has no ultimate basis in objective fact or in reason, but only in sentiment and existing custom."[20]

Because they are not tethered to objective truth, secular ethical systems have no way of answering this vital question: "Should some acts be intrinsically unthinkable, no matter how much overall happiness is derived from them?" For example, suppose there is a city with 1,000 residents, and 975 of them would be enormously happy if the remaining 25 were forced to serve them as slaves. Does maximizing the happiness for the greatest number make enslaving those 25 people good? Some readers might think that is an outrageous example. Slavery has been abolished; there is no need to worry that it might make a comeback. Yes, Christian abolitionists motivated by Christian morality abolished slavery in Christian nations. But anyone who has read the *Gulag Archipelago* knows that slavery was alive and well in Russia within living memory. And anyone who reads the headlines knows there are enslaved Uyghurs in China at this very moment.[21] The fact that there is near-universal abhorrence of slavery among twenty-first century Americans creates an illusion that secular moral systems produce objective morality. As Feser points out, this illusion is at the bottom of all secular ethical systems:

> Certain values tend to be widespread, and this generates the illusion that morality is objective, but of course, the fact that an illusion is widespread does not make it any less an illusion. And if those values should for whatever reason become less widespread, then all we can say is that what we count as morality has changed. It has not moved either farther away from what is objectively good or closer to it, for there is no such thing as objective goodness. The now-widespread horror of slavery cannot on this view be counted a moral advance . . . And should most people sincerely come to believe that it would be good to kill unwanted infants, or unwanted toddlers or teenagers, or unwanted old or sick people, or unwanted anyone for that matter—Jews, blacks, Catholics, Muslims, whomever—then

that too, on this view, would simply be a different set of subjective moral evaluations, objectively neither better nor worse than any other.[22]

Infanticide was a common practice in the pre-Christian world. Fast forward several centuries, and the practice of killing babies had all but ended. What changed? Well, it certainly was not the widespread adoption of John Stuart Mill's utilitarian ethics. After all, the pagans were *implementing* utilitarian ethics. Being rid of unwanted babies maximized their happiness, so that is what they did. Too bad for the baby. As Davidson explains, the brutal practice of exposing babies did not change until Christian ethics began to infuse ancient cultures:

> What our secular society today considers to be "universal human rights" are in fact based entirely on Christian moral precepts that are universal only insofar as Christianity is a universal faith, intended for all people in all places. But the moral precepts themselves are uniquely Christian, and chief among them is perhaps the doctrine of *Imago Dei*, the foundational belief that every human being is created in the image and likeness of God and therefore not only possesses inherent dignity and worth but also has the capacity, through human reason and free will, to know and love God, to be transformed by God's grace, and to participate in the divine life.[23]

The Christian doctrine of *imago Dei* would not only undermine the pagan practice of infanticide; it would also elevate the status of women from little more than property to humans with inherent dignity and value. And in the fullness of time, it would become the philosophical core of the American experiment in government of the people, by the people, and for the people.

Eric Harris was not a madman.[24] He was not out of touch with reality. He knew exactly what he was doing and understood that most people would say he was evil. He simply didn't care because he did not believe in the concept of evil. As mentioned earlier, he took his materialism very seriously, and under materialism, it was no more objectively evil for Harris to kill his classmates than it is for a lion to kill a gazelle. A human is just another kind of animal, after all, and Harris's classmates had the same inherent dignity as a gazelle, which is to say, none whatsoever. Fortunately, the overwhelming majority of materialists do not take their materialism as seriously as Harris did.[25] It is one of the great ironies of the modern age that materialists live their everyday lives as if their most deeply held metaphysical beliefs are false. Recall the exchange between Konstantin Kisin and Richard Dawkins that I quoted earlier in which Dawkins admitted this.[26] Nevertheless, the fact that most materialists are not homicidal monsters does not mean that the widespread rejection of objective moral truth will not have dire consequences for our culture.

The Bible says, "Where there is no vision, the people cast off restraint."[27] When people reject the transcendent moral order grounded in God's being, they lose their moral and spiritual compass, and society descends into moral chaos. For a long time, it has been fashionable among Western elites to assert that morality grounded in objective truth is a myth. What happens when that view spreads more broadly? Common sense suggests that Feser is right when he says that "if this attitude were ever to prevail in society at large, the result could not fail to be a widespread corruption of the moral sensibility."[28]

That is exactly what is happening in America. Nearly 2,000 years of moral progress based on the Christian idea of *imago Dei* is unraveling before our eyes in a riot of moral chaos. Perhaps most alarming is that we find ourselves rapidly sliding down the slippery slope toward the normalization of killing people, especially babies and the elderly. Internationally renowned Princeton "bioethicist"[29] Peter Singer has been advocating killing "defective" babies for many years.[30] One wonders what Singer would say about Derick Hall, who was born at twenty-three weeks' gestation with no heartbeat and a bleeding brain. He was placed on life support for a week, after which doctors told his mother that he would remain in a vegetative state for the rest of his inevitably short life.[31] Singer says his mother had the right to kill him. But if she had, he would not have survived to one day be drafted into the NFL by the Seattle Seahawks. Don't get me wrong.

Even babies who have no chance to ever play in the NFL should not be murdered.[32] My point is that when Singer says that certain babies are "life unworthy of life," his argument is indistinguishable from a Nazi who muttered *Lebensunwertes Leben* ["life unworthy of life"] as he turned the valve to release the gas. He is an evil man.

Attitudes toward abortion are becoming ever more radical. Recently, Bill Maher made headlines when he said:

> I scold the left when they say "Oh, you know what? They just hate women, people who aren't prochoice . . ." They don't hate women. They just made that up. They think it's murder. And it kind of is. I'm just OK with that. I am. I mean there's eight billion people in the world. I'm sorry, we won't miss you. That's my position on that.[33]

In the 2024 debate between President Trump and Vice-President Harris, the moderator asked Harris: "Would you support any restrictions on a woman's right to an abortion?"[34] Harris refused to name a single restriction she would support. Later, the following exchange occurred:[35]

> Trump: You should ask, "Will she allow abortion in the eighth month, ninth month, seventh month?"
>
> Harris: Come on.
>
> Trump: OK. Would you do that?

Harris refused to respond to the question, which, of course, is answer enough. In a breathtakingly short amount of time, we have gone from Bill Clinton's "safe, legal and rare," to Kamala Harris's refusal to limit abortion in any way up to the moment of birth. That is the law in six states (Alaska, Oregon, Colorado, New Mexico, New Jersey, and Vermont)[36] where a perfectly healthy baby can be legally killed the day before it is born. Those states have all but legalized infanticide.

Unplanned and difficult pregnancies are frightening and disrupt your life plans. I get it. In 1985, I was working part-time while carrying a full course load in law school. One day, my wife called me at work from her OB/GYN's office and told me she was pregnant. I said "Oh, that's great!" I did not really feel like it was great. We were just barely hanging on financially. We had no insurance and had to take out a student loan to pay the doctor bills. But we buckled down and resolved to make the best of it. A few months later, I got another call at work. My wife was calling from her OB/GYN's office again, but this time, she couldn't stop crying. I couldn't get her to tell me what was wrong; she just wanted me to drop whatever I was doing and come to her. I rushed to the doctor's office, and when I arrived, I received a shock. The doctor explained that a prenatal test had come back, and it was very bad news: our baby was almost certainly going to be born with a severe mental defect and would never live a normal life. The doctor said he could run more tests, but there wasn't much hope, and we needed to consider "terminating."

If you had asked me before that time, I would have said I was pro-life, but I had never really given the abortion issue much serious thought. Now, it was staring us in the face. What would we do if the additional tests confirmed the diagnosis? Over the next several days, while we waited for the tests to come back, I thought of little else. One day, I was mowing the lawn. I turned the matter over and over in my mind as I pushed the mower back and forth. In a moment of startling clarity, the answer came to me. I turned off the mower and went inside to talk to my wife. Not knowing how she would react to what I was about to say, I said, "The law says this is your decision, but here's what I think: We are not God. We don't get to decide who lives and who dies. I want you to know that I will be OK whatever happens with the baby. We get what we get, and even if the baby isn't normal, we can still love it and take care of it." She did not push back. Her reply was very simple. She said, "I know. That's what we are going to do." The rest of the story is that the additional tests came back negative, and a few months later we received a healthy happy baby. Decades later, my daughter is one of the most intelligent and beautiful women I know.

A few years ago, the actress Michelle Williams won a Golden Globe award. To the raucous applause of the Hollywood elites in the audience, Williams turned her acceptance speech into an abortion get-out-the-vote rally. She said, "I'm grateful for the acknowledgment of the choices I've made, and I'm also grateful to have lived at a moment in our society where choice exists . . . I wouldn't have been able to do this without employing a woman's right to choose, to choose when to have my children and with whom."[37] Ms. Williams is a true disciple of John Stuart Mill. She did not try to justify killing her baby as a tragic necessity. No, killing the baby allowed her to "maximize her happiness," and for that reason it was an affirmatively good thing to do. Shout your abortion! (and don't forget to vote). In a just society, some tradeoffs must be unthinkable. Trading an increase in happiness for another human's life is one of them. I admit that when I was grappling with the issue, that tradeoff was not unthinkable. I grew up in a culture that had conditioned me to consider such options, and consider them I did. If I had been a better man, I would have resisted that cultural conditioning more readily.

If anything, Davidson understated his case in *Pagan America*. As we have seen, if God does not exist—if the universe consists solely of matter and energy in space/time—it is a cold, hard fact that William Provine was correct: No inherent moral laws exist, and there is no ultimate meaning in life. Davidson's thesis (and thus the title of his book) is that as the West abandons Christianity, it is inevitable that pre-Christian pagan morality (or, more accurately, amorality), which is fundamentally based on power dynamics and the radical autonomous self, will move in to take its place. The postmodern moral vision is a mixture of ecological radicalism, the embrace of sexual deviancy, and racist and sexist identity politics.[38] These aspects of postmodern morality are already being forced upon us through insults and cancel culture in private life, as well as through laws, public policy, and funding decisions in the public sphere. They are constantly reinforced by the institutions controlled by the cultural elite: global corporations, the medical and educational establishments, Hollywood, Big Tech, the corporate media, and the political class.[39]

The very survival of our civilization depends on reversing course and returning to Christianity. That said, I urge you to believe in the claims of Christ because those claims are true, not because Christianity is useful in saving our civilization. As I will discuss in chapter eight, Jordon Peterson has an instrumentalist[40] approach to Christianity. He does not believe the claims of historical Christianity are true. Yet, like Davidson, he recognizes that our civilization is sliding into moral chaos, and Christianity is almost certainly the only way to arrest that slide. Therefore, for Peterson, the widespread adoption of a life informed by Christianity is useful in heading off civilizational collapse, even though he believes those claims are false. Thus, Peterson's solution, which he outlines in his book *We Who Wrestle With God*, is that everyone should act as if Christianity were true even though he personally does not believe it is.

I do not have an instrumentalist approach to Christianity. In fact, my approach is affirmatively anti-instrumentalist. I agree with C.S. Lewis, who wrote: "Christianity is a statement which, if false, is of *no* importance, and, if true, of infinite importance. The one thing it cannot be is moderately important."[41] The point of this book is to urge readers to adopt Christianity because it is *true*, not because it is useful. Thus, in the next chapter, I will set forth reasons why the evidence for God's existence and the truth of Christianity is overwhelming. In the chapter after that, I will respond to many of the objections that are raised against these beliefs. I invite my readers to evaluate the evidence, both pro and con, and make up their minds. A fair hearing is all I ask.

Blaise Pascal famously said that each person must make a wager on one of two outcomes: God exists or he does not exist.[42] Choosing not to wager isn't an option because even if a person does not wager, it remains the case that God either does or does not exist. Therefore, refusing to wager is a tacit bet on "does not exist." Pascal argued that the only rational wager is to bet on God's existence. If you bet on God and lose, you have not lost much. Your body goes into the ground, and you cease to exist. But if you bet on God and win, you have gained everything (eternal blessing in heaven). On the other side of the bet, if you wager that God does not exist and win, you win nothing at all (you still go into the ground), and if you wager against God and lose, you lose everything (through eternal separation from God).

Pascal's Wager is not a formal argument for the existence of God. It is a call to approach the question with the utmost seriousness, as literally everything hinges on making the right choice. Pascal understood that a person cannot force himself to believe what he does not believe. He knew some would respond to his wager with a plea of, "I cannot believe . . . . What, then, would you have me do?"[43] Surprisingly, his answer was not that the person should try to find more and more proofs for the existence of God. There is already enough evidence for any reasonable person. Evidence is not the issue. Instead, "passion" (a word Pascal uses for deep-set bias) is the problem. Thus, Pascal's answer to the plea was, "Endeavour, then, to convince yourself, not by increase of proofs of God, but by the abatement of your passions." Pascal was convinced that the key to overcoming unbelief is for a person to realize that their unbelief stems from bias rather than from a lack of evidence. Therefore, they should strive to overcome that bias so they can evaluate the evidence fairly.

America, as has often been said, is a shining light on a hill. It is the last and greatest hope for justice and peace in the world. If you have not noticed that light dimming, at first slightly and now drastically, you have not been paying attention. There is good reason to believe that the light may soon be snuffed out altogether. How did this happen? Solzhenitsyn asked a similar question when he surveyed the destruction that had befallen his beloved Russia. His answer:

> If I were asked today to formulate as concisely as possible the main cause of the ruinous Revolution that swallowed up some 60 million

of our people, I could not put it more accurately than to repeat: "Men have forgotten God; that's why all this has happened."[44]

If we have any hope of turning things around, Americans must "unforget God." In a way, Pascal's Wager is the same as he envisioned it 360 years ago when he jotted down his *Pensées*. But the wager applies to us in a way that Pascal never envisioned because he lived in an era where Christian morality was widely taken for granted. Christianity is not merely instrumental. It is, however, true that returning to our Christian roots is the best chance for our survival as a civilization. Like Pascal, I acknowledge that no one can simply choose to believe something they currently do not believe just because believing it would help preserve our way of life. Nevertheless, the high stakes involved can motivate a person to confront their biases and then study, reflect on, and consider the evidence fairly. If this is true at the level of the individual soul, as Pascal believed, it is even more true at the level of a civilization. We are faced with the same wager. But now the stakes are infinitely higher.

I will end this chapter as I started it, quoting Bob Dylan. "You're gonna have to serve somebody." We all know there is a greater good and that our highest calling is to serve that good. Denying the deep intuition that we must serve is not an option. We do, however, have an option as to whom or what we serve. It "may be the devil or it may be the Lord." My plea to everyone reading this book is that they will evaluate the evidence for the claims of Jesus Christ set forth in the following chapters. That evidence bears scrutiny if considered fairly. Dylan was also right about our choices, and there is nothing more important than getting that choice right.

6. The Case for Christianity

The word "science" comes from the Latin word *scientia*, which means simply "knowledge." The word did not take on the specialized meaning we associate with it today until the nineteenth century. Before that, the systematic study of nature was considered a branch of philosophy called "natural philosophy," which was the term used by Francis Bacon, who is widely regarded as the father of the modern scientific method. Bacon was a devout Christian, but he understood that a superficial knowledge of philosophy (which included "natural philosophy" at that time) would "incline the mind of man to atheism," but a deeper understanding would bring him back to God.[1] Bacon famously believed in a "two books" approach to knowledge. He wrote, "let no man . . . think or maintain that a man can search too far or be too well studied in the book of God's word, or in the book of God's works."[2] Thus, he believed that knowledge comes from studying both the Book of Nature and the Book of God's Word.

Bacon was adamant that both books point to God. However, the Book of Nature points only to theism generally. While that book is sufficient to disabuse a person of the error of atheism, it is necessary to follow up with the Book of Revelation to gain knowledge of the Christian faith.[3] I will follow Bacon's example in this chapter.[4] First, I will delve into the Book of Nature and give an overview of the many features of the universe that point to God.[5] I will then discuss some of the most powerful proofs of the Christian faith in relation to the evidence for the veracity of the death, burial, and resurrection of Jesus of Nazareth.

6.1. THE BOOK OF NATURE

6.1.1. Why is there something instead of nothing?

The first feature of the universe that points to God is the universe itself. Materialists insist that everything in the universe is reducible to particles in motion. But those particles cannot account for their own existence, and they cannot explain why they are in motion.[6] As we saw in chapter two, Sean Carroll, one of the world's foremost scientists, admits that every attempt to explain why the universe exists on materialist grounds fails. For materialists like Carroll, the universe is just a "brute fact," and we cannot "demand . . . that there be something we humans would recognize as a satisfactory reason for its existence."[7]

But that is not true, is it? There is a reason for the existence of the universe that is satisfactory to many people, including many of the most prominent scientists in history. God created it. That explanation will probably not be satisfactory to dogmatic materialists like Sean Carroll, but that is not because it is necessarily false or science has precluded it. It is not satisfactory to them because the possibility that God created the universe is ruled out by their metaphysical (i.e., religious) commitments. They have, however, offered us no compelling reason why we should agree with their religious commitments or join them in refusing to countenance the only plausible (indeed, the only *rational*) explanation for the existence of the universe.

The argument from the sheer existence of the universe is called the "cosmological argument."[8] William Lane Craig states a form of the argument[9] as follows:

1. Whatever begins to exist has a cause.
2. The universe began to exist.[10]
3. Therefore, the universe has a cause.

If both premises are sound, the conclusion certainly follows. Some people respond with the rejoinder, "This only pushes the problem back one step to 'What caused God?'" These people do not understand the argument. It does not claim that everything must have a cause. Instead, the first premise is that everything that *begins to exist* has a cause. The argument claims "God is a factually necessary being; that is, God's original factuality is required to explain all the facts of the universe."[11] There are other forms of the cosmological argument. I address one of these, which reasons from the contingency of the universe to the existence of a necessary being, in chapter seven (see section 7.9).

6.1.2. God is a better scientific explanation than materialism for the beginning of the universe.

Scientific evidence cannot prove that God exists with deductive certainty.[12] Nevertheless, the Big Bang provides substantial epistemic support for the hypothesis of a divine creator in the form of an "abductive" inference.[13] We have good reason to believe that God created the universe. Stephen Meyer offers the following syllogism to demonstrate why this is the case:

Major Premise: If theism is true, then we would have reason to expect evidence showing the universe had a beginning.

Minor Premise: We have otherwise surprising evidence that the universe had a beginning.

Conclusion: We have reason to think that theism may be true.[14]

Conversely, materialism offers no explanation for why the universe exists. Any entity that can explain the origin of the universe must, by definition, transcend matter and energy in space/time, and materialism denies that such an entity exists. Therefore, materialism cannot explain the origin of the universe. Thus, an abductive inference is warranted. While we have good reason to conclude that God created the universe, we have no reason at all to conclude that there is a materialist explanation for the origin of the universe. It follows that

God offers a better explanation than materialism for the existence of the universe.[15]

No one understood this better than Fred Hoyle, the astronomer who coined the term "Big Bang," which, ironically, he intended as a derogatory slur. (In a quirk of history, Hoyle's slur caught on as the theory's name.) Hoyle preferred the since-discredited "steady state" theory of cosmology over the Big Bang because the steady state theory does not imply a beginning to the universe. As an atheist, Hoyle did not want to believe the universe had a beginning, as the Big Bang implies. The theological implications of the Big Bang were so obvious to Hoyle that he accused scientists who embraced it of being religious fundamentalists![16] Fred Hoyle, an inveterate atheist, knew that the Big Bang points unmistakably toward God. The rest of us should take him at his word.

6.1.3. Quantum mechanics is fatal to materialism.

Classical Newtonian physics is completely deterministic. Think of billiard balls moving along a table and colliding with one another. The paths of the balls are, in principle, perfectly predictable. Newtonian physics conceives of the entire universe as a grand game of cosmic billiards in which all future events are theoretically completely predictable from past events. The French astronomer Pierre-Simon, Marquis de Laplace famously articulated this concept as follows:

> We ought then to regard the present state of the universe as the effect of its anterior state and as the cause of the one which is to follow. Given for one instant an intelligence which could comprehend all the forces by which nature is animated and the respective situation of the beings who compose it—an intelligence sufficiently vast to submit these data to analysis—it would embrace in the same formula the movements of the greatest bodies of the universe and those of the lightest atom; for it, nothing would be uncertain and the future, as the past, would be present to its eyes.[17]

This idea is very seductive, and it naturally led to the materialist conceit that absolutely everything can be explained by the interaction of particles in motion, leaving no room for God in the equation.[18] It turns out that even materialist scientists have been forced to concede that Laplace was completely wrong.

Laplace died in 1827. Exactly one hundred years later, in 1927, the world's leading physicists gathered in Brussels at the Fifth Solvay Conference, perhaps the most famous gathering of scientists in history. Of the 29 attendees, 17 had or would win the Nobel Prize. The topic of the conference was the new quantum theory that had swept through the scientific world with breathtaking speed. Quantum theory forever destroyed the idea that we live in the perfectly predictable billiard-ball universe envisioned by Laplace. The new theory revealed that, at the subatomic level, nature is not deterministic but *probabilistic*. It is difficult to overstate how earth-shattering the probabilistic nature of small-scale reality was to some scientists who continued to insist on classical physics's rigid determinism. This included Einstein himself, who famously wrote a letter to Max Born in which he said:

> Quantum mechanics is very impressive. But an inner voice tells me that it is not yet the real thing. The theory produces a good deal but hardly brings us closer to the secret of the Old One. I am at all events convinced that *He* does not play dice.[19]

Quantum mechanics did more than sound the death knell for the determinism of classical Newtonian physics. More importantly for our purposes, it placed *mind*, and not matter, at the center of its explanatory structure. Spencer Klavan describes why this is so:

> Quantum mathematics gave information about how a man could experience a single particle once he measured it. But as for what was happening to the particle when no man was looking—it could not even be spoken of. Particles were not "in many places at once" when described by the Schrödinger wave; they were not in any particular place, *because no one was experiencing their location*.

What's more, Heisenberg's equations showed that experiencing their location put an inherent limit on knowledge of their momentum, a so-called "uncertainty principle" that set bounds to which physical properties could be resolved from potential to reality at any given time.[20]

The pioneers of quantum physics were forced to grapple with the possibility that their discoveries could reduce the building stones of the universe to a "spiritual throb" that comes close to our concept of pure thought.[21] Materialism has no place for the immaterial mind. Indeed, as we have seen, many materialists deny that the mind even exists. Thus, to the extent that mind plays a role in reality, materialism must be false.[22] Klavan argues that what we do at the micro-level, God, in whose image we are created, does at a cosmic level. "For the universe itself is created when consciousness gives shape to time and space."[23]

6.1.4. The fine-tuning of the universe requires a fine-tuner.

About 70 years ago, scientists began to discover that several properties of the universe, such as the values of the fundamental forces of physics and the initial conditions of matter and energy at the Big Bang, among many others, appear to be balanced on a razor's edge to allow for the possibility of life.[24] This has come to be known as the fine-tuning of the universe for the existence of life. Casey Luskin has summarized a few of the fine-tuned properties:

- If the strong nuclear force were slightly more powerful, then there would be no hydrogen, an essential element of life. If it was slightly weaker, then hydrogen would be the only element in existence.
- If the weak nuclear force were slightly different, then either there would not be enough helium to generate heavy elements

in stars, or stars would burn out too quickly and supernova explosions could not scatter heavy elements across the universe.
- If the electromagnetic force were slightly stronger or weaker, atomic bonds, and thus complex molecules, could not form.
- If the value of the gravitational constant were slightly larger, one consequence would be that stars would become too hot and burn out too quickly. If it were smaller, stars would never burn at all and heavy elements would not be produced. . . .

The following gives a sense of the degree of fine-tuning that must go into some of these values to yield a life-friendly universe:

- Gravitational constant: 1 part in 10^{34}
- Electromagnetic force versus force of gravity: 1 part in 10^{37}
- Cosmological constant: 1 part in 10^{120}
- Mass density of universe: 1 part in 10^{59}
- Expansion rate of universe: 1 part in 10^{55}
- Initial entropy:[25] 1 part in $10^{(10^{123})}$

Theists and atheists alike agree the universe appears to be fine-tuned for life.[26] For example, atheist Stephen Hawking admitted: "The remarkable fact is that the values of these numbers seem to have been very finely adjusted to make possible the development of life."[27]

The likelihood of any of these parameters, let alone all of them, landing precisely where they needed to be for the existence of life by sheer coincidence is virtually zero. The fine-tuning of the universe has obvious implications that astronomer Fred Hoyle understood very well. "A common sense interpretation of the facts suggests that a superintellect has monkeyed with physics, as well as with chemistry and biology, and that there are no blind forces worth speaking about in nature."[28]

Stephen Meyer has developed the following syllogism as an abductive proof of the fine-tuning argument for the existence of God:

Major Premise: If God acted to design the universe, we would expect evidence of fine-tuning from the beginning of the universe.

Minor Premise: We have evidence of fine-tuning from the beginning of the universe.

Conclusion: We have reason to think that an intelligent agent that transcends the universe—also known as God—acted to design the universe in a way that makes it conducive to life.[29]

Conversely, materialism has no way of explaining why the initial conditions of the universe and the laws of physics are fine-tuned for the existence of life. Materialism *presupposes* matter/energy, space/time, and the laws of physics. Thus, it has nothing to say about how the initial conditions of the universe and the laws of physics came to be.[30] Once again, theism is a far better explanation for fine-tuning than materialism.

6.1.5. Materialists have to believe crazy things.

In their textbook, *College Physics*, Paul Peter Urone and Roger Hinrichs write: "One of the most remarkable simplifications in physics is that only four distinct forces account for *all known phenomena*."[31] Keying off this insight, Granville Sewell, emeritus professor of mathematics at the University of Texas El Paso, writes that one must believe some crazy things in order not to believe in design in the universe. Specifically, "you must believe that a few unintelligent forces of physics alone could have rearranged the fundamental particles of physics into computers and science texts and jet airplanes and nuclear power plants and Apple iPhones."[32]

Wait a minute, I imagine some readers are thinking. Computers and iPhones are built by people, not mindless forces rearranging fundamental particles. But remember Materialism 101 in chapter two. Materialism posits that after the Big Bang, gravity pulled the lighter elements together into stars, and the heavier elements were fused in the nuclear furnaces in the center of those stars. When those stars burned out after billions of years, planets coalesced from those heavier elements, and eventually, simple life forms arose on one of those planets. Humans evolved from those original simple life forms. Thus, as Sagan wrote, "the iron in our blood, the calcium in our teeth, the carbon in our genes were produced billions of years ago in the interior of a red giant star."[33] We are, in our essence, simply an amalgamation of "starstuff." Materialists insist that a person's mind is reducible to his material brain, and the particles in his material brain can, in principle, be traced all the way back to the Big Bang. Thus, by definition, the materialist believes that everything that happened from the moment of the Big Bang to the moment that a brain arose *in utero* and matured to its present state was a result of the four forces of physics acting on the fundamental particles.

Sewell was not exaggerating even slightly. Materialists literally believe that the four blind undirected forces of physics alone rearranged the fundamental particles into computers and science texts and jet airplanes and nuclear power plants and Apple iPhones. That is a preposterous idea. It is a category error because it attributes to undirected natural forces that which can only be accomplished by minds. If you agree that minds cannot be reduced to mere physical forces acting on particles, you are well on your way to accepting that there is an Ultimate Mind.

6.1.6. Living things are proof of God's handiwork.

In the previous section, I discussed the ridiculous materialist idea that the four forces of physics spontaneously rearranged the fundamental particles of physics into computers and iPhones. It is actually far worse than that. When it comes to complex information-processing entities, even the simplest living cell is orders of magnitude more complex than the most sophisticated computer. We know this because our current technology allows us to make computers, but we have not come remotely close to making even the simplest living cell. In other words, the people making the computers are infinitely more complex than the computers they are making. Nevertheless, materialists insist that blind physical forces spontaneously made things (i.e., living organisms) that are far beyond the capabilities of our most sophisticated technology. As we shall see, the truly staggering level of specified complexity in living things is best explained not by blind physical forces spontaneously rearranging fundamental particles but by the work of a super-intelligence, namely, God.

Before delving into the particulars of the specified complexity in living things, I will explain what specified complexity is and why it matters. In his groundbreaking book *The Design Inference*,[34] William Dembski developed a conceptually rigorous method for detecting design. There are many sophisticated details that I do not have the space (or, candidly, the mathematical ability) to get into. Fortunately, like many elegant theories, the core idea can be conveyed at a popular level,[35] and Dembski has done that. The essence of Dembski's design detection method is straightforward. If an event meets two criteria, we can conclude that it resulted from the act of an intelligent agent (i.e., it was designed). Those criteria are: (1) the event has an extremely low probability, and (2) the event conforms to an easily recognizable pattern known as a "specification."[36]

Imagine a tabletop with 100 fair coins on it. All the coins are facing heads up. This example meets both of Dembski's criteria. The probability that 100 coins will all randomly land heads up if they are tossed on the table is effectively zero. If we tossed coins from the moment of the Big Bang until now, we would not expect to see that happen. Additionally, the arrangement of the coins conforms to the easily recognizable pattern "100 coins all heads up." Therefore, we can dismiss the chance hypothesis and conclude that someone arranged the coins on the table. We have detected design.

Dembski's design detection method can be used to identify design in more complex situations than coin-tossing. This can be illustrated using the game of poker, but a bit of math is involved. Understanding the concept doesn't require knowing the exact numbers, so feel free to skip to the next paragraph if math doesn't interest you. There are 2,598,960 possible five-card poker hands. Thus, the probability of being dealt any specific hand is 1 in 2,598,960 or 0.00000038. There is only one way to make a royal flush in spades ("RFS"), so the probability of being dealt that exact hand is also 0.00000038. The probability of getting any sequence of three hands is calculated by multiplying the single-hand probability by itself three times (0.00000038 × 0.00000038 × 0.00000038). When we do that, we find that the probability of any particular three-hand sequence is 000000000000000057 (5.7×10^{-17}). That's a vanishingly small number—about 1 in 17.56 quintillion. The probability of being dealt a RFS three times in a row is *exactly the same* as any other three-hand sequence.

Suppose you are playing poker with a friend. Your friend is the dealer and he deals himself a RFS on the first hand. Is he cheating?[37] We know that the chance of that happening is low, but we also know that although it is uncommon, people occasionally get RFS's dealt to them through random chance. You might think it is a little fishy, but you cannot rule out the possibility that your friend just got lucky.

Now, suppose your friend deals twice more and gives himself a RFS in each of those hands as well. You complain, and he says, "Quit your bellyaching. The probability of that three-hand sequence is identical to the probability of any other three-hand sequence." Your friend is right about two things: (1) If he had dealt himself any of the millions of three-hand sequences that looked "normal," you would not have batted an eye; and (2) as we saw above, the probability of each of those millions of other sequences is exactly the same as the one that was actually dealt. Since your friend is right about those two things, are you wrong to complain? Of course not. So, what is it about this event that confirms your commonsense intuition that you have been cheated?

The ingredient that was missing from your friend's analysis is the specification "three RFSs in a row."[38] Think of "combinatorial space" as an ocean that represents the total possible outcomes. Imagine the entire surface of the Earth is covered by a vast ocean except for a few tiny islands. In our example, the ocean is 17.56 quintillion possible three-hand sequences. The specification "three RFSs in a row" is an island the size of a postage stamp in that ocean. If a rock descends from space, there are 17.56 quintillion *minus one* ways for it not to land on the island and only one way for it to land on the island. If the rock lands on the island, it is not reasonable to conclude that it did so by chance. Someone aimed it at the island. Dembski's design detection method works by comparing large oceans of combinatorial space to tiny islands of specification.[39]

6.1.6.1. *The origin of life.*

Dembski's design detection methods have been employed to infer design in living things. To illustrate this, I will begin at the beginning—the origin of life (often abbreviated as "OOL"). Honest materialist biologists candidly admit that Dembski's first criterion—extremely low probability—is met. At least, that is what three Nobel Prize–winners say. Francis Crick, co-discoverer of the DNA double helix, wrote that an honest man could only state that "the origin of life appears at the moment to be almost a miracle."[40] Jacques Monod won his Nobel Prize for his role in discovering the genetic regulation system. He believed that the probability of the origin of life is so astronomically low that it almost certainly occurred only once in the universe, and thus, man "knows that he is alone in the unfeeling immensity of the universe."[41] Nobel Prize–winning chemist Ilya Prigogine wrote that the probability of life arising by chance is "vanishingly small."[42] Award-winning Harvard Professor of Chemistry George M. Whitesides sums up the improbability of the spontaneous emergence of life as follows:

> The complexity of the simplest cell eludes our understanding – how could it be that any cell, even one simpler than the simplest cell we know, emerged from the tangle of accidental reactions occurring in the molecular sludge that covered the prebiotic earth? We . . .

do not understand. It is not impossible, but it seems very, very improbable.[43]

The second criterion for Dembski's design inference—a specification—is also met. A cell is a combination of molecules. The overwhelming majority of combinations of molecules are non-living. Thus, the first living cell consisted of a special type of molecular combination that distinguished it from all other combinations. Just as the pattern "three royal flushes in spades in a row" is an easily recognizable pattern in the combinatorial space of possible three-hand sequences, the pattern "living combination of molecules" is an easily recognizable pattern in the combinatorial space of ways molecules can be combined. In other words, in our "ocean," almost all combinations of molecules will be non-living. Thus, the specification "living combination of molecules" represents a microscopic island in a vast ocean of combinatorial space.

Note that materialist OOL researchers cannot appeal to "evolution" or "natural selection" to help them climb the mountain of improbability. Darwinian theory states that natural selection could get started only after the first self-replicating cell appeared. As biologist Theodosius Dobzhansky famously observed, "Prebiotic natural selection is a contradiction in terms."[44]

There are two competing claims as to how life began. Chance and design.[45] But Whitesides says that scientists have no testable hypotheses about how life might have emerged through the operation of blind material forces, only "guesses and intuitions.[46] Indeed, in a moment of candor, he admitted materialist scientists have "no clue" how that might have happened.[47]

Professor James Tour is a synthetic organic chemist at Rice University. His scientific research areas include nanoelectronics, graphene electronics, silicon oxide electronics, and carbon nanovectors for medical applications. He has over 650 scientific publications and 200 patents. He is one of the most highly cited scientists in the world. The H-index is a measure of a scientist's productivity and citation impact, and a value above 100 is exceptional and would place a scientist among the elite in his field. Professor Tour's H-index is 129. Tour was named "Scientist of the Year" by *R&D Magazine* in 2013 and ranked one of the top 10 chemists in the world in 2009. He has been the recipient of dozens of prestigious awards, including the Royal Society of Chemistry's Centenary Prize for innovations in materials chemistry with applications in medicine and nanotechnology and the Feynman Prize in Nanotechnology.

Tour is a Christian, and he agrees with Whitesides. Tour writes that, "synthetic chemists—and scientists in general—remain *clueless* about life's origins."[48] Tour is so confident in that assertion that in 2023, he challenged ten of the world's leading OOL researchers to prove him wrong. He spotted them all of the basic building blocks of life, and then he said that if within 60 days they could answer even one of the five most basic questions about the origin of life, he would take down all of his internet content and never criticize them again. None of them rose to the challenge.[49] A fideistic, grit-your-teeth commitment to materialism is the only reason anyone would believe life spontaneously arose by chance. Therefore, we can conclude with a high level of confidence that, by far, the best explanation for the origin of life is "design."

6.1.6.2. *DNA, the language of life.*

Life is not merely material. It absolutely depends on something immaterial: information. The DNA molecule stores information by specifically arranging chemicals called nucleotide bases along the spine of its helical strands. Scientists represent these four nucleotides with the letters A, T, G, and C (for adenine, thymine, guanine, and cytosine). Just as the letters in this sentence and the digital characters in a computer code convey information depending on how they are arranged, these chemical letters convey the information necessary for building proteins in the cell.[50] *This is not controversial.* Arch-materialist Richard Dawkins says the following regarding the information content conveyed by DNA:

After Watson and Crick, we know that genes themselves, within their minute internal structure, are long strings of *pure digital information*. What is more, they are truly digital, in the full and strong sense of computers and compact disks, not in the weak sense of the nervous system. The genetic code is not a binary code as in computers, nor an eight-level code as in some telephone systems, but a quaternary code, with four symbols. The machine code of the genes is uncannily computerlike. Apart from differences in jargon, the pages of a molecular-biology journal might be interchanged with those of a computer-engineering journal.[51]

Bill Gates agrees. He writes, "Human DNA is like a computer program but far, far more advanced than any software ever created."[52] In *Signature in the Cell,* Stephen Meyer provides a lengthy explanation confirming the commonsense conclusion that DNA and the digital information processing system that reads it satisfy Dembski's two criteria for design detection.[53]

Materialists, on the other hand, must believe that blind, unguided physical forces wrote the most sophisticated digital code in the known universe. Yet, no one has ever seen undirected physical forces write digital code, and no one has ever provided a remotely plausible explanation for how that is even possible. Note that the chemicals themselves (i.e., the adenine, thymine, guanine, and cytosine) are not the source of the information. Information is immaterial. Saying that the chemical letters are the source of the information is like saying that the information in a book comes from the ink and paper used to print it.

So, what is the explanation for the "pure digital information" Dawkins assures us is inside of every living cell? We can answer that question by asking another question. What do we know about the source of specified information—information like that in an English sentence or a digital code—when that source has actually been observed producing the information? Based on countless billions of examples, we know that in every single such case, that source was the mind of an intelligent agent. It was designed. The specified information inside every cell in your body was also designed by the Ultimate Designer.

6.1.6.3. *Functional protein folds are very tiny islands in a vast ocean.*

Proteins are large molecules that the nanomachines[54] inside each cell make from amino acids. The sequence of amino acids in a protein folds up to form a very complex, three-dimensional structure, which can take on many different shapes. There are 20 standard amino acids, so for any given chain, the number of possible combinations is 20 raised to the power of the number of acids in the chain. For example, a protein consisting of a sequence of 153 amino acids has 20^{153} possible combinations of acids, an astronomically large number. Here is the important thing to keep in mind: Of all those possible combinations, almost all of them lead to folded shapes that are *nonfunctional*. Derek Muller at the YouTube channel *Veritasium* has an excellent video with animations showing how protein-folding works.[55]

Douglas Axe, a professor of molecular biology at Biola University, has done important work on these proteins,[56] specifically one of the domains making up an enzyme called beta-lactamase, a sequence that is 153 amino acids long. Axe's goal was to calculate the probability of evolution stumbling upon one of the very few functional amino acid sequences through random chance. His findings were startling. "Of the possible genes encoding protein chains 153 amino acids in length, only about one in a hundred trillion trillion trillion trillion trillion trillion is expected to encode a chain that folds well enough to perform a biological function!"[57] In a vast ocean of combinatorial space consisting of "all sequences of 153 acids" there is a microscopic island called "functional sequences." And the beta-lactamase sequence landed on that island. Unsurprisingly, Axe made a design inference. It is far more likely that a functional protein fold results from an act of an intelligent agent than from random chance. Dembski reviewed Axe's work in *The Design Inference* and confirmed that design is the only reasonable conclusion that can be drawn from Axe's data. [58]

6.1.6.4. *The irreducible complexity of living things points to God.*

Michael Behe is a professor of biochemistry at Lehigh University. In his book *Darwin's Black Box*,[59] Behe used several "irreducibly complex" biological systems to illustrate the impossibility of the evolution of these systems through stepwise materialist mechanisms. An irreducibly complex system consists of several interacting parts that contribute to the system's function, and the removal of any one of these parts causes the system to stop functioning altogether. Behe used a mousetrap to demonstrate this concept. The trap has five basic components (the base, hammer, spring, catch, and holding bar). If one of those components is removed, the trap does not function poorly. It does not function at all. This poses a significant challenge to materialist accounts of evolution, which posit the gradual step-by-step evolution of all biological systems. If the mousetrap were a living thing, it could not have evolved through a step-by-step process because all of the parts would have had to be there at once for it to function at all. There is no stepwise path for the evolution of an irreducibly complex system.

Most famously, Behe highlighted the flagellum motor as an example of an irreducibly complex biological system. The flagellum motor is a rotary engine that single-cell bacteria use to move around. This nanomachine has many parts that are analogous to parts found in human technology. It has a rotor, a stator, a drive shaft, a U-joint, bushings, bearings, and a whip-like tail that functions as a propeller. Each of those parts must be present for the motor to work at all. Remove one, and it stops working. Thus, the flagellum motor could not have evolved in a gradual, stepwise fashion. A better explanation is that all of the parts were there at the beginning, which implies that an intelligent designer was there to put them together.

There are numerous irreducibly complex biological systems. Behe discusses the blood-clotting cascade, the immune system, cellular transport systems, and others to illustrate that such systems appear to be the rule rather than the exception in living things. In other words, it appears to have been impossible for most complex biological systems to have evolved in a gradual, stepwise fashion. In summary, material processes appear to be incapable of creating irreducibly complex systems. On the other hand, we know from countless billions of observations that intelligent agents routinely create such systems. Once again, the best explanation for these systems is design, which implies a Designer.

6.1.6.5. *Summary*

There are numerous other examples from biology that declare the glory of God. As the Psalmist wrote, "I praise you because I am fearfully and wonderfully made; your works are wonderful, I know that full well."[60] I will arbitrarily cut off the discussion here. Otherwise, I could go on about the biological proofs for the rest of the book. The point has been made. God's creatures declare God's glory, and only a willfully blind person denies that.

6.1.7. Objective moral truth exists; therefore, God exists.

I am broken. You are, too. The whole world and everyone in it is broken. We have a deep intuition that things are not the way they are supposed to be. How did our awareness of the world's brokenness come to be? Does it reflect an underlying reality, or is it an illusion? For Christians, these are easy questions. We believe in a transcendent, objective moral standard rooted in God's nature. God has not merely established the good. He *is* the good, and all goodness flows from him. Each of us innately understands that goodness exists and that we all fall short of measuring up to it. The doctrine of original sin should not be controversial. Of all the doctrines of Christianity, it is the one that is supported by indisputable empirical evidence from our personal day-to-day experience and thousands of years of recorded history.[61] For the materialist, on the other hand, it seems that the question is all but unanswerable. If Dawkins is correct—if there really is no evil and no good—there is no reason to believe the world is broken. As C.S. Lewis said, a man does not call a line crooked unless he has some idea of a straight line,[62] and materialists deny that straight lines exist.

Nevertheless, that nagging awareness of our own and the world's brokenness persists even for materialists. The standard Darwinist line is that the moral impulse is an evolutionary adaptation, and they delight in making up just-so stories[63] about why this or that altruistic behavior is adaptive, that is when they are not making up stories for why the opposite of that behavior is also adaptive. After all, if, as materialists insist, there is a physical explanation for everything, then that explanation has to explain every sort of behavior and the opposite of that behavior as well. Under the materialist paradigm, honoring a woman as a human being with inherent dignity is adaptive, and so is raping and murdering her.

This brings me to one of the most powerful proofs of God—the undeniable existence of objective moral truth. The basic argument is fairly simple.

> *Major Premise*: If a personal God does not exist, then objective moral values do not exist.
>
> *Minor Premise*: Objective moral values do exist.
>
> *Conclusion*: A personal God exists.[64]

Only the minor premise of this syllogism is the least bit controversial. As we have seen, Richard Dawkins, for example, denied that objective values exist when he wrote that, "The universe we observe has precisely the properties we should expect if there is, at bottom, no design, no purpose, *no evil and no good*, nothing but blind, pitiless indifference."[65] To be sure, Dawkins uses the word "evil" all the time. But he does not mean objective evil. He means a "sense" of right and wrong derived from our Darwinian past.[66]

Is the minor premise true? Do objective moral values exist? We know that some objective truths exist. Suppose you say that two plus two equals four, and all eight billion other people on the planet insist that two plus two equals five. If objective truth were a matter of nose-counting, it would be 8,000,000,000 to 1, and you would have to concede that they are right and you are wrong. But objective truth is not a matter of nose-counting. We know as an absolute certainty that if you were the only person in the world who said two plus two equals four, you would be right, and everyone else would be wrong. It is simply not possible for two plus two to equal five.

Now, suppose you believe that at all conceivable times and places, the wanton slaughter of six million innocent men, women, and children is objectively evil. Richard Posner is your neighbor, and one day, while chatting across the fence, you share your views on the Holocaust with him. Posner says that while he feels strongly that the Holocaust was a bad thing, and he would have stopped it if he could, he cannot agree that it was an "objectively" bad thing because that implies an objective moral standard that does not exist.[67] After all, he might add, we cannot call another culture "immoral" unless we add "by our lights."[68]

Posner would be wrong. His commitment to materialism blinds him to the obvious truth. The statement "the Holocaust was evil" is true in the same way that "two plus two is four" is true. If it were not the case, the universe would descend into absurd incomprehensibility. Even if everyone else in the world disagreed with the statement, they would all be wrong, and you would be right. If you concede that it is inconceivable for the statement to be false, then you believe in objective moral values. As demonstrated in the syllogism above, once you take that step, the conclusion, "God exists," is logically compelled.

6.1.8. Consciousness destroys materialism.

The only thing you really need to know about consciousness is something you already know: You are conscious. Indeed, it is impossible for you not to know that you are conscious. It is the primordial datum. Your consciousness has many properties that cannot be reconciled with materialism. I will mention four.

- You have a deep sense that when you use the pronoun "I," you are referring to an immaterial something that is not just your physical body. You are referring to the unique "self" that makes you, well, you. This is "subjective self-awareness."
- You are a "subject" that perceives other things as an "object" of perception. This sense of an immaterial "me" perceiving a "that" over there is called "subject-object duality."
- You experience immaterial mental states directed towards objects. This "aboutness" is called "intentionality."
- Your immaterial self has qualitative experiences of things that cannot be objectively communicated. These experiences are called "qualia."

There is a vast literature on the "mind-body" issue and what philosopher David Chalmers calls the "hard problem of consciousness."[69] Space limitations preclude me from going into that literature in much detail.[70] I will limit myself to discussing an area that gives materialists fits: qualia. As mentioned, qualia are the qualitative, subjective experiences of quantitative, objective phenomena, like the tanginess of a pickle, the sadness of depression, the pain of a toothache, or the warmth of the color red. That subjective experience cannot be communicated to another person. To see this, think about how you could convey "red" to a person who has been blind from birth? You can tell them that red light has a wavelength between 625 and 740 nanometers. But that does not convey to them any information at all about what red is "like," i.e., the subjective experience of redness. You might struggle to find a way to communicate that experience, but you will ultimately give up because it is impossible. "Red" is an objective phenomenon that can be communicated as light of a certain wavelength. The experience of red—"redness" if you will—can only be subjectively experienced. Qualia are a problem for materialists who insist that all mental activity can be accounted for as a state of a physical brain. Atheist philosopher of mind Thomas Nagel candidly acknowledges that all attempts to account for mental states like qualia as properties of physical brains have failed.[71]

As we discussed earlier, some materialists try to dismiss consciousness as an illusion, a trick our brains play on us. However, the very effort to dismiss consciousness in this manner demonstrates consciousness. Two elements are necessary for any illusion to exist: that which is deceived and that which deceives. The statement "My brain deceives me into believing I am conscious" is incoherent because it implicitly acknowledges the subject-object duality it seeks to deny.

All four features of consciousness I described above are indisputably true. In fact, it is absurd to contest them. Those who attempt to dispute them are so desperately committed to materialism that they deny the undeniable—their own consciousness.[72] Atheist Thomas Nagel says that consciousness is the most conspicuous obstacle to a comprehensive naturalism because it implies that "physics and chemistry" may not account for everything. According to Nagel, consciousness "threatens to unravel the entire naturalistic world picture."[73] It is not hard to understand why Nagel says this. The realization that immaterial phenomena that defy explanation on materialist grounds exist is only one step away from the realization that God exists.

6.1.9. Miracles happen.

David Hume famously claimed to have disproved the existence of miracles. He wrote: "And as a uniform experience amounts to a proof, there is here a direct and full *proof*, from the nature of the fact, against the existence of any miracle; nor can such a proof be destroyed, or the miracle rendered credible, but by an opposite proof, which is superior."[74] Hume's argument has been justly criticized as circular. How do you know that miracles do not happen? Because our uniform experience is that miracles do not happen. What about all of the accounts of miracles? We can disregard those accounts because miracles do not happen. How do you know that miracles do not happen? Because our uniform experience is that miracles do not happen. Lather, rinse, repeat.

There have been numerous accounts of miracles over the centuries. To reject every one of these accounts à la Hume as counter to "uniform experience" is to assume a conclusion. Unlike Hume, I am not willing to assume that conclusion because I personally know that miracles do not contradict uniform human experience. I have witnessed one.

When my sister Robin was about ten, she became very sick. The doctors diagnosed her with myasthenia gravis and prescribed the drug Mestinon. But after taking the drug for a while, she seemed to be getting worse, not better. One day, while my father was at work, he was thinking about Robin when three words popped into his head like a thunderclap: "Stop the medicine." The message was so clear that he was convinced it came from God, and he spent the rest of the day worrying about how to tell my mother that he believed they needed to stop giving Robin medicine prescribed by her doctor. That same morning, my mom was at home when a thought struck her with powerful force: "Stop giving Robin that medicine." While she was pondering that thought, the phone rang. She picked it up and it was Robin, who was visiting my grandmother and calling from her house. Robin blurted out, "Momma, God told me I have to stop taking the medicine I've been taking."

That evening, when dad got home from work, my mom was standing on the porch waiting to meet him. He wondered what was happening because she never did that. Before he could say a word, mom said, "Ed, I got a word from the Lord, and he told me we have to stop giving that medicine to Robin." That settled it. My parents decided to stop the medicine. Mom took Robin to the doctor to explain their decision. Predictably, he blew his stack. He literally cussed at her and threatened to report her for child abuse. This shook mom, but she calmed down when, on the way out of the doctor's office, my 10-year-old sister took her hand and said calmly, 'Don't worry momma. We do not walk in the counsel of the ungodly.'"

Of course, my parents did not stop medical treatment for Robin altogether. Instead, they switched to another doctor. When they did that, it soon came to light that the first doctor had misdiagnosed Robin. She had spinal meningitis, not myasthenia gravis. The new doctor told my parents that if she had continued taking the prescribed medicine instead of being treated for the disease she actually had, she would have died. Robin was still sick. This is not a story about a miraculous healing. But the miracle prevented her from dying and set her on a path to get proper care. The disease caught up to her in the end. She still died, but that was 50 years later, and in the meantime, she got married, had a son, and lived to see her beautiful grandchildren. Yes, I believe in miracles. I have seen one.

6.1.10. The evidence is more than sufficient.

I could add several more topics to this section. Proofs of God's existence are everywhere, and there are numerous books and articles that go into the topic at a much deeper level than I have. I have cited many of them, including work done by William Lane Craig, Douglas Groothuis, William Dembski, Stephen Meyer, Michael Behe, Edward Feser, C.S. Lewis . . . The list goes on and on. That body of work is so extensive that I must impose an arbitrary cutoff at some point. Otherwise, this book would be about nothing but those proofs.

The sampling that has been provided is sufficient to demonstrate that Paul was telling the truth in his letter to the Christians in Rome when he wrote, "For since the creation of the world God's invisible qualities—his eternal power and divine nature—have been clearly seen, being understood from what has been made, so that people are without excuse."[75] From the level of the unimaginably small revealed by quantum mechanics to the world of the incomprehensibly vast revealed by cosmology—and everywhere in between—the evidence for God's existence is overwhelming. There is indeed no good excuse for not acknowledging and accepting that evidence.

6.2. THE BOOK OF GOD'S WORD

6.2.1. "God" is not comparable to "gods."

There is overwhelming evidence for the existence of God. The next question is "which God?" Here again, every person must evaluate the evidence and make up his own mind. Unsurprisingly, I will argue that the evidence points to the Christian God who became incarnate in the person of Jesus Christ. Before we get to that evidence, we need to consider a common atheist argument I call the "You are an atheist concerning one more god than I am" argument. Atheist Ricky Gervais made the argument as follows:[76]

> Since the beginning of recorded history, which is defined by the invention of writing by the Sumerians around 6,000 years ago, historians have cataloged over 3700 supernatural beings, of which 2870 can be considered deities. So next time someone tells me they believe in God, I'll say "Oh which one? Zeus? Hades? Jupiter? Mars? Odin? Thor? Krishna? Vishnu? Ra? . . ." If they say "Just God. I only believe in the one God," I'll point out that they are nearly as atheistic as me. I don't believe in 2,870 gods, and they don't believe in 2,869.

Like many things atheists say, the argument has a kind of first blush plausibility, but it does not hold up on even a moment's reflection. As David Bentley Hart explains, Gervais has made an elementary category error. In other words, he has compared things that are not comparable. Hart writes:

> Belief or disbelief in fairies or gods could never be validated by philosophical arguments made from first principles; the existence or nonexistence of Zeus is not a matter that can be intelligibly discussed in the categories of modal logic or metaphysics, any more than the existence of tree frogs could be; if he is there at all, one must go on an expedition to find him, or at least find out his address. The question of God, by contrast, is one that can and must be pursued in terms of the absolute and the contingent, the necessary and the fortuitous, potency and act, possibility and impossibility, being and nonbeing, transcendence and immanence. Evidence for or against the existence of Thor or King Oberon would consist only in local facts, not universal truths of reason; it would be entirely empirical, episodic, psychological, personal, and hence elusive. Evidence for or against the reality of God, if it is there, saturates every moment of the experience of existence, every employment of reason, every act of consciousness, every encounter with the world around us.[77]

In summary, Hart is saying that, properly understood, the "God" of the monotheistic faiths is not in the same category as the "gods" in the Greek, Norse, Indian or other pantheons—which are all contingent creatures. God is pure being that is the source of all being. He is the necessary being. A necessary being is not comparable to contingent beings. Thus, to lump the God of the monotheistic faiths in with Odin demonstrates that you understand neither God nor Odin.

Think of it this way. Gervais says something like this: "There are a bunch of oranges, and I disbelieve in all of the oranges without exception. You, on the other hand, admit that you also disbelieve in all of the oranges, except for that last little orange that you irrationally insist on clinging to." No, Ricky, just like you, I disbelieve in all of the oranges without exception. But I do believe in an apple. Why should I stop believing in that apple just because I don't believe in oranges?

6.2.2. The claims of Christianity are supported by overwhelming evidence.

Gervais was right about one thing. Belief in the thousands of gods in the pagan pantheons is irrational. A personal monotheistic God is really the only rational game in town.[78] Each of the three great monotheistic religions – Christianity, Islam, and Judaism – espouses such a God. Of these, the God of Christianity is, by far, the one that is most supported by the historical evidence.[79] That word "historical" is very important. The Christian faith has always been self-consciously grounded in its claim that certain historical facts—actual events at a particular time and place— occurred. C.S. Lewis said that if those events did not actually happen, Christianity is worthless, but if they did happen, it is the most important thing in the world.[80] Of all of those historical facts, the resurrection is the central event upon which everything else hangs. Concerning the resurrection, Paul wrote the following in a letter to the Christians at Corinth:

> [I]f Christ has not been raised, then our preaching is in vain, your faith also is in vain. Moreover, we are even found to be false witnesses of God, because we testified against God that He raised Christ, whom He did not raise, if in fact the dead are not raised. For if the dead are not raised, then not even Christ has been raised; *and if Christ has not been raised, your faith is worthless; you are still in your sins.*[81]

The Christian faith stands or falls on the veracity of its historical claims about Jesus of Nazareth. Fortunately for Christians, those claims are among the most verified historical facts. Hundreds of books have been written about the evidence supporting the resurrection. Space limitations prevent me from presenting more than a summary of that evidence. I will draw heavily from Douglas Groothuis's *Christian Apologetics*, which I highly recommend for those interested in a more in-depth review of the evidence. Additionally, the following books are classics in the field: *The Resurrection of the Son of God* by N.T. Wright, *Did Jesus Rise from the Dead?*

by William Lane Craig, *Resurrection of God Incarnate* by Richard Swinburne, *The Case for Christ* by Lee Strobel, and *Evidence That Demands a Verdict* by Josh McDowell and Sean McDowell.

The following historical facts are best explained by the actual physical resurrection of Jesus:[82]

Fact 1: The Crucifixion. It is widely acknowledged that the crucifixion took place in the early 30s AD. Regardless of one's beliefs about the *significance* of the crucifixion, there is no good reason to deny the substantial Biblical and extra-Biblical evidence that it indeed occurred.[83] The non-Biblical evidence includes Cornelius Tacitus's *Annals* written in approximately 116 AD. In Book 15, Chapter 44, Tacitus writes, "Christus, from whom the name [i.e., Christians] had its origin, suffered the extreme penalty during the reign of Tiberius at the hands of one of our procurators, Pontius Pilatus."[84] The *Testimonium Flavianum* is another non-Biblical confirmation of the New Testament accounts. The *Testimonium* appears in Book 18, Chapter 3 of *Antiquities of the Jews*, written in the late first century by the Jewish historian Flavius Josephus. While the exact text of the passage is disputed, there is general agreement among scholars on an authentic core in which Josephus reported the basic fact that Pilate condemned Jesus. Josephus also confirms the historical existence of several other New Testament figures, including John the Baptist and Jesus' brother, James.

From the beginning, Christians have taken great pains to keep the memory of Jesus' death by crucifixion alive. At a certain level, this makes no sense because crucifixion was both horrible and shameful. So, why would the early Christians emphasize the fact that Jesus died such a death? Groothuis explains: "If Jesus had been crucified and stayed dead, there is little reason to think his followers would have gloried in his agonizing and shameful death. By Jesus' day, thousands of criminals and insurrectionists had been crucified, died, and were buried. We know little about any of them. But we divide history by the birthdate of Christ."[85] The best—indeed the only rational—explanation is that he did not stay dead. Jesus triumphed over his death on the cross. That was a reason for hope, not shame,[86] and that is why the early Christians kept the memory of the triumph alive.

Fact 2: A Known Tomb. Significant, uncontroverted evidence supports the fact that Jesus was buried in a tomb owned by Joseph of Arimathea, a member of the Jewish court that sentenced Jesus. This fact is corroborated by the gospel accounts of Matthew, Mark, Luke, and John and, later, by Paul. It is unlikely that the early Christians would have made this story up because it makes no sense for a man to suffer the horrible, shameful death of a common criminal only to be given a dignified burial in a tomb owned by a wealthy member of the religious elite who was also a member of the very court that condemned him.[87]

Fact 3: An Empty Tomb. The four gospels state that Jesus' tomb was discovered empty on the Sunday following his crucifixion and death. These accounts are credible for several reasons, the first of which may not be apparent to twenty-first-century Westerners who have long been accustomed to according equal dignity to women. All the gospel writers have women reporting that the tomb was empty. This is the last thing they would have done if they were fabricating the story because in the first century, the testimony of women was held in low regard.[88] Next, the Jewish leaders opposing the early Christians claimed that Jesus' disciples stole his body. This claim presupposes that the tomb was empty.[89] It is important to keep in mind that the early Christians started telling people that Jesus had been resurrected almost immediately. The Jewish leaders and the Romans had an obvious interest in discrediting that story, and doing so would have been simple if they had been able to retrieve Jesus' body from his tomb and display it. But they couldn't, and that is why they made up the "stolen by his disciples" story.[90]

Fact 4: The Post-Resurrection Appearances of Jesus. The New Testament records that Jesus made twelve post-resurrection appearances over a forty-day period:

1. Mary Magdalene (Jn 20:10-18)

2. Mary and the other women (Mt 28:1-10)
3. Peter (Lk 24:34; 1 Cor 15:5)
4. Two disciples on the road to Emmaus (Lk 24:13-35)
5. Ten apostles (Lk 24:36-49)
6. Eleven apostles (Jn 20:24-31)
7. Seven apostles (Jn 21)
8. All of the apostles (Mt 28:16-20)
9. Five hundred disciples (1 Cor 15:6)
10. James (1 Cor 15:7)
11. Again to all the apostles (Acts 1:4-8)
12. The apostle Paul (Acts 9:1-9; 1 Corinthians 15:8; 9:1)[91]

Paul wrote a summary of Jesus' appearances in a letter to the church in Corinth:

> For I handed down to you as of first importance what I also received, that Christ died for our sins according to the Scriptures, and that He was buried, and that He was raised on the third day according to the Scriptures, and that He appeared to Cephas, then to the twelve. After that He appeared to more than five hundred brothers and sisters at one time, most of whom remain until now, but some have fallen asleep; then He appeared to James, then to all the apostles; and last of all, as to one untimely born, He appeared to me also.[92]

Some try to dismiss the resurrection as a Christian legend that arose long after Jesus was crucified, but this is obviously false. Paul's letter to the Corinthians is widely dated only a few years after Christ was crucified, and by that time, the fact of his resurrection was so firmly established that Paul could already speak of it as one of the core tenets of Christianity.[93] Note that Paul says that as of the time of his writing, most of the hundreds of eye witnesses to Jesus' post-resurrection appearances were still alive. If anyone had doubts about the truth of his claims, they were free to interview those witnesses for themselves.

Fact 5: The Post-Resurrection Transformation of the Disciples. After the crucifixion, Jesus' disciples were a motley group of scattered, dejected, dispirited, and grieving followers of a crucified rabbi in whom they had placed such high hopes. But just a little while later, they were transformed into men who confidently proclaimed the gospel of Jesus Christ. Their confidence was such that they were willing to endure persecution, hardship, and even martyrdom for the sake of Jesus.[94] The best explanation for this remarkable transformation—again, the only rational explanation—is that they witnessed Jesus' post-resurrection appearances, which, to them, validated Jesus' claim to be God incarnate.

Fact 6: The Early Worship of Christ. Gaius Plinius Caecilius Secundus, better known to history as Pliny the Younger, was the Roman governor of the province of Bithynia-Pontus on the southern coast of the Black Sea under Emperor Trajan. In a famous letter to Trajan from around 112 AD (*Epistulae* X.96), Pliny informed the emperor that he had been routinely executing Christians but a particular case had arisen on which he desired advice. He had received an anonymous accusation naming many people as suspected Christians and after torturing two deaconesses of the local church as part of his investigation, he found no further information. He wanted to know how much further he should push the matter.[95] Trajan replied that crediting anonymous accusations was a bad idea and if anyone accused of being a Christian worshiped a Roman God, they should be pardoned.[96] Importantly for our present purposes, in his letter to Trajan, Pliny said that his investigation revealed a number of Christian practices, including the following:

> [T]hey had been in the habit of meeting together on a stated day, before sunrise, and of offering in turns a form of *invocation to Christ, as to a god*; also of binding themselves by an oath, not for any guilty purpose, but not to commit thefts, or robberies, or adulteries, not to break their word, not to repudiate deposits when called upon . . .[97]

Pliny's letter demonstrates that by a very early date, Christians in a province over six hundred miles from Jerusalem were worshiping Jesus as God. This tradition could not have arisen, especially among the zealously monotheistic Jews, unless Jesus' claim to be God incarnate had been supremely vindicated by his resurrection from the dead.[98]

Fact 7: The Lord's Day. Very soon after Jesus' death, the early church began worshiping him on Sunday. To understand how striking this is, it is necessary to understand that almost all of the early Christians were Jews, and one of the core doctrines of their faith was to worship on Saturday. "Such a transformation would not occur for frivolous reasons. This deep change in spiritual observance is best explained by their belief in the resurrection of Jesus on Sunday, which, in turn, is best explained by the resurrection itself."[99]

Fact 8: The Martyrdom of the Apostles. No one suffers torture and execution defending a lie that they know is a lie.[100] Yet, many of the early Christians went to their deaths rather than recant their faith. This is powerful—indeed, practically irrefutable—evidence of the resurrection. Groothuis provides the following formal argument:

1. People do not die for what they know to be a lie apart from some extraordinary situation.
2. All the apostles were willing to suffer and die for their faith, and there is good reason to believe that at least four of them – Peter, Paul, and both James – were martyred for their faith.
3. Therefore (a), it is very likely the apostles willingly suffered, and some died, for their belief that Jesus rose from the dead.
4. Therefore (b), the testimony of the apostles is very likely reliable.
5. Therefore (c), the resurrection very likely occurred.[101]

Conclusion: Jesus Rose From the Dead. Groothuis wraps up his survey of the evidence for and against the resurrection as follows: "This chapter has argued that the resurrection of Jesus is well established historically. The alternative naturalistic theories of the resurrection fail to account for commonly agreed-on facts relating to Jesus and the early church. Along with Christ's saving death, this unparalleled divine intervention by resurrection in history is the rock on which the church stands."[102]

Is there room to doubt that Jesus rose from the dead? Of course there is. As we shall discuss in the next chapter, there is room to doubt anything. That is why "Can it be doubted?" is the wrong question. The right question is, "What is the most reasonable conclusion to draw from the evidence?" Groothuis is surely correct. Christianity started with a rag-tag group of ten fishermen and a former tax collector in a backwater province on the edge of the Roman empire telling anyone who would listen that a poor carpenter-turned-itinerant-rabbi had been crucified and buried only to rise from the dead because he was God incarnate. Within a few centuries, Christianity transformed that empire. The explosive growth of Christianity would not have been possible if those men had not been convinced beyond the slightest doubt that they had seen the risen savior. Thus, the most reasonable conclusion to draw is that their testimony is true. Jesus rose from the dead. Christianity stands or falls on the veracity of the resurrection. And it stands.

7. Objection!

There are many common arguments for rejecting theism in general and Christianity in particular. In this chapter, I will address some of the more common objections. My response to each objection could be its own stand-alone chapter, but space constraints dictate that my replies be in summary form. I will include references to more detailed resources for those who want to explore these topics further.

7.1. When Darwin explained the emergence and evolution of life, he left no room for God.

As I discussed in chapter one, the explosive growth of materialism was closely linked with Charles Darwin's discovery[1] of natural selection and the publication of *Origin of Species* in 1859. According to Richard Dawkins, by seemingly solving the problem of the overwhelming appearance of design in living things without invoking a designer, Darwin made it possible to be an intellectually fulfilled atheist. Over 165 years later, one still frequently hears the claim that the "fact" of evolution makes belief in God untenable.[2] But is it true that evolution is an unassailable fact that necessarily shatters belief in God? The answer is that the claim is not merely false; it is, as we shall see, preposterous.

Let's start by addressing whether science has demonstrated that evolution is a "fact." It might surprise you to learn that I readily acknowledge that, depending on what one means by the word "evolution," the science of paleontology has demonstrated that evolution is a fact. Indeed, in a certain sense, evolution is so obviously true that every reasonable person—from the most fervent young Earth creationist to the most hardboiled materialist atheist—acknowledges it. This is easy to demonstrate. Go to the nearest window and look outside. I guarantee you will not see a T-Rex running around waving its tiny arms as it chases your neighbor's dog down the street. Yet, no rational person denies that T-Rexes once roamed the Earth. So, if by "evolution" one means simply that the biosphere today is different from the biosphere in the past, then evolution is an undeniable fact. I will go one step further. No reasonable person denies that neo-Darwinian[3] evolutionary theory has been empirically verified as the explanation for small-scale variations such as the development of antibiotic resistance in bacteria, the loss of sight in cavefish, and variation in beak size in some birds.

Still, we have not come close to the end of the story when it comes to answering the question of whether evolution is a demonstrated "fact." The much more interesting questions are: (1) Is it a "fact" that materialist scientists have a plausible explanation for how life evolved from dead matter?[4] and (2) Is it a "fact" that neo-Darwinian theory explains how things like fish and birds came to exist in the first place? It turns out that the answer to question (1) is: Scientists do not have the first clue how life arose from non-life. And the answer to Question (2) is: Many scientists—including leading materialist biologists—do not believe that standard neo-Darwinian theory is up to the task of explaining how large-scale body plans came to exist. Famous neo-Darwinian biologist Theodosius Dobzhansky used the term "microevolution" to refer to small-scale changes within species and "macroevolution" to refer to large-scale changes such as the development of new species or organs. I will use those terms in the same way in the discussion below.

Let's start with the materialist origin of life ("OOL") project. Darwin did not think deeply about how life arose from non-life,[5] but we can be certain that had he done so he would have failed to appreciate the mind-boggling complexity of the cell. Victorian scientists simply did not have the tools necessary to investigate matter at scales that small. Hence, they believed the cell was relatively simple. For example, Darwin's great popularizer, Ernst Haeckel,[6] wrote: "Each of us was, at the beginning of his existence, a *simple globule of protoplasm*, surrounded by a membrane, about 1/120 of an inch in diameter, with a firmer nucleus inside it."[7]

In the mid-twentieth century, as research tools improved, scientists launched an intensive OOL research project that continues to this day. That project has been a spectacular failure. Professor James Tour, whom we met in chapter six, says that scientists are "clueless" about life's origins."[8] Atheist Richard Dawkins agrees with Tour. He says, "We don't know how [life] started, and that's still a mystery. And it may always be a mystery because it happened a very long time ago, and we may never know exactly what did happen."[9] Materialist Harvard chemist George Whitesides also agrees: "[The problem of the the origin of life] is one of the big ones in science. It begins to place life, and us, in the universe. Most chemists believe, as do I, that life emerged spontaneously from mixtures of molecules in the prebiotic Earth. How? *I have no idea.*"[10] In 2024, *Nature,* which claims to be the world's leading multidisciplinary science journal, published an article admitting that origin of life research is moribund.[11] The authors reported that the field is "beset with over-claims" and pleaded with their fellow researchers to stop "cherry-picking" the data.[12] In summary, OOL researchers themselves do not claim that any materialist account of how the first living thing arose from dead matter is a fact. There is no reason that we should either.

In chapter six, we discussed the coded digital information in DNA, protein folds, molecular machinery, irreducible complex organic systems, and other features of living things that exhibit a staggering degree of specified complexity, and we concluded that design is the best explanation for these features. Unlike with OOL research, materialists seldom acknowledge a complete lack of understanding about how the blind physical forces of nature created these features.

However, in a development that would have been unthinkable until recently, candid materialists are now admitting that standard neo-Darwinian theory has significant explanatory shortcomings.

Design theorists are way ahead of them. In his book *Darwin's Doubt*,[13] Stephen Meyer explained some of the numerous explanatory deficits of neo-Darwinian theory. It is not widely known that Darwin himself understood that the fossil record does not support his theory. There are two particularly thorny problems with the fossil record from a Darwinian perspective: (1) the Cambrian explosion in which many animal groups appeared in the record all of a sudden instead of gradually over eons of time as his theory predicts; and (2) the general absence of the vast number of transitional fossils his theory predicts. In *Origin of Species*, Darwin candidly admitted these problems existed. He addressed them by appealing to the incompleteness of the fossil record. He suggested the problems would evaporate as the record was developed more fully. In the intervening 165 years, paleontologists have worked frenetically to find Darwin's missing fossils. Meyer convincingly demonstrates that they have largely not succeeded in finding those fossils, and it is becoming increasingly clear they never will. The problems with the fossil record are real, and those problems remain unsolved to this day.

Meyer has also shown that neither the neo-Darwinian mechanism of natural selection acting on random mutations, nor more recently-proposed mechanisms of evolutionary change (species selection, self-organization, neutral evolution, natural genetic evolution, etc.) are sufficient to generate the biological *information* that arose in the Cambrian period. Therefore, those theories cannot, in principle, explain the data. A general debunking of neo-Darwinian theory is beyond the scope of this book. My point from this brief sketch is that neo-Darwinian theory (as opposed to evolution in some general sense) is not an indisputable "fact," as is often claimed. Indeed, it is almost certainly not a fact at all, at least insofar as its claim to explain macroevolution goes.

Materialist evolutionary biologist Bret Weinstein agrees that neo-Darwinian theory is "broken" and credits Meyer with spotting that the neo-Darwinian mechanism is not powerful enough to explain the things Darwinists say it explains.[14] Weinstein is also critical of his fellow Darwinists for exaggerating how much the theory has explained and downplaying what it has yet to explain, which he characterizes as a sort of lying. He says:

> In my opinion, the mainstream Darwinists are telling a kind of lie about how much we know and what remains to be understood. So by reporting that yes, Darwinism is true, and we know how it works, and people who aren't compelled by the story are illiterate or ignorant or whatever, they are pretending to know more than they do. So all that being said, let me say, I think modern Darwinism is broken.[15]

Weinstein's comments demonstrate that one needn't be a theist to recognize that the neo-Darwinian evolutionary account is not a demonstrated "fact." Prominent atheist consciousness scholar Thomas Nagel also has his doubts. Nagel is resolute in his atheism. He once wrote, "It isn't just that I don't believe in God and, naturally, hope that I'm right in my belief. It's that I hope there is no God! I don't want there to be a God; I don't want the universe to be like that."[16] Despite his atheism, Nagel is honest enough to admit that the materialist neo-Darwinian conception of nature is almost certainly false because it simply does not explain the data. He writes:

> "[T]he prevailing doctrine—that the appearance of life from dead matter and its evolution through accidental mutation and natural selection to its present forms has involved nothing but the operation of physical law—cannot be regarded as unassailable. It is an assumption governing the scientific project rather than a well-confirmed scientific hypothesis.[17]

Nagel is caught on the horns of a dilemma of his own making. On the one hand, his strident atheism prevents him from believing in God. On the other hand, his unflinchingly honest assessment of the evidence causes him to reject the absurd conclusion that living things in general, and consciousness in particular, arose from blind physical forces spontaneously rearranging the fundamental particles. Nagel tries to resolve that dilemma by proposing the "teleological hypothesis," which posits that "life, consciousness, and the value that is inseparable from them" are "determined not merely by value-free chemistry and physics but also by something else, namely a cosmic predisposition to [their] formation."[18] Nagel does not speculate about the nature and source of this "cosmic predisposition." With all due respect to Nagel, who has been one of the brightest stars in the firmament of consciousness studies for over fifty years, his cosmic-woo-of-the-gaps hypothesis is more than a little sad.

Weinstein and Nagel are far from the only ones who believe neo-Darwinism is an inadequate explanation for the data. In 2008, sixteen prominent materialist biologists (who came to be known as the "Altenberg 16"[19]) gathered in Vienna at the Konrad Lorenz Institute for Evolution and Cognition Research to discuss whether, given neo-Darwinism's explanatory deficits, an "extended evolutionary synthesis" is necessary.[20] In 2010, the participants published a collection of essays challenging key components of neo-Darwinism, including the theory's "dogmatic" insistence on "the gene as the sole agent of variation and unit of inheritance,"[21] and, most spectacularly, the theory's insistence on "gradualism."[22] This is stunning because if there is a core idea in *Origin of Species*, it is that natural selection works on slight, barely perceptible variations over millions of years. Darwin himself believed this idea was essential to his theory, going so far as to say that without it, "my theory would absolutely break down."[23]

The Royal Society of London is the world's oldest and most prestigious scientific academy. (Isaac Newton himself served for many years as president.) In 2016, a group of biologists met at the Royal Society to discuss the extended evolutionary synthesis.[24] Professor Gerd Müller, one of the meeting's organizers, listed five "explanatory deficits" of standard neo-Darwinian theory. The theory does not adequately explain.

- phenotypic complexity
- biases in generation of variation
- phenotypic novelty [i.e., macroevolution]
- non-gradual forms of transition
- non-genetic factors of change[25]

In a follow-up article published by the Royal Society's publishing arm, Müller noted that "[neo-Darwinian] theory lacks a theory of organization that can account for the characteristic features of phenotypic evolution, such as novelty, modularity, homology, homoplasy or the origin of lineage-defining body plans."[26] In other words, according to this group of materialist biologists, when it comes to macroevolution, standard neo-Darwinian theory does not explain the very thing it is supposed to explain.

On January 13, 2025, *Nature* published a review[27] of *Evolution Evolving*, a 2024 book calling for new thinking in the field of evolutionary biology. The article's lede is a stunning rebuke to the conventional materialist narrative that all important questions in evolutionary theory have been settled:

> It's rare that researchers question theories that make up the backbone of whole fields. But in *Evolution Evolving*, Kevin Lala and four other eminent evolutionary biologists do just that. Their philosophically informed discussion challenges the textbook version of evolutionary theory, known as the Modern Synthesis, which has been regarded by many scientists as sacrosanct since its conception in the mid-twentieth century. This shift in thinking —which amounts to a new way of unifying the life sciences—is long overdue.

In 2022, *The Guardian* published an article entitled "Do we need a new theory of evolution?"[28] The author candidly admits up front that, "Strange as it sounds, scientists still do not know the answers to some of the most basic questions about how life on Earth evolved." To illustrate this, he relates the standard Darwinian narrative concerning the evolution of the eye, and then he writes:

> This is the basic story of evolution, as recounted in countless textbooks and pop-science bestsellers. The problem, according to a growing number of scientists, is that it is absurdly crude and misleading. For one thing, it starts midway through the story, taking for granted the existence of light-sensitive cells, lenses and irises, without explaining where they came from in the first place… And it isn't just eyes that the traditional theory struggles with. "The first eye, the first wing, the first placenta. How they emerge. Explaining these is the foundational motivation of evolutionary biology," says Armin Moczek, a biologist at Indiana University. "And yet, we still do not have a good answer. This classic idea of gradual change, one happy accident at a time, has so far fallen flat."

Why should it sound "strange" to the author that scientists do not know the answers to some of the most basic questions about evolution? Because even though some of the world's leading materialist scientists question the explanatory power of neo-Darwinian theory, one would never know this from most popular reporting on the subject. The standard narrative is that the Modern Synthesis is a fact that has the same scientific standing as the theory of gravity.[29] Why does the actual status of the theory vary so widely from its reported status? To answer this question requires a knowledge of medieval European castles. Allow me to explain. A motte-and-bailey castle, as its name suggests, has two main features: a motte, which is a strong keep built on the high ground, and a bailey, which is a courtyard surrounded by a wooden wall. A motte is easy to defend and a bailey much less so.

The motte-and-bailey logical fallacy is named after the castle. The fallacy is an argument in which an easily defended proposition is conflated with a proposition that is much harder to defend, and the arguer hopes his audience will not notice the difference. In the evolution debate, the "motte" is the proposition that the biosphere today is different from the biosphere in the past. The "bailey" is the assertion that materialist science has definitively explained *how* life arose from non-life and the *mechanism* by which the biosphere changed over time. As we have seen, the motte is easily defended. Everyone acknowledges the biosphere is different today than it was in the past. The bailey is not so easily defended because all honest scientists acknowledge that how life arose from inanimate matter is a mystery, and many of them also question the standard neo-Darwinian explanation of macroevolution.

Readers might have been surprised to learn that scientists do not have the first clue about how life began or that neo-Darwinian theory has been called out for its explanatory deficits by even many materialist scientists. After all, the popular media constantly bombard us with headlines such as "Discovery boosts theory that life on Earth arose from RNA-DNA mix,"[30] and "Amazing 30-year experiment captures evolution happening in real time."[31] But as Professor Tour has demonstrated,[32] the study referred to in the first article did not come remotely close to demonstrating how first life began. As for the second article, the researchers themselves admit that there was no evolutionary novelty. Instead, the organism (a kind of snail) tapped into "genetic diversity that was *already present* in their population" or perhaps arose through crossbreeding with other snails.[33]

What is going on here? Why do the media fail to show the slightest curiosity about or skepticism toward materialist scientists' claims about OOL and evolution research? Why do they mindlessly parrot the claims of the researchers when even the slightest scrutiny would reveal the claims are wildly overblown?

The answer to all of these questions is the same: Religion. Recall our earlier definition of religious belief as "a belief held as a matter of faith on account of one's metaphysical commitments." The researchers who produce the studies and the reporters who write the articles about those studies share a common religion: Metaphysical materialism. Darwinism is the creation myth of the materialist religion, and just as there are Christian and Islamic fundamentalists, there are materialist fundamentalists. Richard Lewontin, who was a professor of biology at Harvard and one of the most prominent scientists in the second half of the twentieth century, was such a fundamentalist. In a famous review of Carl Sagan's The *Demon-Haunted World* in *The New York Review of Books*, Lewontin wrote:

> We take the side of science in spite of the patent absurdity of some of its constructs, in spite of its failure to fulfill many of its extravagant promises of health and life, in spite of the tolerance of the scientific community for unsubstantiated just-so stories, because we have a prior commitment, **a commitment to materialism**. It is not that the methods and institutions of science somehow compel us to accept a material explanation of the phenomenal world, but, on the contrary, that we are forced by our *a priori* adherence to material causes to create an apparatus of investigation and a set of concepts that produce material explanations, no matter how counterintuitive, no matter how mystifying to the uninitiated. Moreover, that materialism is absolute, for we cannot allow a Divine Foot in the door.[34]

One of the consequences of a fervent religious commitment to materialism such as that seen in this passage, is the belief that *any evidence* is a stunning confirmation of the materialist origins myth. Phillip Johnson pointed out that if materialism is true, "then some materialistic theory of evolution has to be true simply as a matter of logical deduction, regardless of the evidence. That theory will necessarily be at least roughly like neo-Darwinism, in that it will have to involve some combination of random changes and law-like processes."[35] If your religion tells you that materialist evolution just has to be true, any evidence at all—no matter how weak and inconclusive it is to the rest of us—will confirm it.[36]

I call the uncritical acceptance and hyping of extremely weak or even non-existent evidence the "Peppered Moth Syndrome," after the 1950s work of British naturalist Bernard Kettlewell. Peppered moths in the UK come in dark and light varieties.[37] Kettlewell claimed to have demonstrated that when pollution darkened the moths' environment (and thus provided superior protection for dark moths from predators), dark moths became more common. In an article written for *Scientific American*, Kettlewell called his findings "Darwin's missing evidence."[38] For decades, Kettlewell's story (often illustrated with photos of light and dark peppered moths on tree trunks) was featured in many biology textbooks as absolutely compelling evidence for evolution.[39]

It turns out that Kettlwell's methods were, shall we say, suspect. He conducted his experiments under conditions that do not occur in the wild (for example, putting the moths on tree trunks where they normally do not rest), and he staged some of the famous photographs.[40] But a moment's reflection reveals that even if the story were completely true, it would not move the needle one iota toward proving the neo-Darwinian theory of macroevolution. Kettlewell never claimed that dark moths turned into light moths. Both light and dark moths existed before pollution, and both light and dark moths existed after pollution. At best, Kettlwell's story showed that natural selection can shift the proportions between *already existing varieties*!

Kettlewell did not show that anything evolved into anything else. Yet, for decades, his work was touted as a stunning confirmation of the neo-Darwinian mechanism in action. The decades-long hyping of the peppered moth story can only be explained by religiously motivated confirmation bias. If, like Lewontin, you insist on your religion above all other considerations, any evidence—and even non-evidence—will confirm your beliefs. The same thing explains science reporters' uncritical hyping of OOL and evolution studies. Long ago, the universal acid dissolved the reporters' capacity for curiosity and skepticism.

How to account for the astonishing complexity of living things without invoking God was one of the great mysteries of the ages that vexed materialists since the days of Lucretius. After 1859, materialism took off because there was a widespread belief that the mystery had finally been solved and only the details needed to be filled in. But I wonder if Darwin would be a Darwinist today. He could not have conceived of the marvelous nano-machinery researchers have recently discovered in the cell. At the Youtube channel *Veritasium*, Derek Muller has provided a fantastic animation of these molecular machines in action.[41] By the way, "nanomachine" is not my word; that is what *materialist* scientists call them.[42] Darwin also could not have begun to appreciate the complex digital information encoded into every strand of DNA.

Today, there is more reason to question the materialist explanation for the origin and development of life than at any time in the past 165 years. Darwin and his followers were profoundly mistaken. Science does not rule out the necessity of a designer. In fact, as we discussed in chapter six, the evidence points in the opposite direction. Despite the countless millions of dollars invested in OOL research, researchers are as far from an answer today as they ever were. And with each new discovery of complex machinery and digitally encoded information within the cell, the likelihood that it can all be explained by blind, directionless, material forces diminishes a little further. Since the mid-nineteenth century, materialist intellectuals have scoffed at those who "cling to their religion." The tables have turned. Perhaps the real clingers are those who insist on holding onto a Victorian analog theory that is (not very successfully) trying to make its way in a digital age.

7.2. Science has proved that God does not exist.

The claim that science has proved God does not exist need not detain us long. Even arch-materialist Carl Sagan knew science has done no such thing. He wrote:

> An atheist is someone who is certain that God does not exist, someone who has compelling evidence against the existence of God. I know of no such compelling evidence. Because God can be relegated to remote times and places and to ultimate causes, we would have to know a great deal more about the universe than we do now to be sure that no such God exists.[43]

Richard Dawkins, the world's most famous atheist, agrees and concedes that science has provided no absolutely definitive answer to the question of whether God exists.[44] Indeed, he has flatly admitted that science "can't disprove that there is a God."[45] Neil DeGrasse Tyson does not believe that God exists, but he insists that everyone should keep an open mind about the question.[46] He would hardly say that if science had proven God does not exist. If three of the most famous materialists in the world concede that science has not proven the nonexistence of God, we can consider the matter fairly well settled.

In addition to scientists, honest atheist philosophers also concede that there is no absolute proof that God does not exist. Bertrand Russell was perhaps the most famous philosopher of the twentieth century. Many people believe he was an atheist but that is not true. Like Dawkins, he was vehemently anti-religious, but, also like Dawkins, he knew that dogmatic atheism cannot be supported. He said that an atheist claims to know for certain something that cannot, in principle, be known for certain, i.e., that there is no God. Thus, his position was that the existence of God is improbable but not impossible.[47]

7.3. There is no evidence that God exists.

In a recent appearance on Joe Rogan's podcast, evolutionary biologist Bret Weinstein said, "I'm open to a universe with intelligence behind it, but I've seen *no evidence* of that universe myself."[48] Weinstein took a stance I have seen materialists take many times over the years when they say there is "no evidence" that God exists. After 38 years of practicing law, I have learned a thing or two about evidence, and I can assure you that they are quite mistaken about the evidence issue.

Before we can determine if there is any evidence for God's existence, we must first understand what evidence is. "Evidence" has a commonsense definition. It means anything offered to prove something.[49] Whether the evidence offered actually proves that thing is a separate question. Suppose I represent Bill in a case in which he says that Ted ran a red light and injured him. At trial, I call three witnesses who testify they saw Ted blow right through that light and hit Bill. Ted's lawyer also calls three witnesses, and they say the light was definitely green when Ted went through the intersection. The judge then instructs the jury that Bill has the burden of proving that Ted ran the light and injured him. The judge will tell the jury that if Bill met his burden, their verdict must be for him, but if Bill failed to meet that burden, their verdict must be for Ted. Let's say the jury deliberates and returns with a verdict for Bill. This means that for whatever reason, the members of the jury did not credit the testimony of Ted's witnesses as much as they credited the testimony of Bill's witnesses. Does that mean that Ted's lawyer failed to put on any evidence at all? Of course not. Evidence that does not convince the jury is still evidence.

All of this is obvious, which is why the claim that there is no evidence for the existence of God is ridiculous. People who make this claim are confused. They seem to believe that "evidence that does not convince me" is the same thing as "no evidence." Of course, there is evidence for God's existence. In chapter six, I presented some of that evidence for your consideration. I would be very happy if that evidence persuaded you that God exists. But if you reject that conclusion, you cannot justify your decision by asserting there is no evidence for God's existence.

7.4. You cannot "prove" that God exists.

Now let's turn to the matter of proof. Before one can speak cogently about whether it is possible to prove that God exists, one must first clarify what one means by the word "prove." The first thing to know about proof is that it is not a discrete yes/no concept. Rather, proof falls on a continuum. In the law, that continuum looks like this:

Proof beyond a reasonable doubt	Proof that is so convincing that a person would not hesitate to rely and act on it in making the most important decisions in his life
Proof by clear and convincing evidence	Proof that is highly probable and leaves no serious doubt[50]
Proof by a preponderance of the evidence	Proof that is more likely than not
Probable cause	A fair probability but not a preponderance[51]
Reasonable suspicion	More than an unparticularized suspicion or "hunch" but something less than the level of suspicion required for probable cause[52]

The level of proof required varies depending on the stakes. Criminal cases involve the highest stakes, sometimes literally life and death. That is why the highest standard—beyond a reasonable doubt—applies in such cases. In the vast majority of civil cases, the preponderance standard applies.

Did the evidence I presented in chapter six prove that God exists? That depends on whom you ask. Whether something has been proven is a subjective determination. Evidence that convinces one person will not necessarily convince someone else. That is why when I am advising a client about whether to settle a case, I never say the jury will do this or that if we reject a settlement and go to trial. Instead, I use what I call the "ten-jury" rule to explain the difficulties of making predictions about jury trials. I tell my client that no one can predict with certainty how his case will turn out if he goes to trial. If we were to try the case ten times in front of ten juries, the results would certainly fall on a spectrum. The best I can do is make my best prediction about what that spectrum looks like based on my assessment of the law and the evidence. For example, if we have a good but not perfect case,[53] I might estimate that three juries would return a defense verdict, while seven would likely return a plaintiff's verdict.[54]

In my view, the evidence presented in chapter six is sufficient to prove beyond a reasonable doubt that God exists. No reasonable person believes the universe created itself from nothing. And no reasonable person can look at the undeniable exquisite fine-tuning of the universe for the existence of life and not agree with astronomer Fred Hoyle, who wrote that "A commonsense interpretation of the facts suggests that a superintellect has monkeyed with physics, as well as chemistry and biology."[55] At the very least, I do not see how a reasonable person can review the evidence and say it does not preponderate in favor of God's existence.

Other people review the evidence and come to different conclusions. In *The God Delusion*, Richard Dawkins included a chart that he called the "spectrum of probabilities" for God's existence.[56] Dawkin's spectrum has seven points designating various levels of certainty ranging from totally certain God exists to totally certain God does not exist. Dawkins places himself at point 6 (God is highly improbable).

The point of all of this is that if you say the existence of God cannot be proven, you are not stating an objective fact. Even Dawkins admits that God's existence cannot be rejected with one hundred percent certainty.[57] Instead, you are saying that after evaluating the evidence for and against God's existence, you personally remain unconvinced. Many highly intelligent people have evaluated that same evidence. Some of them agree with you, and some of them disagree.

Before we leave the issue of proof, I should mention a final standard of proof known as "apodictic proof." This is proof that a proposition is necessarily or logically certain, such as a mathematical proof. Apodictic certainty is the kind of unquestionable certainty where something is so undeniably true that it is not rational to question or doubt it. The law does not use this standard of proof. Indeed, judges sometimes tell juries that the prosecution is not required to prove their case with "mathematical certainty." This is the judge's way of saying that the prosecution's burden of proving a case beyond a reasonable doubt is not the same as proving the case beyond *all doubt* because that is impossible. It seems to me that many times when people say that it is not possible to prove God exists, they jump right to this standard. And if that is your standard of proof, you are correct. It is not possible to prove God exists to an apodictic certainty. But by the same token, it is not possible to prove the nonexistence of God to an apodictic certainty. The best one can do is evaluate the evidence and draw a conclusion.

7.5. Evil exists. Therefore, God does not exist.

Materialists often argue that if God exists, he would not permit evil to exist, and since we know evil exists, we can conclude that God does not. Let's see whether that argument holds up. Good arguments depend on the unambiguous use of language. The argument from evil is no exception. It requires a clear definition of the word "evil," and materialists face a difficult challenge from the start because they deny the existence of evil. Dawkins, for example, writes that "The universe we observe has precisely the properties we should expect if there is, at bottom, no design, no purpose, *no evil and no good*, nothing but blind, pitiless indifference."[58] If Dawkins is correct and there is no evil, it would seem to be impossible to argue that the existence of evil disproves the existence of God.

But that is not necessarily the case because when Dawkins says there is no good and no evil, he means there is no *objective* transcendent morality. In other words, he is saying that in a universe governed by blind, physical forces, stuff just happens for no reason, and it is neither good nor evil in the sense of "conforming to an objective transcendent moral code." However, Dawkins himself uses the word "evil" all the time to describe certain things or people. For example, he believes that discrimination and religion and Hitler and Stalin are evil.[59] There is no contradiction here because when Dawkins uses the word "evil," he means a "sense" of right and wrong derived from our Darwinian past.[60] Remember our discussion of morality from chapter two. Materialists agree that we feel strong urges to do certain things (which we call good) and not do other things (which we call evil). For the materialist, those urges are reducible to the electrochemical processes of our physical brains, and our brains, like all of our other organs, are the product of evolutionary processes. We have an appendix because, at some point in our evolutionary history, it gave our ancestors an advantage in the Darwinian struggle for relative reproductive success, and we have strong feelings of revulsion about the Holocaust for the same reason.

Given all this, we arrive at the materialist definition of evil: "That which blind, physical evolutionary forces have programmed me not to prefer." Now that we have the definitional issue out of the way, we can go on to the argument, which is straightforward and amounts to the following syllogism:

Major Premise: If God exists, he would prevent "evil"—i.e., that which blind, physical, evolutionary forces have programmed me not to prefer – from happening.

Minor Premise: Things often happen that blind, physical, evolutionary forces have programmed me not to prefer.

Conclusion: God does not exist.

Thus, we see that if "evil" means what materialists say it means, the argument from evil is absurd. A subjective sense of revulsion caused by evolutionary forces cannot be the basis for asserting God does not exist. To avoid this problem, the materialist must smuggle into the argument an objective meaning of "evil." But then the argument hits another insurmountable problem. Objective evil can exist only if it is possible to transgress an objective, transcendent moral code.[61] But as Arthur Leff explained, an objective, transcendent moral code exists only if God exists. Thus, it makes no sense to argue that God does not exist because things happen that transgress a code that only he could create. The argument eats itself. Objective evil is possible *only* if God exists. Therefore, the existence of objective evil, far from disproving the existence of God, actually confirms it.

There is no *logical* contradiction between God's existence and the fact that he permits evil to exist, for it could be the case that an all-powerful, all-knowing and omnibenevolent God has good reasons for allowing evil to exist and persist.[62] This is not a controversial conclusion among philosophers. Both theist and atheist philosophers widely agree that Alvin Plantinga's Free Will Defense[63] demolished the logical argument from evil. Professor Chad Meister writes:

> Most people writing at the popular level aren't aware that professional philosophers of religion, theists and atheists alike have agreed in recent years that this version of the problem of evil [i.e., that the existence of evil logically precludes the existence of God] has been decisively rebutted and is therefore unsuccessful. That kind of consensus doesn't come very often in philosophy![64]

Well-known atheist philosopher Paul Draper agrees. He writes, "Logical arguments from evil are a dying (dead?) breed."[65]

7.6. If God is good, he would not allow innocent people to suffer.

While the logical argument from evil is dead, the "evidentiary" version of the argument from evil is another matter. This argument asserts that the existence of evil[66] and suffering makes it highly improbable that God exists. This appears to be the version of the argument Neil DeGrasse Tyson uses to reject the existence of God.[67] William Lane Craig has provided a detailed and persuasive response to the evidentiary problem, which he summarizes as follows:

> As finite persons, we are limited in time, space, intelligence, and insight. But the transcendent and sovereign God sees the end from

> the beginning and providentially orders history so that his purposes are ultimately achieved through human free decisions. In order to achieve his ends, God may have to put up with certain evils along the way. Evils which appear pointless to us within our limited framework may be seen to have been justly permitted within God's wider framework.[68]

Craig then argues that when all of the evidence (not just the existence of evil) is considered as a whole, including all of the evidence for God's existence that we examined in chapter six, the existence of God is the most reasonable conclusion.[69]

Craig's argument is consistent with the Biblical story of Job. Job was, we are told, a very righteous man. Yet, God allowed almost unbearable pain to fall on him. In the midst of his anguish, Job insisted on his innocence and demanded that God explain why he had required him to endure such torment. He shouted, "Let the Almighty answer me!"[70] But God declined to give an account of himself to Job. Instead, he reminded Job of his unimaginably awesome power and wisdom as demonstrated in creation, and he reminded Job of his own comparatively limited intelligence and perspective.[71] God expected Job to trust him even when he could not understand him.

The Christian faith is a reasoned and reasonable one grounded in a sober assessment of several lines of evidence. However, as we saw above, apodictic certainty is unattainable. Some degree of doubt will always be possible, and God requires us to trust Him[72] in the face of that doubt. Sometimes that can be hard, especially when we are suffering or we see the ones we love suffer. Fyodor Dostoevsky, for example, was a Christian, but his faith was sorely tested by doubts that arose when he contemplated innocent suffering, especially the suffering of children.

Dostoevsky explored these themes in *The Brothers Karamazov*, widely regarded as one of the greatest novels of all time. The novel is written mainly from the perspective of a young Russian Orthodox novice,[73] Alexei Fyodorovich Karamazov, nicknamed Alyosha. Dostoevsky contrasts Alyosha's beliefs with those of his brother, an atheist intellectual named Ivan. In the chapter entitled "Rebellion," Ivan offers, in the words of Professor Gary Saul Morson, "the strongest case against God ever made."[74] Ivan recounts several gut-wrenching stories of children who endured almost unimaginable suffering at the hands of sadistic torturers. (These accounts are all the more horrifying because Dostoevsky based them on actual newspaper reports.) Ivan rejects God because even if God somehow eventually harmonizes all of creation so that we can see how it all makes sense in the end, the price—innocent suffering—is too high. Ivan declares:

> I don't want harmony, for love of mankind I don't want it. I want to remain with unrequited suffering. I'd rather remain with my unrequited suffering and my unquenched indignation, even if I am wrong. Besides, they have put too high a price on harmony; we can't afford to pay so much for admission. And therefore I hasten to return my ticket.[75]

Ivan is angry with God for allowing children to suffer, and his anger drives him to reject God unequivocally. His rage is so incandescently hot that he says he rejects God "even if I am wrong." In other words, he acknowledges that he could be mistaken and God might have morally justifiable reasons for permitting innocent suffering. It does not matter. Ivan will have nothing to do with a God that allows innocent suffering.

The most important thing to understand about Ivan's declaration is that it is not a logical *argument* that God does not exist. It is a visceral emotional rejection of God. This is not uncommon among atheists. For example, one commentator said that New Atheist Christopher Hitchens's atheism could be summed up with a single sentence: "There is no God and I hate Him."[76] Ivan has not offered an intellectual argument for his atheism, so it does no good to offer counterarguments. As William Lane Craig has said, those who reject

God for emotional reasons do not need a philosopher; they need a counselor.

What would a Christian counselor say to Ivan? First, I don't think a counselor would dismiss Ivan's anguish and doubts out of hand. At a certain level, anger at God can be understandable (even if it is ultimately unjustified), and even the most faithful sometimes harbor doubts about God's goodness in the face of great pain and suffering. Dostoevsky himself was candid about his struggles with doubt. Near the end of this life, he wrote, "It is not as a child that I believe and confess Jesus Christ. My hosanna is born of a furnace of doubt."[77] It is hardly surprising that the man who put in Ivan's mouth "the strongest case against God ever made" was tormented by doubt.

As Alvin Plantinga writes, while both the logical and the evidentiary argument from evil have been defeated, "this is cold and abstract comfort when faced with the shocking concreteness of a particularly appalling exemplification of evil."[78] This does not mean that the counselor has nothing to say to Ivan. Again, Job is our example for getting to the other side of the doubt that understandably springs from suffering. In the depths of his misery, pain, and confusion, when he desperately searched for God and could not find him, Job clung to his faith that God was there and that, in the end, he would bring him through.[79]

A Christian counselor would also tell Ivan that he is being unfair to God. In his intellectual hubris, Ivan thinks of God solely in abstract intellectual terms, as if he were a cosmic trolley operator standing above the fray pulling levers[80] as he calmly computes an optimal overall outcome. But that is not who God is. Instead, in the person of Jesus Christ, God entered into his creation and shared in its sufferings in order to redeem it to himself. God does not stand at the lever directing trolleys. He placed himself on the track and allowed the trolley to hit him so that he could save us all. Plantinga writes:

> As the Christian sees things, God does not stand idly by, coolly observing the suffering of his creatures. He enters into and shares

our suffering. He endures the anguish of seeing his son, the second person of the Trinity, consigned to the bitterly cruel and shameful death of the cross.... Christ was prepared to endure the agonies of hell itself; and God, the Lord of the universe, was prepared to endure the suffering consequent upon his son's humiliation and death. He was prepared to accept this suffering in order to overcome sin, and death, and the evils that afflict our world, and to confer on us a life more glorious than we can imagine. So we don't know why God permits evil; we do know, however, that he was prepared to suffer on our behalf, to accept suffering of which we can form no conception.[81]

Where does all of this leave us? On the one hand, God does not force himself on anyone. We must approach him in faith, a reasoned and reasonable faith to be sure, but faith nevertheless. God does not give us absolute certainty. There will always be room for doubt, and that doubt intensifies in the face of suffering. On the other hand, there are compelling reasons to believe that God exists, that He loves us, and that he sent his son, Jesus Christ, to suffer, die, and rise again to save us.

7.7. Unlike Christians, we materialists believe only scientifically verified claims.

Several years ago, my wife and I had the pleasure of inviting a Chinese college student into our home for a few weeks while he visited the United States during his summer break. This brilliant young man was studying at the Harbin Institute of Technology, one of China's most prestigious universities.[82] One evening, our conversation turned to philosophical matters, including the most basic question of all: Why is there something rather than nothing? I shared my perspective, and he summed up his own views when he said, "I can choose 'God,' or I can choose 'science.' I choose science." Sadly, our young friend had failed to lash himself to the mast, and the siren song of scientism caused him to steer the ship of his soul onto the shoals.

Most materialists I have encountered are like our Chinese friend. They believe everyone falls into one of two camps: (1) smart people who hold only beliefs grounded in the deliverances of empirical science and (2) deluded people who hold irrational beliefs grounded in religious superstition, emotions, wishful thinking, or what have you. Naturally, they take the side of science and usually assume an air of smug intellectual superiority as they do so. However, materialists' smug attitude is misplaced, even ironic, for two reasons. First, they are mistaken in believing that the methods of science offer the only valid way of knowing. Second, their attitude reveals an acute lack of self-awareness regarding their own belief system because just a little probing inevitably reveals that they believe things that have not been scientifically proven.

"Scientism" is the belief that science is the only reliable source of knowledge. This belief fails to meet the most basic requirement of any belief system: coherence. It is easy to demonstrate this incoherence because the statement "science is the only reliable source of knowledge" is not itself a scientific statement; rather, it belongs to the realm of philosophy, specifically epistemology.[83] Not only is scientism incoherent, but it is also demonstrably false because we all accept certain truths that cannot be scientifically proven. In a famous debate with the atheist scientist Peter Atkins, William Lane Craig effectively dismantled the claims of scientism in less than two minutes in the following exchange:

> Atkins: Do you deny that science [can] account for everything?
> Craig: Yes, I do deny that science can account for everything.
> Atkins: So, what can't it account for?
> Craig: . . . I think there are a good number of things that cannot be scientifically proven but that we're all rational to accept.
> Atkins: Such as?
> Craig: Let me list five.
>
> [1] Logical and mathematical truths cannot be proven by science. Science presupposes logic and math, so that to try to prove them by science would be arguing in a circle.

[2] Metaphysical truths, like there are other minds other than my own, or that the external world is real, or that the past was not created five minutes ago with an appearance of age are rational beliefs that cannot be scientifically proven.

[3] Ethical beliefs about statements of value are not accessible by the scientific method. You can't show by science whether the Nazi scientists in the camps did anything evil as opposed to the scientists in Western democracies.

[4] Aesthetic judgments, number four, cannot be accessed by the scientific method because the beautiful, like the good, cannot be scientifically proven.

[5] And finally, most remarkably, would be science itself. Science cannot be justified by the scientific method. Science is permeated with unprovable assumptions. For example, in the special theory of relativity, the whole theory hinges on the assumption that the speed of light is constant in a one-way direction between any two points A and B. But that strictly cannot be proven. We simply have to assume that in order to hold to the theory. . . .

So none of these beliefs can be scientifically proven and yet they are accepted by all of us, and we're rational in doing so.[84]

Craig was undoubtedly correct. Let's consider just one of his examples of a truth we are rational to accept even though it cannot be scientifically proven—the belief that the external world we perceive through our senses is real. Anyone who has seen the movie *The Matrix*[85] is familiar with this example. In the film, Neo lives a dull existence in what he believes to be a real world. Then, he meets Morpheus, who gives him the opportunity to have a red pill moment. When Neo takes the red pill, he is disconnected from the Matrix, a vast computer simulation that connects directly into the minds of almost everyone alive, and he realizes that the external world he perceived his entire life is not real but a computer-generated illusion. The movie becomes truly mind-blowing the moment one realizes that it is impossible to prove one is not in the Matrix at this very moment. Yet, as Craig says, even though we cannot scientifically prove the reality of the external world we perceive, it is eminently rational to assume that it exists.

7.8. God is not necessary because there is a material explanation for why the universe exists.

Our Chinese friend made a second mistake regarding the specific question of how the universe began. He assumed there is a faith-based theistic answer and a rational scientific answer, and one must choose between them. This is incorrect. There is no rational materialist answer to why the universe exists, and honest materialists admit this, as Neil DeGrasse Tyson did in an interview with Piers Morgan.[86]

> Morgan: What was there before the beginning of the universe? Everyone asks this question. What's the simple answer?
>
> DeGrasse Tyson: Well, I am delighted I can respond to you. We don't know. But we've got top people working on it. OK, there may have been a multiverse.
>
> Morgan: You know what, I like that. I like the honesty. We genuinely don't know. People just don't know, right?
>
> DeGrasse Tyson: We don't know. There might have been a multiverse that's birthing universes and we're one of them. But that just pushes the question one step further before that. What was around before the multiverse? So, we just don't know. It's a frontier question right now.

DeGrasse Tyson says that scientists are working on the problem, and he implies there may one day be a materialist answer to the question of how the universe began. His optimism is, however, surely misplaced because there cannot, in principle, be a rational materialist answer to how a material universe came into being. To see why this is so, we must consider the three potential explanations for the existence of the universe:

1. A supernatural being created the universe *ex nihilo*.[87]
2. The universe has always existed.
3. The universe created itself.

As we saw in chapter six, the theistic possibility is supported by several lines of evidence. While accepting this explanation requires a leap to a necessary being (an uncreated creator), the explanation itself is not irrational, as I will discuss in the next section. In contrast, the two materialist possibilities are not only unsupported by the evidence, but they are also fundamentally irrational.

An eternal universe is irrational because of the contingency problem. Something is "contingent" if its existence can be explained as the result of something else. For example, an apple is contingent because we know it came from a tree, and the tree is contingent because it grew from a seed planted in soil, and the soil is contingent because it resulted from the gradual breakdown of rocks and organic matter. The chain of contingent explanations for the apple could, in principle, go back to the Big Bang.

In contrast, something is "necessary" if it could not possibly have not existed and therefore depends on nothing prior to it for its existence."[88] *Every material thing is contingent.* It follows that saying the material universe is eternal is another way of saying there is an infinite regress of contingent things. The principle of sufficient reason requires that there be at least one necessary being that starts the series of contingent things.[89] To say otherwise is to confess that there is ultimately no reason for the series to exist or to be the way that it is. And to say something exists for no reason is to give up on the principle of sufficient reason, which is irrational.

What about self-creation? In *The Grand Design*, Stephen Hawking said, "Because there is a law such as gravity, the universe can and will create itself from nothing."[90] While I will grant that Hawking was brilliant in his field of expertise— theoretical physics—when he ventured into metaphysics, he was just another layman. And in this one sentence, Hawking committed two egregious logical blunders. First, he committed the error of "reification" when he ascribed concrete properties to an abstract concept. The law of gravity does not "do" anything. It is not an agent. Like all laws of physics, the law of gravity is a mathematical model of observed regularities. Why those regularities are the way they are and how they came to be in the first place is a question of metaphysics beyond the realm of science—and thus not within Hawking's area of expertise. Hawking's error is all the more inexplicable because he knows that the law of gravity has no creative power. In an earlier book, he wrote:

> What is it that breathes fire into the equations and makes a universe for them to describe? The usual approach of science of constructing a mathematical model cannot answer the question of why there should be a universe for the model to describe. Why does the universe go to all the bother of existing?[91]

Hawking also committed the error of "equivocation"—the use of ambiguous language to obscure rather than illuminate the truth.[92] The question to be answered is, "Did the universe create itself from nothing?" The word "nothing" in that sentence has a particular meaning. It means "absolute non-being." Absolute non-being means the absence of anything at all. Hawking claimed that because we have something (the law of gravity), the universe can create itself from nothing. Well, sure, if we redefine "nothing" to mean "something," then Hawking's assertion might be true (whether it is true is a separate matter). However, "nothing" does not mean "something," so Hawking's statement is obviously false. Nothing comes from nothing, and to suggest otherwise is irrational.

Nature has not always existed and it did not create itself. Thus, as is often said, nature points to something beyond nature. And that something is God.

7.9. "God created the universe" just pushes the problem back to "who created God?"

In his book *Five Proofs of the Existence of God*, Ed Feser explains why there must be one necessary being. The following is a simplified summary of his argument.[93]

1. The principle of sufficient reason states that there is an explanation for the existence of all things. Rejecting the principle of sufficient reason is irrational. In fact, it is arguably the most irrational stance one can take, because rejecting the principle implies that events can happen for no reason at all. Science itself depends on the principle of sufficient reason because it assumes there are explanations for why things happen.

2. As discussed in the previous section, everything is either contingent or necessary. There is no third option.

3. No contingent thing, or any series of contingent things, can explain why contingent things exist in the first place. However, the principle of sufficient reason means that the existence of contingent things must have an explanation. The only possible explanation left is the existence of a necessary being.

4. Thus, there must be at least one necessary being to explain why contingent beings exist. This necessary being is the cause of everything except itself. This necessary being is God.

In summary, rationality itself absolutely depends on there being one necessary being, which is God. God was not created. Rather, he is the necessary ground of all being. Therefore, asking "Who created God" is seeking a contingent explanation for a necessary being. The question reflects a basic category error. The only way to avoid the conclusion that a necessary being exists is to assert that the universe consists of an infinitely long chain of contingent things,[94] which is irrational.

7.10. The multiverse explains everything.

Does the multiverse explain absolutely everything? Yes, it does, and that is why it explains nothing.

The multiverse is a materialist God-substitute,[95] but Neil DeGrasse Tyson has already told us why the multiverse can never be an ultimate explanation for the existence of the universe. The multiverse itself is contingent. He said, "There might have been a multiverse that's birthing universes and we're one of them. But that just pushes the question one step further before that. What was around before the multiverse?"[96]

Materialists' attempts to invoke the multiverse as an explanation for the fine-tuning of the universe also fail. Elie Feder and Aaron Zimmer explain the basic argument of those who place their faith (I use that word advisedly) in the multiverse as follows:

> Since there are an infinite number of universes—each with different laws, constants, and initial conditions—every possible universe must exist somewhere in the multiverse—including a universe that's as fine tuned, designed, and ordered as our own. And, of course, we shouldn't be surprised to find ourselves in a universe hospitable to intelligent life, because there simply aren't any observers in universes that aren't hospitable to life.[97]

The first problem with this theory is, as physicist Alan H. Guth explains, "In an eternally inflating universe, anything that can happen will happen; in fact, it will happen an infinite number of times."[98] Imagine you are playing poker with a friend. He deals himself a royal flush ten times in a row, and you say, "Hey, something fishy is going on here." Suppose your friend responded, "Relax, I admit that getting ten royal flushes in a row is highly improbable, but we live in an infinite multiverse where anything that can happen will happen, and it's just your bad luck that you live in a universe where I get ten royal flushes in a row." Would you be satisfied with that explanation and pull out your wallet and settle up? No? Well, substitute "fine-tuning of the physical constants" for "ten royal flushes in a row," and you have the materialist explanation for fine-tuning. The multiverse can be invoked to explain anything, no matter how vanishingly small the odds that it will happen may be. Therefore, it explains nothing. A theory that accounts for every conceivable scientific observation in this universe—and the opposite of every conceivable scientific observation in the universe next door—is the ultimate science killer. Notice that even though you don't believe your friend's explanation for his lucky streak, it is impossible to disprove it. The explanation is intrinsically irrefutable because any apparent contradictory evidence can be dismissed by saying, "It has to occur in one universe in the multiverse, and apparently, we're in that universe."[99]

Multiverse theorists attempt to prevent the theory from killing science by invoking the "typical universe premise." This is the claim that from the infinite subset of universes that have intelligent observers, our universe is typical.[100] The idea is that the multiverse does not explain everything (and therefore nothing). It only explains observations in "typical" universes. If this premise is true, multiverse theory predicts that we should observe a typical universe.[101] Here, the theory smacks into another problem—the prediction appears to be false. This is the case for at least two reasons that Feder and Zimmer call the Boltzmann Brain problem and the Grand Universe problem.[102]

The Boltzmann Brain problem compares two probabilities. The first one is the probability that the process I described in chapter two happened—the Big Bang occurred billions of years ago, galaxies and planets formed, life arose on one of those planets, and over eons of time, humans evolved so that they could observe the universe. The second probability is the probability that five minutes ago particles spontaneously coalesced into a disembodied brain that falsely believes it is observing an orderly universe. Scientists refer to such a brain as a "Boltzmann Brain," after the man who first conceptualized it at the end of the nineteenth century. It turns out that in an infinite multiverse where every possible thing happens an infinite number of times, the probability of a Boltzmann Brain (astronomically unlikely but simple) is much higher than the probability that humans evolved over eons in a universe with trillions of stars (astronomically unlikely but complex).[103] The Grand Universe problem arises from the fact that our galaxy contains at least a hundred billion stars, and the universe has hundreds of billions of galaxies. But wouldn't a more typical universe with observers be much less grand? Why are all those trillions of stars necessary to explain the fact that humans can observe the universe? These two problems demonstrate that we do not live in the "typical" universe predicted by the theory.[104]

The multiverse theory is not a scientific theory if, by "scientific theory," one means a hypothesis about reality that can be empirically tested and potentially falsified. By definition, all of our empirical tests must be performed in this universe. Except in science fiction, all other universes are inaccessible to us. As a matter of empirical observation, we will never know whether any other universe exists. If the multiverse is not science, what is it? As I said at the beginning of this section, it is a metaphysical God substitute, and it would have horrified William of Ockham. Ockham's razor is often stated as "of two competing theories, the simpler explanation is to be preferred." However, the classic Latin formulation is "*Entia non sunt multiplicanda praeter necessitatem*," which means "entities must not be multiplied beyond necessity."[105] Multiverse theory posits infinite entities (i.e., infinite universes) in an effort to escape the conclusion that one God exists. There are many insurmountable problems with multiverse theory, not the least of which is that it is literally the most egregious violation of Ockham's razor it is possible to imagine.

7.11. Invoking a creator commits the "god of the gaps" fallacy.

Critics of intelligent design argue that invoking an intelligent agent as an explanation is wrong because it amounts to an argument from ignorance. They contend that filling gaps in our understanding of nature with "God did it" explanations is especially misguided because science will eventually provide natural explanations for those gaps.

Stephen Meyer has convincingly refuted this objection. He points out that a true God of the gaps argument from ignorance would assert that the failure of materialist explanations, *standing alone*, must mean that God is the explanation, but that is not what the modern design argument does.[106] Rather, the design argument has both negative and positive components. First, it demonstrates that no materialist cause accounts for the data. Second, it demonstrates that intelligent causes have demonstrated the power to account for the data. It then concludes that, of the two explanatory options, design is the best, most causally adequate explanation.[107]

Thus, the design argument is not an argument from ignorance. It is an argument from knowledge. It is an argument from the knowledge that one explanation (the materialist explanation) has not been shown to be able to account for the data, and a second explanation (design by an intelligent agent) has been. Therefore, only a metaphysical bias against intelligent causes as explanations prevents the latter from being accepted as the current best explanation. This does not foreclose the possibility that, someday, a materialist answer will be found that will explain the data. However, for now, design is the best explanation we have. That is how science is supposed to work—all scientific explanations are tentative and subject to revision if new data come to light. In his highly influential book, *The Logic of Scientific Discovery*, Karl Popper put the matter this way:

> The bold structure of [science's] theories rises, as it were, above a swamp. It is like a building erected on piles. The piles are driven down from above into the swamp, but not down to any natural or 'given' base; and if we stop driving the piles deeper, it is not because we have reached firm ground. We simply stop when we are satisfied that the piles are firm enough to carry the structure, at least for the time being.[108]

Let's consider how this works with a specific example—the origin of life. As discussed above, James Tour challenged ten of the world's leading OOL researchers to answer any one of five basic questions. One of those questions was, "Account for the origin of specified information (rather than Shannon information) embedded in sequences in polypeptides, polynucleotides or polysaccharides, whichever you think arose first."[109] None of the researchers was able to respond to Tour. That is because even the best OOL researchers in the world remain utterly "clueless" about how to answer even the most basic questions concerning the origin of the first living cell.[110]

Now, suppose a design theorist were to respond to Tour as follows: "No one can explain how blind physical forces could create the vast amounts of complex specified information in the first cell; therefore, it must have been placed there by God." If they did that, they would be committing the God of the gaps fallacy. But that is not what design theorists do. Instead, they examine the causal-adequacy and the causal-existence criteria for an inference to the best explanation. The causal-adequacy criterion asks, "Does the the proposed cause have the power to produce the observed phenomenon?" The causal-existence criterion asks, "Has the proposed cause been observed to exist?"

In the context of OOL research, materialist theories fail both tests. There is no reason to believe that blind material forces have the power to spontaneously generate the staggering specified complexity observed in even the simplest imaginable cell. Moreover, there is no direct evidence that purely natural processes lacking guiding intelligence ever have produced such specified complexity. While there is no known natural source of complex specified information, our consistent experience over centuries has demonstrated that, whenever the origin of such information is known for certain, it has always been the product of a mind.[111] Therefore, the design explanation is the current best explanation.

Meyer's conclusion is based on what we *know*, not on what we do not know. He has not committed the God of the gaps fallacy.

Furthermore, the fact that he has proposed a tentative solution does not foreclose further work in the area. As Popper stated, all scientific conclusions are provisional, and if someone comes up with a plausible explanation for how blind material forces created complex specified information, their solution will supplant Meyer's (and earn them a Nobel Prize to boot). In the meantime, Tour is certainly correct. No one has a clue about how blind material forces created the first life, and it does no one any good to pretend otherwise. It is especially dishonest for OOL researches to continue to pretend they are on the verge of a solution when nothing could be further from the truth. Nobel Prize–winning physicist Richard Feynman once wrote that the "first principle" is that a scientist must not fool himself about his work, and he should always be careful not to fool laymen when talking about science.[112] For far too long, OOL researchers have been violating Feynman's first principle.

7.12. Invoking a creator is a science stopper.

Materialists often say that invoking God as an explanation is a "science stopper." The idea is that science continually strives to find natural explanations and that work stops if we just throw up our hands and say, "God must have done it," every time we encounter a seemingly intractable problem like the origin of life. History shows that this objection is not valid.

Isaac Newton is the best example of this. In his book *Opticks*, Newton contemplated whether irregularities in planetary orbits might be apt to increase over time until the "System wants a Reformation."[113] Newton's rival, Gottfied Wilhelm Leibniz, accused Newton of holding the view that God needs to wind up the watch of the solar system from time to time.[114] The story has come down through the centuries that Newton did not have a natural explanation for how the planetary orbits would remain stable, and so he invoked a tinkering God to address the problem, and perhaps that is true.[115] But even if it is true, it was by no means a science stopper. Scientists continued to work the problem, and Laplace and Lagrange eventually demonstrated how planetary orbits remain stable.

As discussed above, materialist chemist George Whitesides and theist chemist James Tour agree that today, materialist scientists do not have a clue about how life began. From a materialist perspective, the problem appears to be hopelessly intractable. Imagine a "metaphysically neutral" person, i.e., someone who does not insist that materialism must be true. If that person knew the OOL data, there is not the slightest doubt that they would conclude that, by far, the best explanation for the origin of life is that an intelligent designer created it. Why shouldn't everyone else honestly admit that? If we admit that, must attempts to find a natural explanation for OOL come to a screeching halt? Of course not. Perhaps the biological counterparts of Laplace and Lagrange will someday come up with a solution. They clearly have a strong incentive to do so, because if the problem is ever resolved, the person who solves it can immediately book their ticket to Stockholm, where a shiny prize (and a large check) will be waiting for them. And when they return from Sweden, they will be able to bask in the universal adulation of their peers for the rest of their life. Until that time, it would be nice if OOL researchers would stop misleading us about how close they are to a solution.

7.13. Science and religion are at war.

Heroic atheists dragged the world out of the Dark Ages and kickstarted the scientific revolution, all while fighting obscurantist clerics who were busy burning Galileo at the stake and insisting that the Earth is flat. Right? No. Almost everything you have been told about the "war" between Christianity and science is false.[116]

For example, how many times have you heard that Columbus had to overcome the opposition of benighted flat-earther churchmen to gain funding for his voyage from the Spanish Crown? The story is pure nonsense. The ancients knew the Earth is a sphere, and the ancient Greek mathematician Eratosthenes even made a remarkably accurate estimate of its circumference as early as 230 BC.[117] That knowledge was never lost, and the late *atheist* paleontologist Stephen J. Gould, who was certainly no Christian apologist, had the integrity to tell the real story. In his essay "Columbus and the Flat Earth: An Example of the Fallacy of Warfare Between Science and Religion," Gould wrote:

> Greek knowledge of the sphericity never faded, and all major medieval religious scholars accepted the Earth's roundness as an established fact of cosmology. Ferdinand and Isabella did refer Columbus's plans to a royal commission headed by Hernando de Talavera, Isabell's confessor and, following the defeat of the Moors, Archbishop of Granada. This commission, composed of both clerical and lay advisors, did meet at Salamanca among other places. They did pose some sharp intellectual objections to Columbus, but no one questioned the earth's roundness. As a major critique, they argued that Columbus could not reach the Indies in his own allotted time, because the earth's circumference was too great. Moreover, his critics were entirely right. Columbus had "cooked" his figures to favor a much smaller earth, and an attainable Indies. Needless to say, he did not and could not reach Asia. Americans are still called Indians as a legacy of his error.[118]

Columbus seriously underestimated the length of the westward route to the Indies. If he and his crew had not accidentally discovered the Americas, they would have starved to death long before reaching their intended destination. Columbus was wrong, and the clerics were right. Yet, for generations, American students were taught the flat-earth myth as unimpeachable truth.

How did this happen? The source of the myth is a work of *fiction* funneled through an academic who was angry at Christian opposition to Darwin. In 1828, Washington Irving published *The Life and Voyages of Christopher Columbus*, a work of historical fiction based on Columbus's voyages. In his fictionalized account of the Council of Salamanca, Irving had the clerics attempting to rebut Columbus's accurate geographic calculations with specious citations to the Bible and the church fathers.[119] As Gould explained, that did not happen. Enter chemist-historian John William Draper. In 1860, Draper traveled to Oxford to speak about Darwinism at a meeting of the British Association. Bishop Samuel Wilberforce and Thomas Huxley also attended the meeting, and after Draper's talk, they had a legendary exchange in which Wilberforce attacked, and Huxley defended, Darwin. The confrontation between Wilberforce and Huxley engendered in Draper the view that religion and science are at war,[120] and in 1875, he published a book entitled *History of the Conflict Between Religion and Science*. In his book, Draper decided to smear Christianity with the flat earth myth. His source? Irving's fictionalized account of Salamanca, which he lifted almost word for word from Irving's book.[121]

A few years later, Andrew Dickson White, the first president of Cornell University, published *A History of the Warfare of Science With Theology*. White, also a fervent defender of Darwin,[122] further perpetuated the flat-earth myth. He wrote:

> Many a bold navigator, who was quite ready to brave pirates and tempests, trembled at the thought of tumbling with his ship into one of the openings into hell which a widespread belief placed in the Atlantic at some unknown distance from Europe. This terror among sailors was one of the main obstacles in the great voyage of Columbus.[123]

The Draper-White "warfare thesis" continues to be influential to this day, which is unfortunate because not only were they wrong about Columbus specifically, but they were also wrong about the supposed "war" between science and religion generally. Indeed, they were more than merely wrong; as we shall see, their warfare thesis is ridiculous. Far from being at odds with Christianity, modern science was largely built on a Christian foundation, and many of the greatest scientists from the beginning of the Scientific Revolution until the present time have been Christians who obviously saw no conflict between their science and their faith.

We have already met James Tour, who is simultaneously a devout Christian and one of the world's leading chemists. Let's consider another example. Professor Henry F. Schaefer is the Graham Perdue Professor of Chemistry at the University of Georgia, where he is also the director of its Center for Computational Chemistry. He has written over 1,600 scientific papers and is one of the most highly cited chemists in the world. Professor Schaefer's major awards include the American Chemical Society Award in Pure Chemistry (1979, "for the development of computational quantum chemistry into a reliable quantitative field of chemistry and for prolific exemplary calculations of broad chemical interest"); the American Chemical Society Leo Hendrik Baekeland Award (1983, "for his contributions to computational quantum chemistry and for outstanding applications of this technique to a wide range of chemical problems"); the Schrödinger Medal (1990); the Centenary Medal of the Royal Society of Chemistry (London, 1992, as "the first theoretical chemist successfully to challenge the accepted conclusions of a distinguished experimental group for a polyatomic molecule, namely methylene"); the American Chemical Society Award in Theoretical Chemistry (2003, "for his development of novel and powerful computational methods of electronic structure theory, and their innovative use to solve a host of important chemical problems"). In 2003, he also received the annual American Chemical Society Ira Remsen Award. The Remsen Award citation reads, "For work that resulted in more than one hundred distinct, critical theoretical predictions that were subsequently confirmed by experiment and for work that provided a watershed in the field of quantum chemistry, not by reproducing experiment, but using state-of-the-art theory to make new chemical discoveries and, when necessary, to challenge experiment." Professor Schaefer has been nominated for a Nobel Prize five times.

Impressed? I know I am. Dr. Schaefer is one of the foremost scientists in the world. He is also a committed Christian. In his essay

"How Have Christians Helped to Advance Science?"[124] Schaefer notes that the Scientific Revolution occurred in Christian Europe and nowhere else.[125] One reason for this is the Christian belief that God created an intelligible universe. Schaefer quotes Dr. Keith Ward:

> Thus appeal to the general intelligibility of nature, its structuring in accordance with mathematical principles which can be understood by the human mind, suggests the existence of a creative mind, a mind of vast wisdom and power. Science is not likely to get started if one thinks that the universe is just a chaos of arbitrary events, or if one thinks there are many competing gods, or perhaps a god who is not concerned with elegance or rational structure. If one believes those things, one will not expect to find general rational laws, and so one will probably not look for them. It is perhaps no accident that modern science really began with the clear realization that the Christian God was a rational creator, not an arbitrary personal agent...[126]

Schaefer then discusses many of the Christians who created and sustained the scientific revolution over the centuries.[127] These include Francis Bacon, the discoverer of the scientific method. As we saw above, Bacon believed there were two "books," the book of nature and the book of God's work, and the books were equally important. Johannes Kepler, who discovered the laws of planetary motion, was a devout Lutheran who wrote that his purpose was to think God's thoughts after him. Blaise Pascal, who made discoveries in both mathematics and physics, also contributed to theology in his *Pensées*. Robert Boyle was the first true chemist, and he also wrote a book entitled *The Wisdom of God Manifested in the Works of Creation*.

Sir Isaac Newton deserves special mention, as many consider him to be the greatest scientist who ever lived. Did you know that Newton wrote more words on theology than on physics? Michael Faraday discovered benzene and electromagnetic induction, invented the generator, and was a pioneer in the theory in electromagnetism. On his deathbed, Faraday praised Jesus and quoted the Bible. James Clerk Maxwell's equations—which form the foundation of classical electromagnetism, classical optics, and electric and magnetic circuit theory—are one of the great achievements of the human intellect. On June 23, 1864, Maxwell wrote:

> Think what God has determined to do to all those who submit themselves to his righteousness and are willing to receive his gift [the gift of eternal life in Jesus Christ]. They are to be conformed to the image of His Son, and when that is fulfilled, and God sees they are conformed to the image of Christ, there can be no more condemnation.[128]

Dozens more of the most famous scientists in history who were also Christians could be named, including Nicolaus Copernicus, a canon of the Catholic Church who proposed heliocentric cosmology. In modern times, a Catholic priest, Georges Lemaître, discovered that the universe is expanding, which led to the Big Bang theory. Schaefer goes on to name many other twenty-first-century scientists who are Christians,[129] such as Nobel Prize–winner William Phillips, who sings in a gospel choir, teaches Sunday school, and leads Bible studies.[130] Scientists who profess faith are the rule, not the exception. Schaefer cites a poll of 3,300 members of the scientific professional society Sigma Xi. Half of the scientists who were polled regularly participate in religious activities.[131]

All of that's fine, you might say, but what about all the guys the church burned at the stake because of their scientific views? There were none. That's right. Despite what you may have heard, there were exactly zero scientists burned at the stake because the church disagreed with their scientific views.[132]

What about Galileo? Galileo's main mistake was picking a fight with the Pope, openly ridiculing him, and making him look like an enemy of science. At a time when the Pope wielded great temporal power, that was unwise. I will not deny that the Catholic Church treated Galileo badly when it placed him under house arrest and banned his books. But even if that is true, it does not come remotely close to proving the warfare thesis. The warfare thesis must be evaluated in light of the *totality of the evidence*, not an isolated incident involving a single man hundreds of years ago. The totality of evidence includes the fact that natural philosophy (later called "science") was fostered in the universities, a Christian invention. The first university in the world opened in Bologna in 1088, and dozens more had opened by 1450. The totality of evidence includes the fact that Christianity provided the metaphysical foundation for science, as discussed above. The totality of evidence includes the fact that from medieval times through the present day, scientists, including arguably the greatest scientists of all time, were Christians. The totality of evidence includes the fact that Galileo himself, despite his run-ins with ecclesiastical authorities, remained a committed Christian until the day he died. After he first observed the moons of Jupiter through his telescope, he said, "I render infinite thanks to God for being so kind as to make me alone the first observer of marvels kept hidden in obscurity for all previous centuries."[133]

I could go on, but you get the point. Conflict thesis advocates have Galileo (sort of). Non-conflict advocates have pretty much all of the rest of history up to and including the present moment. There is an atheist slogan I have heard many times: "Science flies men to the moon. Religion flies planes into buildings."[134] That slogan (as slogans often do) obscures rather than illuminates the truth, which is that the overwhelming historical evidence demonstrates there is no war between science and Christianity. Christians have been doing great science—including much of the most important science of all time—for hundreds of years and continue to do so to this day.[135]

7.14. The universe is big; therefore, God does not exist.

If you looked at the title of this section and your first thought was that the conclusion clearly does not follow from the premise, you are right. Whoever said God cannot create a big universe? Moreover, for proponents of the multiverse, this objection is not only logically incoherent but also a contradiction. As we saw above, multiverse theory predicts that grand universes are *typical*. So, to assert this objection, a multiverse proponent would have to say that God can't create a big universe, but the multiverse generator, if it exists, has done it many times, maybe even an infinite number of times. It makes no sense.

In fairness, I take it that the materialists' "big universe" objection is not a strictly logical one. Instead, it is an argument from incredulity, i.e., claiming that a proposition is false simply because someone has difficulty believing it. For instance, imagine you are transported back to 1753, one hundred fifty years before the Wright brothers' first powered flight, and you find yourself in an auditorium debating someone about the future of technology. With the advantage of being a time traveler, you assert that one day, metal machines hundreds of feet long will carry hundreds of passengers tens of thousands of feet in the air and transport them across oceans. Suppose your debate opponent responds, "You're crazy. Metal can't even float; that's why we build ships out of wood. Now you're saying that a metal machine will someday fly through the air like a bird? Insane." Your opponent would be arguing from incredulity. They would, of course, be wrong, but they would nevertheless almost certainly be declared the winner of the debate because no one in the audience would believe you, either. I never claimed that arguments from personal incredulity aren't effective. They certainly are. They just aren't logical, and they can lead us astray.

Those who assert the big universe argument are relying on a dynamic similar to your debate opponent. The argument goes like this. The ancients had no conception of the scale of the universe and the Earth's place in it. It was easy for them to imagine that the universe is kind of small and that the Earth is at the center of it. But Copernicus came along and demolished the idea that the Earth is special, and in the 1920s, we discovered that there are millions of other galaxies out there,[136] and that knowledge demolished the cozy little universe idea. The cold hard facts are that Earth is an insignificant speck in an insignificant galaxy in a vast universe. There is no reason to believe that a God exists who cares about humans wandering around on that tiny speck.

Carl Sagan presented a classic example of the big universe argument while reflecting on an image of Earth taken by Voyager I[137] from billions of miles away:

> Look again at that dot. That's here. That's home. That's us. On it everyone you love, everyone you know, everyone you ever heard of, every human being who ever was, lived out their lives... Our posturings, our imagined self-importance, the delusion that we have some privileged position in the Universe, are challenged by this point of pale light. Our planet is a lonely speck in the great enveloping cosmic dark. In our obscurity, in all this vastness, there is no hint that help will come from elsewhere to save us from ourselves.[138]

Sagan's argument boils down to the assertion that he cannot imagine why God would care about creatures who live on a tiny speck in a vast universe. But a critical, unanswered question is: "Why should the poverty of Carl Sagan's imagination concerning God's motivations matter to us?" But like your debate opponent, while Sagan's argument is not logical, it is undeniably powerful, and many people refuse to believe that God exists because of arguments like it. There are many problems with Sagan's argument, not the least of which is that he is glaringly wrong when he says there is "no hint" that God exists. There are far more than hints that God exists. As we demonstrated in chapter six, there is overwhelming evidence that he exists.

Let's consider the first premise of the big universe argument—the ancients believed we live in a cozy little universe. The problem with the premise is that it is pure bunkum, as anyone with the faintest grasp of the history of cosmology knows. Ptolemy's *Almagest* was, by far, the most influential book on cosmology ever written if one measures influence by time. Ptolemy published the *Almagest* around 150 AD, and his geocentric model remained the standard model of cosmology for nearly 1,400 years until Copernicus *De revolutionibus orbium coelestium* was first printed in 1543.[139] That was 482 years ago. Copernicus has over 900 years to go before his span of influence matches Ptolemy's.

While Ptolemy's geocentric model was ultimately displaced, that doesn't mean he was wrong about everything. For example, he knew the Earth is a sphere.[140] Another thing he knew is that the scale of the universe is mind-bogglingly vast. He wrote: "Moreover, the earth has, to the senses, the ratio of a point to the distance of the sphere of the so-called fixed stars."[141] Thus, according to Ptolemy, the earth has no "perceptible size in relation to the distance of the heavenly bodies."[142]

Ptolemy was not the only ancient who knew the universe is vast. The Psalmist was fully aware of his insignificance in relation to the cosmos. Writing circa 1,000 BC, he said:

> When I consider thy heavens, the work of thy fingers, the moon and the stars, which thou hast ordained;
> What is man, that thou art mindful of him? and the son of man, that thou visitest him?
> For thou hast made him a little lower than the angels, and hast crowned him with glory and honour.[143]

It is hard to believe that Sagan was unaware that the ancients knew about the vastness of the cosmos. After all, in *The Demon-Haunted World*, he cited Ptolemy's demonstration that the Earth is a sphere,[144] which occurs only a couple of pages before the text I quoted. C.S. Lewis might have been on to something about materialist coverups when he related the following conversation he had with one of his friends:

> Friend: The whole picture of the universe which science has given us makes it such rot to believe that the Power at the back of it all could be interested in us tiny little creatures crawling about on an unimportant planet! It was all so obviously invented by people who believed in a flat earth with the stars only a mile or two away.
> Lewis: When did people believe that?

Friend: Why, all those old Christian chaps you're always telling about did. I mean Boethius and Augustine and Thomas Aquinas and Dante.

Lewis: Sorry, but this is one of the few subjects I do know something about. You see this book, [handing over the *Almagest*] You know what it is?

Friend: Yes, it's the standard astronomical handbook used all through the Middle Ages.

Lewis: Well, just read that.

Friend: "The earth, in relation to the distance of the fixed stars, has no appreciable size and must be treated as a mathematical point!" Did they really know that then? But—but none of the histories of science—none of the modern encyclopedias—ever mention the fact.

Lewis: Exactly. I'll leave you to think out the reason. It almost looks as if someone was anxious to hush it up, doesn't it? I wonder why.

Lewis: At any rate, we can now state the problem accurately. People usually think the problem is how to reconcile what we now know about the size of the universe with our traditional ideas of religion. That turns out not to be the problem at all. The real problem is this. The enormous size of the universe and the insignificance of the earth were known for centuries, and no one ever dreamed that they had any bearing on the religious question. Then, less than a hundred years ago, they are suddenly trotted out as an argument against Christianity. And the people who trot them out carefully hush up the fact that they were known long ago. Don't you think that all you atheists are strangely unsuspicious people?[145]

The first premise of the "big universe" argument cannot hold up under scrutiny. What about the second premise, the idea that Copernicus demonstrated that the Earth is not the center of the universe (sometimes called the "Copernican principle" or the "mediocrity principle")? It turns out that this idea has not held up well either.

First, the ancients did not think of the Earth as occupying an honored place at the "center" of the universe. Rather, it is more accurate to say that the Earth's "sublunar" position is the nasty bottom of the universe.[146] More importantly, in their groundbreaking book, *The Privileged Planet*, Guillermo Gonzalez and Jay Richards convincingly demonstrate that the Earth is special after all. Gonzalez and Richards discuss many of the parameters that must be simultaneously balanced for a planet to exist that supports life that is capable of observing the universe. The parameters for such a planet include:[147]

- It orbits an early G dwarf star that is at least a few billion years old
- It orbits a star in the in the galactic habitable zone
- It orbits a star near the corotation circle and with a low eccentricity galactic orbit
- It orbits a star outside spiral arms
- It orbits a star with at least one terrestrial planet in the circumstellar habitable zone
- It is one of the terrestrial planets in the circumstellar habitable zone
- It orbits a star with no more than a few giant planets comparable in mass to Jupiter in large, circular orbits
- It has a low eccentricity orbit and is outside the region where giant planets would destabilize its orbit
- It is near enough to the inner edge of the circumstellar habitable zone to allow high oxygen and low carbon dioxide concentrations in atmosphere
- It is in the right mass range
- It has a proper concentration of sulfur in its core
- It has a large moon and the right planetary rotation period to avoid chaotic variations in its obliquity
- It has the right amount of water in crust
- It has steady plate tectonic cycling
- It is a planet where life appeared
- It had a critically low number of large impacts

- It was exposed to a critically low number of transient radiation events
- It is a planet where complex life appeared
- It is a planet where technological life appeared
- It is a planet where technological civilization has not destroyed itself

Gonzales and Richards assign a (almost certainly too high) chance of ten percent for each of the factors. Multiplying the combined probability of only the first 13 factors by the number of stars in the Milky Way, Gonzales and Richards calculate that the total expected number of habitable planets in the Milky Way is 0.01. In other words, it turns out that it is highly unlikely that even one planet in the Milky Way is habitable at all, much less that it hosts a technological civilization that can observe the universe. The Earth beat the odds and is a privileged planet after all, and that giant crashing noise you hear is the second premise of the "big universe" argument falling down like the first.

What about the possibility of other life forms in the universe? Even if the probability of life is much lower than we thought, what if it is discovered? C.S. Lewis also contemplated this issue. This is his response:

> Christianity says what God has done for Man; it doesn't say (because it doesn't know) what He has or has not done in other parts of the universe. [You] might recall the parable of the one lost sheep. If Earth has been specially sought by God (which we don't know) that may not imply that it is the most important thing in the universe, but only that it has strayed. Finally, challenge the whole tendency to identify size and importance. Is an elephant more important than a man, or a man's leg than his brain?[148]

Lewis's final point is particularly significant. An implicit assumption of the "big universe" argument is that in a vast universe, the physical insignificance of Earth implies its metaphysical insignificance as well. But why should that be? Size and importance have no logical connection.[149] A diamond is many times smaller than a ten-ton boulder, yet it is also many times more valuable. It seems to me that until materialists can demonstrate (rather than merely assert) that the size of the Earth is necessarily linked to its value to God, they should be more modest in making their claims.

7.15. Materialists can be good people.

In chapter six, I presented the argument from objective morality to the existence of God. Materialists often respond to that argument by asserting that atheists can be good people, and, therefore, the argument fails because God is not necessary for a person to do good. That response is misguided for a number of reasons. First, Christians never say that materialists cannot do good. Indeed, they insist that they can. The Bible teaches that God has written a transcendent moral code on every person's heart, and everyone—believer and unbeliever alike—has a conscience that accuses him when he transgresses that code.[150]

Ironically, it is materialists —not Christians—who really deny that materialists can do good. That might sound strange because I just said that Christians insist atheists can do good. Once again, confusion arises from ambiguous language. As we have discussed before, materialists and Christians mean completely different things by the word "good." When a Christian says an act is good, he means that it conforms to God's transcendent, objective moral code. Christians argue that code is written on the atheist's heart even if he denies its existence, and because it is written on his heart he can act in accordance with it.

Materialists, on the other hand, deny that objective good exists.[151] It follows that they must deny that they (or anyone else) can do good in the sense of "objectively good." Sure, if materialism is true, a person can do good in the sense of doing those things that blind, physical, evolutionary forces programmed them to prefer. Indeed, on materialism, free will does not exist, and the materialist is deterministically compelled to do what evolution has programmed him to do. Thus, it does not make sense for a materialist to take credit for doing "good" when his metaphysical premises compel the conclusion that it was not possible for him to do anything other than what he did. In summary, the materialist's response that "atheists can do good, too" is based on a fundamental misunderstanding of the argument from objective morality.

Finally, even if one grants the premise that materialists can do good, they cannot point to any objective foundation for valuing the good in the first place. In other words, if materialism is true, there is no objective reason to prefer one set of moral values over another. William Lane Craig writes that on atheism, "an atrocity like the Holocaust was really morally indifferent. You may think that it was wrong, but your opinion has no more validity than that of the Nazi war criminal who thought it was good."[152] This is another way of saying that materialists can never escape Arthur Leff's "sez who?" problem that we discussed in chapter one. Common sense suggests that the lack of an objective foundation for morality makes a difference in our ethical choices. Edward Feser describes that difference as follows:

> [O]ur understanding of the grounds of morality can hardly fail to influence the seriousness with which we try to practice it.... Would you be more inclined rigorously to abide by policy X if you were truly convinced that God or nature unconditionally commands it, or if instead you were sure it was just something we feeble humans have cooked up because it is "mutually advantageous" (even if you don't see much advantage in following it yourself just now)? To ask this question is to answer it.[153]

7.16. Christians can be horrible people.

Some years ago, I took a case to trial in which my client claimed her employer had discriminated against her due to her religious expression. I put my client on the stand, and she shared her story. I doubt I will ever forget the other lawyer's cross-examination. He stood up and asked my client, "Do you know how many people have been killed in the name of religion?" I immediately jumped to my feet. The lawyer side of my brain intended to say something like, "Objection! Inflammatory, prejudicial, irrelevant." But when I opened my mouth, the human side of my brain took over, and "That's outrageous!" came out of my mouth. The judge said, "Sustained."[154] While the other lawyer did not get away with it, he was trying to take advantage of a prejudice many people hold against religious people. In this section, I will examine whether that lawyer's objection is a valid reason to doubt Jesus Christ's message of love and peace.

It is indeed true that wars have been started in the name of Christianity. The European Wars of Religion fought in the sixteenth and seventeenth centuries were particularly terrible. There are two standard responses to this objection. First, the Wars of Religion were at least partially, if not mainly, driven by competition over economic, political, dynastic, and social issues among the warring kings, princes, and emperors, and religion merely served as a convenient banner under which to advance those rulers' secular ambitions. The second response is to observe that while those wars were indeed terrible, if one wants an example of slaughter on a truly industrial scale, the death toll of the militantly atheist totalitarian regimes in the twentieth century was orders of magnitude worse.[155]

But deflections and whataboutisms do not address the core of the objection, which is that Christians often do not act like Christ. In response, I will ask if you can name one good thing that evil men have not corrupted. You cannot? Neither can I. The message of Christ is no exception to this seemingly universal rule. Part of Christ's message is "love your neighbor." Who is our neighbor? Perhaps you are familiar with Jesus's parable of the Good Samaritan. Before I share that story, a bit of background knowledge is helpful. First-century Jews harbored a deep antipathy toward Samaritans. If they were on a journey to the other side of Samaria, they would add many miles to the trip by walking around the region instead of through it to avoid risking defilement from contact with Samaritans. The ethnic hatred was so intense that one influential rabbi remarked that eating Samaritan bread was like eating pig flesh.[156]

Against this cultural backdrop, Jesus told the following story.[157] While traveling from Jerusalem to Jericho, a man was assaulted by robbers who beat him, took his possessions, and left him for dead by the side of the road. One after another, two religious leaders walk by, but when they notice him, they cross to the other side of the road to avoid helping him. Then, a Samaritan arrives at the scene. The Samaritan knows that the man would almost certainly despise him under normal circumstances. However, moved by compassion, he tends to the man's wounds, places him on his donkey, and takes him to an inn to care for him. The next day, he gives the innkeeper money and says, "Look after him, and if it costs more, I'll pay you when I come back."

The point of the story isn't primarily about helping people; it's about who does the helping. The Samaritan, an outsider and enemy, showed compassion when the religious insiders did not. The story is a radical call to love beyond boundaries, to act with kindness even toward those you are "supposed" to hate. Jesus commands us to love our enemies and to do good to those who hate us.[158] This does not mean that we are required to have warm feelings of affection for our enemies. You cannot force yourself to feel a certain way, but, like the Samaritan, you can set your feelings aside and will yourself to do good to the downtrodden. That is what Jesus calls us to do.

Radical self-denying love is at the heart of Jesus' message, and he exemplified that love on the cross. In the greatest act of love in the history of the world, the sinless one allowed himself to be crucified so that he could bear the penalty for our sins. Christians are called to follow Christ. This means following his example of self-sacrificial love. For 2,000 years, Christians, including this one, have both succeeded and failed in varying degrees to follow that example. There is a long list of good things that Christians have done over the centuries, including the elevation of the status of women, ending infanticide, the abolition of slavery, the civil rights movement, universities, hospitals, humanitarian aid, building the moral and intellectual foundation of liberal democracy—the list goes on. At a more personal level, there can be no doubt that countless millions of Jesus' followers have heeded his message of love and mercy and have become better people as a result. But none of these good things excuses the evil committed by Christians and people who call themselves Christians (there is a difference), and I will not try to defend that evil.

This brings me back to the objection. The charge is that Christians do bad things. I plead guilty. That's why I'm not asking anyone to follow Christians, including this one. I'm asking you to follow Christ. Do you object to Christianity because Christians have done bad things? I understand why you would do that. However, if you're looking for a religion, ideology, or philosophy whose followers have always been pure and blameless, you are bound to be disappointed. None exists. Do not look to Christ's followers; even the best among them have feet of clay. It is even more true that you should not look to wicked individuals who claim to be Christ's followers yet act as if they have never heard his message of radical love.

Finally, as Tom Holland has pointed out, this objection is ultimately circular and, therefore, incoherent. Yes, he writes, many Christians "have themselves become agents of terror. They have put the weak in their shadow; they have brought suffering, and persecution, and slavery in their wake. Yet the standards by which they stand condemned for this are themselves Christian."[159] Holland's point is similar to the refutation of the argument from the existence of evil. One can hardly argue that God does not exist on the ground that people who claim to serve Him do not measure up to a standard that does not exist unless God exists. One can hardly argue that Christianity is false because Christians do not measure up to a standard that would not exist but for the existence of Christianity.

The bad news is that history reveals that many times fallen men have failed to act in accordance with Christ's message. There is no denying that. The good news is that those failures do not defeat the message. The gospel of Jesus Christ is very simple. God loved the world so much that he gave his son to suffer, die, and rise again. He offers forgiveness of sin and everlasting life to whoever believes in him. If the gospel is true, the horrible things Christians (and those who call themselves Christians) have done do not make it untrue. There is good reason to believe that it is true. Indeed, it is—as it has always been—the hope of the world.

7.17. You are pathetic if the only reason you do good is the fear that God will smack you around if you step out of line.

Richard Dawkins says the following in *The God Delusion*:

> If you agree that, in the absence of God, you would "commit robbery, rape, and murder", you reveal yourself as an immoral person, "and we would be well advised to steer a wide course around you". If, on the other hand, you admit that you would continue to be a good person even when not under divine surveillance, you have fatally undermined your claim that God is necessary for us to be good.[160]

This is complete nonsense. Jesus said that if we *love* him, we will keep his commands.[161] Christians believe God became man and allowed himself to be nailed to the cross to pay the penalty for our sins. The only rational response to that act of supreme sacrificial love is an overwhelming sense of gratitude and to love God in return. That love, then, motivates us to live our lives in a way that is pleasing to him. To be sure, our motivations also include a healthy respect for God as a loving father who disciplines his children.[162] However, it is our love, not our fear, that is our primary motivation for pleasing God by keeping his commandments.

This is one of Dawkins's sillier arguments because it is so easy to refute. I would simply ask him why he obeyed his father's rules when he was growing up. Was it merely because he was terrified of his father's wrath if he were caught breaking a rule? Or did he obey the rules because he loved and respected his father and did not want to disappoint him?

That said, it is just common sense that the belief that we are accountable to God has practical implications that influence behavior. Suppose there are two people. The first person believes that "good" is nothing more than what his DNA tells him to do,[163] and since there is no God, every act, whether good or bad, is ultimately meaningless. The second person believes there is an objective moral code and that if he transgresses that code, he will be held accountable by a righteous God. Which of those two people is more likely to act morally, especially when doing so requires him to sacrifice his own strongly felt personal interest? The answer to that question is obvious.

Christabel Bielenberg wrote of a conversation she had with an SS soldier she met on a train. The soldier, who had been a member of one of the death squads, told her the following story:

> Do you know what it means—to kill Jews, men, women, and children, as they stand in a semicircle around the machine guns? I belonged to what is called an *Einsatzkommando*, an extermination squad—so I know. What do you say when I tell you that a little boy, no older than my youngest brother, before such a killing, stood there to attention and asked me "Do I stand straight enough, Uncle?" Yes, he asked that of me; and once, when the circle stood round us, an old man stepped out of the ranks, he had long hair and a beard, a priest of some sort I suppose. Anyway, he came towards us slowly across the grass, slowly step by step, and within a few feet of the guns he stopped and looked at us one after another, a straight, deep, dark and terrible look. "My children," he said, "God is watching what you do." He turned from us then, and someone shot him in the back before he had gone more than a few steps.[164]

The old rabbi stood before the SS troops, looked them in the eye, and told them that God was watching them. Then, one of the troops shot him. There is one thing about which we can be absolutely certain. The SS soldier who shot the rabbi did *not* believe he was being watched by a righteous God who would judge and punish him for cold-blooded murder.

People behave differently when they believe they are being watched by someone with the power to punish them if they do wrong. As Dennis Prager says, this is just common sense: "Do people drive as carefully when there is a police car driving next to them or no police car? Clearly, if you think that you are being watched, you act differently. That should go without saying. But we live in the age of secular foolishness where people deny the obvious."[165] As if studies were needed to demonstrate the glaringly obvious, science confirms Prager's commonsense observation.[166] Ironically, given the passage I quoted at the start of this section, even Dawkins agrees. He obviously does not believe religion is true, but he once told *The Times* that abolishing it would be a bad idea because "People may feel free to do bad things because they feel God is no longer watching them."[167]

7.18. The "fact" that artificial intelligence has or will soon become conscious proves that humans are meat robots.

What do the following have in common?

I, Robot
Her (2013)
Bicentennial Man
Ex Machina
Chappie
Westworld
I am Mother
Blade Runner
The Matrix
2001: A Space Odyssey,
Wall-E
Star Trek, the Next Generation
A. I. Artificial Intelligence

All of them are at some level propaganda for the "machines can be conscious" cult. The primary objective of the cult is to undermine human exceptionalism by promoting the materialist superstition that the human mind is a meat computer that can, in principle, be replicated by silicon computers.[168] But despite all of the hype we have heard from AI doomsayers in recent years, it is actually fairly easy to demonstrate that computers cannot become conscious.[169]

Robert J. Marks, II, is the Distinguished Professor of Electrical and Computer Engineering at Baylor University. In his book *Non-Computable You*, Professor Marks shows that there are certain aspects of human consciousness that simply cannot be replicated by a computer. "Computers only do what they're programmed by humans to do, and those programs are all algorithms—step-by-step procedures contributing to the performance of some task."[170] Such algorithms have inherent constraints on what they can accomplish. Computers run algorithms. That's all they do. Therefore, if something cannot be reduced to an algorithm—i.e., it is non-computable—it is beyond the reach of computers and thus AI.[171]

There are many things the human mind can do that are not computable. Therefore, it is impossible, in principle, for AI to replicate the human mind. The materialist conceit underlying fictional characters like Commander Data on *Star Trek* turns out to be so much hogwash. Computers can never, for example, experience "qualia," the subjective experience of objective phenomena, like the taste of a fine wine, the pain of a papercut, or the mustiness of a wet dog. Imagine someone connects a spectrometer to a computer and points it at the western horizon. They write a program (an algorithm) that instructs the computer as follows: "when light with a wavelength of 650 nanometers is detected, print this statement: 'Oh, what a beautiful sunset.'" At the same moment the computer prints this statement, I look at the horizon and say, "Oh, what a beautiful sunset." The computer and I said the same thing. Does this mean we experienced the sunset in the same way? Of course not. The computer did not "experience" the sunset at all. An algorithm cannot replicate my subjective experience of the sunset. The "redness" I experienced is in a different conceptual category from the "red" detected by the spectrometer.

To be sure, AI applications like ChatGPT and Grok are getting better at mimicking the responses of a conscious person all the time. Someday, that mimicry might become so good that we cannot tell the difference between talking to an AI and talking to a real person. The AI will have passed the so-called "Turing test."[172] When that happens, and it probably will, it will be easy to lose sight of the fact that the AI is not truly conscious and is inherently limited by its algorithmic nature. Philosopher John Searle famously demonstrated this with his "Chinese Room" thought experiment. Suppose a person who does not speak Chinese is in a room that has a slot at the door. A person outside the room writes a question in Chinese and puts it through the slot. The person in the room then follows a set of instructions by which he matches the symbols on the paper with potential responses filed away in file cabinets and passes the response back through the slot. The person in the room did not know what the question meant; nor did he know what the response meant. He was just following a set of instructions (which is the essence of an algorithm). But from the perspective of the person outside the room, something or someone with an understanding of Chinese answered his question. When you ask ChatGPT a question, you are playing the role of the person outside the room. ChatGPT plays the role of the person in the room. It runs an algorithm in the same way the person in the room ran an algorithm (just at an incredibly faster speed) and gives you a response. ChatGPT does not "know" what your question meant, nor does it "know" what the answer it provided meant. If you believe otherwise, you have been fooled.

In summary, even the most powerful computers running the most sophisticated AI programs do nothing but what the algorithms written by their human programmers tell them to do. They are simply very fast Chinese rooms. The human mind, on the other hand, is not computable. Our brains are not meat computers. Another prediction of materialism fails.

7.19. Infinite monkeys typing on keyboards will eventually type out the complete works of Shakespeare.

How many times have you heard someone say something like, "Infinite monkeys typing on typewriters will eventually produce the complete works of Shakespeare." People who say this are usually trying to justify their belief that some wildly implausible event happened by pure random chance. For example, if someone wants to believe that blind physical forces spontaneously rearranged non-living molecules into a living cell, they might say that given enough time and enough chances, it could happen, just like those monkeys typing out Shakespeare.

"Probabilistic resources" means the number of opportunities for an event to occur. [173] Appeals to infinite probabilistic resources and deep time are a ploy for explaining the otherwise inexplicable. Surprisingly, it works. If one assumes that monkeys can type for infinity, they will indeed type out the complete works of Shakespeare. Indeed, they will type out the complete works of Shakespeare an infinite number of times.

Atheist astronomer Fred Hoyle published a scientific paper pushing a version of infinite monkeys to justify his continued belief in the infinite steady state universe long after it had been discredited by Big Bang cosmology. Hoyle argued backwards from the existence of life to an infinite universe. He estimated the probability of the spontaneous emergence of life to be $10^{-40,000}$. That is an unimaginably small number. He then argued that there is no chance an event that improbable could have happened in the time allowed by Big Bang cosmology for the age of the universe. He reasoned that an event as improbable as the spontaneous emergence of life could have occurred only if the universe were eternal.[174]

There is a fundamental problem with the infinite monkeys gambit. Hoyle was wrong. We don't actually have an infinite number of monkeys. The universe had a beginning. The standard model of cosmology estimates that beginning was about 13.8 billion years ago. Still, that seems like a lot of time, and people sometimes appeal to deep time (even if it is not infinite time) to justify their beliefs in wildly improbable events happening. The problem is that the spontaneous emergence of life is not remotely probable even on a scale of 13.8 billion years, far less 4.7 billion years (the estimated age of the Earth) So, it turns out that "infinite monkeys" is not the solution some materialists think it is.

7.20. Extremely improbable things happen all the time.

Materialists often try to rebut the design argument by claiming that highly improbable events occur all the time without being designed. Therefore, asserting that if something is improbable, it must have been designed is faulty logic. Brown University biochemist Kenneth Miller illustrated this when he argued that a specific sequence of cards dealt from a randomly shuffled deck is a highly improbable event that was not designed. This is a straw man argument. No design theorist has ever argued "X is improbable; therefore X is designed." Miller's argument left out a crucial step in the design inference—a specification.

We can illustrate Miller's error using his own example of a hand of cards. Recall the poker game I discussed in chapter five in which your friend deals himself three royal flushes in a row. Suppose your friend says, "I admit that three royal flushes in a row is a highly improbable sequence of cards, but no less of an authority than Kenneth Brown says that highly improbable events happen all the time, and just because they are improbable does not mean they are designed. He even used dealing cards to illustrate this point. Your design inference is bad logic." Would you be satisfied with this explanation? Certainly not. But what is your friend's error? As we saw, it is true that any given three-hand sequence in poker is astronomically improbable. But when one combines that improbability with the specification "three royal flushes in a row," it is no longer reasonable to attribute the sequence of cards to random chance. Dembski's method for detecting design supports your commonsense intuition that you have been cheated.

Materialists use this same logic when arguing against design in nature. They might say, for example, that just because a particular protein fold is improbable does not mean a design inference is proper. After all, astronomically improbable events that everyone agrees are not designed happen all the time. The error here is that the specification "functional protein," like the specification "three royal flushes in a row," is a vanishingly small subset of the total number of folds that are possible. A design inference is certainly justified.

7.21. There are many religions. How do you know you have the right one?

Jesus said, "I am the way and the truth and the life. No one comes to the Father except through me."[175] Christianity is exclusive, and that exclusivity is a scandal[176] in a pluralistic society such as ours.

The first thing to notice about this objection is that, in a certain sense, it is not really an objection at all. The statement, "I am offended by Jesus' message; therefore, Jesus' message is false," is not a logical deduction. Whether the message is offensive to a pluralistic twenty-first-century Westerner has no bearing on whether it is true. Indeed, the fact that some people are offended by Jesus' message makes it more likely that the message is true, as this is precisely what the Bible predicted would occur.[177] The most important truth claim of Christianity is that the tomb was empty. If that claim is true, Jesus' assertion that he is *the* way, *the* truth, and *the* life does not fill it back up again. If that claim is false, then nothing Jesus said really matters anyway, and you can ignore him.

How do you determine if Jesus' claims are true? In the same way you determine whether any claim is true. You evaluate the evidence and come to a conclusion. Lee Strobel was an atheist investigative journalist for the *Chicago Tribune*. In his book, *The Case for Christ*, Lee Strobel reports on his journey from atheist to Christian as a result of his intensive investigation—an investigation only a trained investigator could have performed— of the claims of the Bible about Jesus. He found that the evidence for the veracity of the claims was so overwhelming that there was only one reasonable conclusion. The claims are true.

There is an unspoken premise to the objection to Christianity's claim of exclusivity. That premise is that if a loving God exists, he will save everyone. The premise has no force because the Bible teaches that God has provided a way of salvation and desires that all should accept that salvation and only those who reject God's offer by their own free choice will not be saved. William Lane Craig writes:

> According to the New Testament, God does not want anyone to perish, but desires that all persons repent and be saved and come to know the truth (11 Peter 3.9; 1 Timothy 2.4). He therefore seeks to draw all men to Himself. Those who make a well-informed and free decision to reject Christ *are self-condemned*, since they repudiate God's unique sacrifice for sin. By spurning God's prevenient grace and the solicitation of His Spirit, they shut out God's mercy and seal their own destiny. They, therefore, and not God, are responsible for their condemnation, and God deeply mourns their loss.[178]

What about those who have been misinformed by other religions or have never heard of Jesus? Craig responds to this objection as well.

> Nor does it seem to me that the problem can be simply reduced to the inconsistency of a loving and just God's condemning persons who are either un- , ill-, or misinformed concerning Christ and who therefore lack the opportunity to receive Him. For one could maintain that God graciously applies to such persons the benefits of Christ's atoning death without their conscious knowledge thereof

on the basis of their response to the light of general revelation and the truth that they do have, even as He did in the case of Old Testament figures like Job who were outside the covenant of Israel. The testimony of Scripture is that the mass of humanity do not even respond to the light that they do have, and God's condemnation of them is neither unloving nor unjust, since He judges them according to standards of general revelation vastly lower than those which are applied to persons who have been recipients of His special revelation.[179]

C.S. Lewis said much the same thing:

> Here is another thing that used to puzzle me. Is it not frightfully unfair that this new life should be confined to people who have heard of Christ and been able to believe in Him? But the truth is God has not told us what His arrangements about the other people are. We do know that no man can be saved except through Christ; we do not know that only those who know Him can be saved through Him. But in the meantime, if you are worried about the people outside, the most unreasonable thing you can do is to remain outside yourself.[180]

We know that God reaches out to people who have never heard the name of Jesus. Lee Strobel tells the story of a Christian in Egypt named Kamal. One day, he was standing in a market when a Muslim woman in traditional garb rushed up to him yelling, "You're the one! You're the one! You were in my dream last night! Those clothes—you were wearing those clothes. For sure, it was you." Kamal asked the woman, whose name was Noor, to tell him about the dream and this is what she reported:

> "Jesus walked with me alongside a lake, and he told me how much he loves me. His love was different from anything I've ever experienced. I've never felt so much peace. I didn't want him to leave. I asked this Jesus, 'Why are you visiting me, a poor Muslim mother with eight children?' And all he said was, 'I love you, Noor. I have given everything for you. I died for you.'" She said that as Jesus turned to leave, he told her, "Ask my friend tomorrow about me.

He will tell you all you need in order to understand why I've visited you." She replied to Jesus, "But who is your friend?" Jesus said, "Here is my friend," and he pointed to a person who was behind him in the dream. "He has been walking with us the whole time we've been together." . . . "Even though you had walked with us around the lake, I hadn't seen anyone but Jesus. I thought I was alone with him. His face was magnificent. I couldn't take my eyes off him. Jesus did not tell me your name, but you were wearing the same clothes you have on right now, and your glasses—they're the same too. I knew I would not forget your smile."[181]

Kamal shared the gospel of Jesus Christ with Noor. Stories like Noor's are becoming common in the Middle East, as reported by Tom Doyle in his book *Dreams and Visions: Is Jesus Awakening the Muslim World?* Joel Rosenberg also reports these events on his podcast.[182]

I personally know a couple who were born and raised in Iran. They were both Shia Muslims and had never heard the gospel. One night, they both had the same dream. Jesus appeared to them and personally invited them to accept him as their savior, and they both responded to that personal invitation. Jesus knows and calls his own, and he promises that he will never lose even one of them, no matter where they are in the world.

7.22. If God exists, then why doesn't he show himself?

The phrase "Divine hiddenness" refers to the hiddenness of God, i.e., the *alleged* fact that God is hidden, absent, or silent.[183] The idea is reflected in the skeptic's cry (or taunt), "If God is there, why doesn't he show himself?" The problem with the objection is that it rests on a false premise. God is not hidden. He is evident in nature, in conscience, in history, in Jesus Christ, and in the Scriptures.[184] Chapter six was devoted to discussing some of the innumerable ways God has made himself evident.

This is not to say that the objection has no force, but I take it that the real objection is not that God is totally hidden but that the skeptic believes he is insufficiently revealed. A reporter once interviewed the famous agnostic philosopher Bertrand Russell, and the following exchange occurred:

> I asked, "Let us suppose, sir, that after you have left this sorry vale, you actually found yourself in heaven, standing before the Throne. There, in all his glory, sat the Lord—not Lord Russell, sir: God." Russell winced. "What would you think?"
> "I would think I was dreaming."
> "But suppose you realized you were not? Suppose that there, before your very eyes, beyond a shadow of a doubt, *was* God. What would you say?"
> The pixie wrinkled his nose. "I probably would ask, 'Sir, why did you not give me better evidence?'"[185]

Russell's response reminds me of a story Jesus told about a rich man and a beggar named Lazarus. The rich man lived a life of extreme opulence and never gave a thought to the plight of the beggar at his gate. Both men died; Lazarus went to Abraham's side, while the rich man went to Hades. The rich man cried out and begged Abraham to send Lazarus back from the dead to warn his brothers to change the course of their lives to avoid the torment he was suffering.

> Abraham replied, "They have Moses and the Prophets; let them listen to them."
> "No, father Abraham," he said, "but if someone from the dead goes to them, they will repent."
> He said to him, "If they do not listen to Moses and the Prophets, they will not be convinced even if someone rises from the dead."[186]

Jesus understood that the "God hides himself" excuse is just that—an excuse. Skeptics refuse to believe not from a lack of evidence but because of the hardness of their hearts.

While the objection of divine hiddenness is ultimately unsuccessful, the impulse behind it is not hard to understand. Yes, God has made himself manifest in many ways, but why not all the way? Why does he insist on an irreducible element of faith? Pascal understood this paradoxical presence and absence as divinely calibrated to the human condition:

> All appearance indicates neither a total exclusion nor a manifest presence of divinity, but the presence of a God who hides himself. Everything bears this character. . . .[187]
>
> If there were no obscurity, man would not be sensible of his corruption; if there were no light, man would not hope for a remedy. Thus, it is not only fair, but advantageous to us, that God be partly hidden and partly revealed; since it is equally dangerous to man to know God without knowing his own wretchedness, and to know his own wretchedness without knowing God.[188]

If God were perfectly obvious, people would not feel their inadequacies and their need for grace and redemption. On the other hand, if God were completely hidden, there would be no reason to hope for grace and redemption.[189] In his grace, God has provided just the right mix of hiddenness and obviousness to accommodate our nature, which he knows perfectly.

7.23. You can always find a stick.

As with proofs for God's existence, I could add many more sections to this chapter. But for a determined skeptic, there are never enough proofs, and there are never enough answers to his objections. They are never struck dumb. They always have something to say, some objection to raise. Some of those objections are silly, such as the objection that there is absolutely no evidence for God's existence. Some of those objections, while ultimately unsuccessful, can cause angst. Whose heart does not ache when they look at a suffering child? Who has not wondered why God would allow that to happen? There are cogent logical answers to the objection from innocent suffering, but there is no sense in denying the emotional force of Ivan Karamazov's case.

Nevertheless, the proofs presented in chapter six are sufficient to convince anyone with an open mind, and all of the objections raised can be answered. However, as I discussed above, apodictic certainty will always be beyond our reach. There is no absolutely airtight case for God's existence. God knows that and intended it. There is no room for reasonable doubt. But there is room for doubt, and if you want to take a whack at the idea of God, you can always find a stick to do it with. But that is not a reasonable thing to do.

8. Can We Fake it Till We Make it?

Is it a good idea to lie to people in pursuit of a "greater good" such as social cohesion? Plato thought so. In *The Republic*, Plato imagines an ideal society rigidly divided into three classes—rulers, guardians, and producers, such as farmers and tradesmen. To reinforce this social stratification, he proposed telling everyone a lie that has come to be known as the "noble lie." The lie he proposed telling the people goes like this: "While all of you in the city are brothers . . . yet God in fashioning those of you who are fitted to hold rule mingled gold in their generation, for which reason they are the most precious but in the helpers silver, and iron and brass in the farmers and other craftsmen."[1] The people were then told that "the first and chief injunction" of the gods is to maintain a strict separation of the metals. Plato understood that it would be difficult to get people to believe this nonsense, but he suggested giving it a go and hoping for the best.

This brings me to Jordan Peterson. Peterson is one of the most important public intellectuals in the world, and I have immense respect for him. I especially admire the integrity and courage he has demonstrated in the face of the Canadian authorities' relentless persecution of him for exercising his right to free speech. Sadly, Peterson cannot bring himself to believe in God.[2] To his credit, Peterson recognizes that materialism has led to a widespread crisis of meaning at the personal level and to nihilistic authoritarianism at the social level. He understands that our civilization is in crisis and would doubtless agree with much of what was said in the first five chapters of this book. He and I part company, however, when it comes to the solution to the crisis. I propose returning to Christianity. Peterson proposes acting as if Christianity were true even though all of the smart people like him know it isn't. Will his solution work? Let's find out.

In a 2022 discussion with Douglas Murray and Jonathan Pageau, Peterson referred to Hume's guillotine,[3] a well-known problem in ethics articulated by the eighteenth-century Scottish philosopher David Hume, which states that one cannot derive an "ought" from an "is." As we have seen, materialism asserts that everything from rocks to humans is composed of burnt-out star stuff. If this is true, there is no hope of establishing a non-arbitrary foundation for ethics. A rock is neither moral nor immoral; it simply is. It makes no sense to say that a rock "ought" to be a certain way. Since a person is made of essentially the same kind of stuff as a rock, it makes no sense to claim there is an inherent "oughtness" that governs human behavior. If materialism is true, William Provine is right. There is no ultimate foundation for ethics and no ultimate meaning to life.

Peterson believes he has a solution to the dilemma posed by Hume—fiction. (If only I were making this up.) Peterson thinks that fiction and mythology are the solution to materialist meaninglessness. He told Murray that "God is the ultimate fictional character," whom we should emulate because "that unites us psychologically and socially." For Peterson, the Bible, though fictional, is important because it provides a sense of meaning and a foundation for ethics. As I mentioned in chapter five, Peterson's is an instrumentalist approach to Christianity. He values it because he thinks it is useful, not because he thinks it is true. His argument boils down to: "God-talk is valuable because it is a soothing noise clever hairless apes make at each other, and the apes need to be soothed."

Peterson develops this theme in his book *We Who Wrestle With God*,[4] where he observes that even materialists behave as if humans possessed intrinsic worth despite their materialism's leading to a contrary conclusion.[5] He writes that this "presumption of intrinsic value reflects a reality that is deep enough—'real' enough—so that we deny it at our practical peril. And, if that presumption is so absolutely necessary, how is it not true? . . . At what point must it be admitted that a 'necessary fiction' is true precisely in proportion to its necessity?"[6] In other words, even though the idea that humans have intrinsic or transcendent value is a fiction, it is a "necessary fiction," and our lives will fall apart if we do not act as if it is were true. Therefore, it is true.

This is nonsense, of course. Just because we feel strongly that everyone should act as if a lie were true does not make it true. Plato felt a need to tell his noble lie, but that didn't make it any less of a lie. Peterson believes the God of the Bible is a "necessary fiction," but the fact that Peterson believes the fiction is necessary does not make it less fictional (if it is fictional, which, of course, I am not conceding). Atheist Alex O'Connor pointed out the obvious problem with Peterson's project. Most people cannot act "as if" God existed if they do not believe that he does. In an interview with Chris Williamson, O'Connor spoke of people like Peterson who cannot get behind the truth claims of Christianity but recognize the utility of having *other people* believe they are true. O'Connor explained why this will not work:

> I will accept your premise wholesale that religion is good, maybe even necessary for society. What do you want me to do if I just don't think it's true. Am I to just lie to my children, raise them believing something that I don't believe is the case, because I think it will somehow be beneficial to society? I don't think it works like that. I don't think people can actually fool themselves. Sure, you can act as if God exists, and that's what someone like Peterson says that people do already. But ultimately, if you just say, "Well I think that, you know, I should just act like a Christian because it's good for me," then when push comes to shove and you really have to make a moral sacrifice, if you're not actually a Christian, you're probably not going to do the actually Christian thing.[7]

Materialists have an explanation for why humans believe in religion.[8] Yuval Noah Harari, whom we met earlier, discusses sociological research that shows that the maximum "natural" size of a group is about 150 people. In groups larger than that, personal communication becomes ineffective.[9] Harari continues:

> How did *Homo sapiens* manage to cross this critical threshold, eventually founding cities comprising tens of thousands of inhabitants and empires ruling hundreds of millions? The secret was probably the appearance of *fiction*. Large numbers of strangers can cooperate successfully by believing in common myths.[10]

Harari's thesis is that the evolutionary development of fiction, including religious fiction, was important because it facilitated large numbers of people acting cooperatively to accomplish group goals. In an interview with Richard Dawkins, Konstantin Kisin referred to Harari's thesis, and they had the following exchange:[11]

> Kisin: [A]s I look around at the world with its inability to agree on what words mean, what people call now the crisis of meaning, where a lot of people are kind of lost. They don't know what the purpose and meaning of their life is. . . . for a lot of . . . people what they actually need is not necessarily the belief in God so much as the social function that religion used to fulfill, which is to bind us together with a set of shared values, and a set of shared morals, and a set of shared ideas about what it means to be human, what it means to relate to other people. And without that we are lost and therefore we create these new religions that sort of tear our society apart.
>
> Dawkins: I think it is very interesting and I am rather persuaded by Harari's argument. But notice what you've just done. You've said maybe humans *need* religion, maybe they need something to bind society together and function as a unit and so on. And maybe they do. *But it doesn't make it true.* . . . And I just want to make a distinction between what is true and what humanity needs. And it may very well be that we do need false ideas in order to flourish and prosper. But I am also interested in what's true. I don't

want to get involved in the sort of snobbish idea that it's OK for us intellectuals' pursuit, but the hoi polloi need religion.

Dawkins has Peterson's number. He is not interested in the snobbish idea that intellectuals should push religion on the brutes in the "hoi polloi" even though the intellectuals "know" it is not true. In contrast, Peterson is OK with foisting the "fiction" of religion on the hoi polloi because he thinks that fiction is necessary for social cohesion. Dawkins called Peterson out to his face in a 2024 discussion mediated by Alex O'Connor.[12] Peterson developed the theme we have been discussing – God is a fiction but we ought to act as if that fiction is true; otherwise everything will fall to pieces. Dawkins responded with a profound question: "Are you saying that Jesus really did die for our sins? I mean do you believe that? Do you believe that as a fact, that Jesus died for our sins?" Dawkins conceded Christianity may have some social utility, but "that doesn't in any way increase my trust in the validity of Christian propositions like the resurrection, the virgin birth, the miracles and Jesus is the son of God." Dawkins then dismissed Peterson's entire project. He said that if Christianity's truth claims are not actually true, it is useless, and he is not impressed by Peterson's attempt to push Christianity for its instrumental value.

Douglas Murray also rejected Peterson's project in the discussion I mentioned earlier. In that discussion, Peterson argued that the Bible's claims about God are "true" in the same sense Dostoevsky's powerful fiction is true. Murray countered this as follows:

> Is it still a fiction, Jordan? For you, this is your version of Schopenhauer. . . . you say, "Is Dostoevsky true" and you need to say, "In what sense?" But then the issue with the Bible, the issue with Christianity, the issue with faith, is that it's obviously different. It must be in a different realm. It's clearly in a different realm because it claims different things for itself. Dostoevsky doesn't demand that we believe that Raskolnikov [the main character in *Crime and Punishment*] lived. The Bible, if you're going to be a believer, you have to be able to say in the words of the Creed, that you believe

in the virgin birth, that you believe, most importantly, in the resurrection.

Murray's assertion that Peterson's "God is fiction" thesis is his version of Schopenhauer is a penetrating insight. Like Peterson, Schopenhauer believed the Bible is false but necessary for mankind to "get on."[13] Unlike Peterson, Schopenhauer understood that the day will arrive when people catch on to the fact that their teacher does not actually believe the doctrines he has taught them, and when that happens, "then there is an end of them."[14] In the long run, people cannot base their lives on an idea that they do not believe is true.

Dawkins and Murray would have probably been surprised if they had known they were in complete agreement with Christian apologist C. S. Lewis, who wrote: "Christianity is a statement which, if false, is of *no* importance, and, if true, of infinite importance. The one thing it cannot be is moderately important."[15] In response to Peterson, Lewis would probably say: "Christianity is a statement which, if false, is of no importance, and, if true, of infinite importance. The one thing it cannot be is merely socially useful."

It is one thing for a secular psychologist like Peterson to treat the God of the Bible as a fictional character. It is far worse when some so-called Christian churches do the same thing. In his book *Religionless Christianity*, Eric Metaxas says the following of the secularization of the faith that has been wrought by many "progressive" churches:

> [W]e must be supremely clear that [the events of Scripture] are also *actual events in time and history*. And this matters infinitely. We cannot relegate them to the merely mythical, as though they happened "once upon a time" – which is to say that they never actually happened at all. This is one of the ways that our "religious" instinct often deals with the parts we don't like. It puts "religious" reality in a separate box from the rest of reality, as though our faith has no bearing on the rest of reality when, of course, the exact opposite is true. If our faith exists apart from the rest of reality, then it is meaningless. This is precisely what dead "religion" always does. . . .

> But real faith in the God of the Bible is exactly the opposite of this. It spreads into the real world in every dimension, because faith in the God of the Bible is faith in the One who called Himself Truth and who created every part of the reality in which we live.[16]

As we discussed in chapter five, from the beginning, the Christian faith has always been self-consciously grounded in its claim that certain historical facts – actual events at a particular time and place – occurred. Of these historical facts, the resurrection of Jesus Christ was, by far, the most important.[17] Paul steadfastly insisted that the resurrection is essential to the faith. This is the scandal of Christianity. The English word "scandal" has its roots in the Greek word *skándalon*, which means something that causes someone to fall, a stumbling block. The Bible uses the word figuratively of the cross. To many, the idea that righteousness can be obtained only by faith in the crucified and resurrected Jesus instead of scrupulous adherence to religious rules is a stumbling block (literally, a *skándalon*) that prevents them from believing.[18] Though the doctrine of the resurrection is a scandal to many, all Christians everywhere have insisted on that doctrine for nearly 2,000 years. It is non-negotiable because it lies at the very core of the faith. The old Christian hymn captures the idea:

> My hope is built on nothing less
> Than Jesus' blood and righteousness
> I dare not trust the sweetest frame[19]
> But wholly lean on Jesus' name
> On Christ the solid rock I stand
> All other ground is sinking sand

The cross is a scandal to Jordon Peterson. He cannot bring himself to believe in the death, burial and resurrection of Jesus of Nazareth,[20] and instead, he offers an ersatz Christianity stripped of its most basic and essential doctrine. This makes me immensely sad. As Metaxas says, "The secular narrative needs to be boldly denounced not merely as false, but as a pernicious lie that has harmed billions of human beings throughout history."[21]

Tragically, the cross has become a scandal even in many so-called churches. John West calls the phenomenon of large swathes of formerly Christian churches abandoning the core tenets of the faith "Stockholm Syndrome Christianity." Those churches have been captured by the culture and, like kidnap victims who come to identify with their captors, have lost their way. West writes:

> But Stockholm Syndrome Christianity isn't a very solid place to try to plant yourself. It's like the proverbial slippery slope. Once you adopt the operating assumptions of those who oppose Christ, you are likely to continue to slide down the slope along with the culture. As the culture slides away from Christ and truth, so will you.[22]

The Christian faith is not a psychological self-help program, as Peterson would have it. Nor is it a club where people with vaguely religious impulses gather, and every view is welcome so long as it would not be embarrassing in the secular culture. Christianity stands or falls on the historical fact of the resurrection. Fortunately, as we discussed in chapter six, there are very good reasons to believe the resurrection occurred, and therefore, the hope that Christianity provides has a firm foundation. But if the resurrection did not occur, Christianity offers nothing that the average Optimist Club does not offer. "[I]f Christ has not been raised, your faith is worthless." So, to answer the question posed in the title of this chapter, we cannot fake it until we make it.

9. Give Love a Chance

Beloved, let us love one another, for love is of God;
and everyone who loves is born of God and knows God.
He who does not love does not know God, for God is love.[1]

God is love. In his very essence, God is ἀγάπη—*agape*—selfless, sacrificial, unconditional love. God's love for humanity is reflected in the gospel message, which is distilled to its essence in the most famous verse in the Bible: "For God so loved the world, that He gave His only Son, so that everyone who believes in Him will not perish, but have eternal life."[2]

God could have created any universe. He chose to create this one. Why? Because he loves us and desires to be loved by us. God knew what would happen not just in the universe he created but also in all possible universes he could have created. Knowing that, he chose to create a universe in which his creatures have free will. He did this to make creaturely love possible. Choosing the good of the other is the essence of love. A creature that has no free will cannot choose and therefore cannot love. God gave his creatures free will so that when he loved them, they could freely choose to love him also. But there was a tragic downside to God's decision. The inevitable consequence of bestowing the gift of free will on his creatures – of allowing them to choose to love – is that often they would choose not to love. And we all know how that turned out.

Before he created the universe, God knew the consequences of our abuse of our free will. He knew there would be terrible pain and suffering. He also knew that to redeem his creation, he would have to step into it, become a man, live a perfect life, die a horrible death by crucifixion while bearing the sins of the world on his shoulders, be buried for three days, and then rise again to offer the gift of eternal life to everyone who believed in him. God loved us so much that he created a universe in which he knew he would suffer and die.

How deep the Father's love for us,
How vast beyond all measure,
That He should give His only Son
To make a wretch His treasure.[3]

In chapter seven, we saw Ivan Karamazov's angry indictment of God for allowing pain and suffering to exist. Dostoevsky's response to Ivan's indictment was not an argument but a person. Alyosha replied to Ivan:

> "you asked just now if there is in the whole world a being who could and would have the right to forgive. But there is such a being, and he can forgive everything, forgive all and for all, because he himself gave his innocent blood for all and for everything. You've forgotten about him, but it is on him that the structure is being built, and it is to him that they will cry out: 'Just art thou, O Lord, for thy ways have been revealed!'"[4]

God gave us free will, and we abused it, and sin and death came into the world. Now, the whole creation groans as if under a heavy weight, and we groan within ourselves.[5] The chaos and pain we see all around us sometimes seem unbearable. But our faith in Christ's finished work on the cross gives us hope. Ours is not a "faith that would necessarily satisfy Ivan Karamazov, but neither is it one that his arguments can defeat."[6] We are not saved by logical arguments. We are saved by grace, and as Hart goes on to say, on that great and glorious day, God "will not simply reveal the sublime logic of fallen nature, but will strike off the fetters in which creation languishes;

and . . . rather than showing us how the tears of a small girl suffering in the dark were necessary for the building of the Kingdom, He will instead raise her up and wipe away all tears from her eyes—and there shall be no more death, nor sorrow, nor crying, nor any more pain, for the former things will have passed away, and He that sits upon the throne will say, 'Behold, I make all things new.'"[7]

The universal acid of materialism corrodes everything it touches, from individual souls to great civilizations. Its message is one of meaninglessness, despair, and nihilism. But we are not helpless against its onslaught. There is hope, but to access that hope requires placing one's faith in Christ's supreme act of sacrificial love. All I am asking is that you give love a chance.

About the Author

Barry Arrington began his professional journey in 1984 with the public accounting firm Ernst & Whinney (now Ernst & Young). He later pursued law, graduating with honors from the University of Texas School of Law in 1986. Barry's practice has included civil litigation in the state and federal courts, nonprofit law, and constitutional law with a particular focus on First and Second Amendment freedoms. Barry served as a member of the Colorado House of Representatives from 1997 to 1998 and co-founded Jefferson Academy, a successful charter school in Colorado. Two of Barry's cases have reached the United States Supreme Court.

Acknowledgments

I had a tremendous advantage growing up. There were hundreds of books lying around our house and hundreds more down the street in my grandfather's study. Most of the people who influenced me – my parents, my grandfather, my uncle – had a book in their face as often as not. My family's idea of a good time was to pack up the car and head out to a used book fair. Nowadays, they call that modeling. To my family, it just what one does. My father's main literary interest was theology, and he had an extensive theological library.

There were all kinds of books in my life, but two hold special memories. When I was about ten, my grandfather gave me a thick book that contained the complete collection of Sherlock Holmes stories: All 56 shorts and all four novels. As I devoured that book over the next few weeks, the world of literary imagination opened up for me. A couple of years later, my father gave me a copy of Dwight Pentecost's *Things to Come*, a classic in hermeneutics and eschatology. Some of my best memories are talking about books with my dad. Dad is getting older, and his body has slowed down a bit, but his mind remains as sharp as ever. To this day, fifty-odd years later, he and I still enjoy discussing the latest book or article we've read.

Dad imparted lessons about the life of the mind that have served me well throughout my life. One in particular was especially significant. Like most teenagers, I was feeling my intellectual oats. So, one day, I chose to take a contrary view on a theological topic that I knew mattered to him. I expected him to power down on me, but he surprised me. Instead of trying to force me into his way of thinking, he took the opportunity to teach me a lesson. I remember his response to my challenge almost verbatim: "Well, son, if you think you need to change your mind on a matter, you need to study up on it and think long and hard. If you have done the hard work and you still aren't happy with your current view, you have to change your mind." My dad taught me I had a right to think for myself. At the same time, he taught me that rights come with responsibilities. He gave me a precious gift that day. Of course, the most important gift that my father and mother gave me was to bring me to a knowledge of the saving grace of Jesus Christ. From an eternal perspective, that is the only gift that truly matters, and I will always be grateful to them.

I want to thank my wife, Lona, for her patience and grace during the months I have been working on this book. Lona has a radiant smile that brightens any room and a special gift for encouraging others. She constantly bestows that gift on me. A few years ago, Lona and I adopted the "three amigos," and they, too, have been patient with a papa who has spent many long hours pounding on a keyboard. I want to thank Bill Dembski for his encouragement and assistance. James Barham comments were particularly valuable, and Jennifer Finley made the book much better. I am also grateful to the people who have read and commented on all or parts of the manuscript, including Denyse O'Leary, Granville Sewell, Gordon Mullings, Gino Geraci, and Gene Malpas.

Notes

1. Introduction

1. Some people might prefer "naturalism," "physicalism," or "monism" to describe this idea, and professional philosophers may quibble that this is an over-simplified definition of a very complex idea. There is no need to get bogged down in that discussion. The basic idea is straightforward: Only material entities exist, and an immaterial God does not.
2. Just how completely Darwin captured the imagination of Victorian elites is reflected in the ecstatic writing of British geologist John Judd, who, in 1912, asserted with supreme confidence that "When the history of the Nineteenth Century. . . comes to be written, a foremost place must be assigned to that great movement by which evolution has become the dominant factor in scientific progress, while its influence has been felt in every sphere of human speculation and effort. . . . At the end of the Century, evolution had not only become the guiding principle of naturalists, but had profoundly influenced every branch of physical science; at the same time, suggesting new trains of thought and permeating the language of philologists, historians, sociologists, politicians—and even of theologians." Judd, *The Coming of Evolution*, 1.
3. Dennett, *Darwin's Dangerous Idea*, 63.

4. As we shall see, the changes quickly extended far beyond biology. As Judd noted in *The Coming of Evolution*, by the end of the nineteenth century, Darwin's ideas had permeated practically every field of intellectual endeavor. See note 2.

5. This is why some Victorians were befuddled by the furor that erupted after the publication of *Origin of Species*. For example, John Judd related an 1871 exchange with the literary critic and poet Matthew Arnold in which Arnold remarked, "I cannot understand why you scientific people make such a fuss about Darwin. Why it's all in Lucretius!" Judd, *The Coming of Evolution*, 3. Professor Arnold was wrong. Darwin is not all in Lucretius. Darwin's ideas gained traction when Lucretius's did not for the reasons discussed in the text.

6. In the fifth century BC, Democritus, a contemporary of Socrates, introduced the term "atom," which he envisioned as tiny, indivisible particles of matter that move through the universe, either bouncing off each other or coming together to form larger clusters. Democritus believed that all phenomena could be explained by the interactions of these atoms. In the fourth century BC, Epicurus founded Epicureanism, a philosophical school that bears his name to this day. Epicureanism is a strictly materialist philosophy that is largely based on the theory of atoms developed by Democritus. Finally, in the first century BC, the Roman poet Lucretius, who was heavily influenced by Epicurean philosophy, proposed that living organisms evolved by trial and error from the random interactions of atoms.

7. Cicero famously derided the atomists' appeal to chance in the first century BC. He wrote:

> Is it possible for any man to behold these things, and yet imagine that certain solid and individual bodies move by their natural force and gravitation, and that a world

so beautifully adorned was made by their fortuitous concourse? He who believes this may as well believe that if a great quantity of the one-and-twenty letters, composed either of gold or any other matter, were thrown upon the ground, they would fall into such order as legibly to form the *Annals* of Ennius. I doubt whether fortune could make a single verse of them. How, therefore, can these people assert that the world was made by the fortuitous concourse of atoms, which have no color, no quality—which the Greeks call no sense? Or that there are innumerable worlds, some rising and some perishing, in every moment of time?

Cicero, *De Natura Deorum (On the Nature of the Gods)*, 78. Many ideas that we consider new actually have an ancient heritage. I suspect that many, perhaps most, people believe Darwin made up the theory of evolution from whole cloth rather than merely tweaking an ancient theory criticized by Cicero 2,000 years ago. In this passage Cicero also anticipated the "infinite monkeys" argument (see chapter seven) and, arguably, the many-worlds interpretation of quantum mechanics (see chapter six,).

8. See note 7. The word "atom" comes from the Greek "*atomos*," which means "indivisible." Yes, there is such a thing as Greek "atomic theory."
9. Darwin, *Origin of Species*, 65–66.
10. Darwin never speculated in his published work about how living things made the leap from non-living matter in the first place. In 1868, he wrote that "the first origin of life on this earth . . . is at present quite beyond the scope of science." Darwin, *The Variation of Animals*, 12. Privately, in a famous 1871 letter to his friend Joseph Hooker, Darwin speculated about how life might have spontaneously arisen on the early earth in "some warm little pond" full of chemicals and energy. February 1, 1871 letter to J.D. Hooker,

Darwin Correspondence Project, available at https://www.darwinproject.ac.uk/letter/?docId=letters/DCP-LETT-7471.xml (accessed December 5, 2024).

11. In a paroxysm of hagiographic excess, Dennett wrote, "If I were to give an award for the single best idea anyone has ever had, I'd give it to Darwin, ahead of Newton and Einstein and everyone else." Dennett, *Darwin's Dangerous Idea*, 21. While the idea was perhaps not *that* important, there is little doubt that the world became a fundamentally different place after 1859. Incidentally, Dennett is not alone in his quasi-religious Darwin worship. Richard Dawkins has said that Darwin's idea "is possibly the greatest achievement that any human mind has ever accomplished." Richard Dawkins, "Richard Dawkins vs John Lennox | The God Delusion Debate," *Larry Alex Taunton Youtube Channel* (Feb. 8, 2017), available at https://www.youtube.com/watch?v=zF5bPI92-5o (at 1:42:08) (accessed February 8, 2025).

12. Dawkins, *The Blind Watchmaker*, 10.

13. Ibid.

14. I discuss this topic in chapter seven.

15. Dawkins, *River Out of Eden*, 134.

16. Nietzsche, *The Gay Science*, 181–182.

17. Nietzsche understood there was a monumental problem facing Western culture. He knew that the "death of God"—i.e., the widespread acceptance of metaphysical materialism—would have cataclysmic cultural consequences, and his life's work was to develop an ethic to replace the Judeo-Christian ethic he believed would inevitably collapse. He failed spectacularly. G.K. Chesterton noted early on that Nietzsche sidestepped the truly consequential questions through metaphor. "He said, 'beyond good and evil,' because he had not the courage to say, 'more good than good and evil,' or, 'more evil than good and evil.'" Chesterton, *Orthodoxy*, 192. (alluding to Nietzsche, *Beyond Good and Evil*.)

18. Leff, "Unspeakable Ethics, Unnatural Law."
19. Id., at 1230.
20. Ibid.
21. Ibid.
22. Id., at 1232.
23. Id. at 1240.
24. Id. at 1249.
25. Herberg, *Judaism and Modern Man*, 91–92.
26. Hemingway, *The Sun Also Rises*, 136.
27. CDC, Facts About Suicide, available at https://www.cdc.gov/suicide/facts/index.html (accessed December 11, 2024).
28. "For me the sole datum is the absurd . . . And carrying this absurd logic to its conclusion, I must admit that that struggle implies a total absence of hope . . ." Camus, *The Myth of Sisyphus*, 31. By "absurd," Camus does not mean "laughably foolish or false." He uses the word in the philosophical sense of "the condition of existing in a meaningless and irrational world."
29. Camus, *The Myth of Sisyphus*, 3.
30. Id., 123.
31. Jean-Paul Sartre's existentialism suggests that we make our own meaning by the way we live our lives. "Man is nothing but that which he makes of himself." Pull yourself up by your bootstraps with Sartre or lean into the meaninglessness with Camus. The options are, in a sense, the same in that they are equally arbitrary.
32. Here I owe a great debt to Critical Theory for helping me to understand the implications of the materialist worldview. Critical Theory is metaphysical materialism applied to human relations. The core ideas of the theory are fairly straightforward: Truth, morals, and rationality itself are socially constructed. The only thing that is real is power, and all human relations play out in power dynamics. The goal of Critical Theorists, like all things rooted in academic

discourse, is often shrouded by an almost impenetrable thicket of academic jargon. However, the goal seems to be to identify and root out "systems of oppression" imposed by those with power on those without power. The only thing the theory lacks is a non-arbitrary reason for preferring those without power to those with power. When I was in law school, I had an opportunity to attend a lecture by one of the founders of Critical Legal Theory, Harvard Law School professor Duncan Kennedy. Naturally, Kennedy was a Marxist (though he called himself a social democrat), and the main thing I remember about his lecture 40 years later is his complaint about how outrageous it was that the janitors at Harvard were paid less than he was. I remember thinking at the time that there was an easy solution to this problem. All he had to do was agree with the janitors to pool their salaries (I was sure they would be OK with that) and split the pool equally. That obvious solution never seemed to have occurred to Kennedy. Like millionaire socialist Bernie Sanders and the elite of the Soviet *nomenklatura*, it apparently never occurred to him that redistributing his own wealth was an option. The immiseration that invariably accompanies Marxism is for the little people.

33. Plato, *The Republic*, Book I, 47. Perhaps the Athenians captured the concept better in their ultimatum to the Melians: "The strong do what they can, and the weak suffer what they must." Thucydides, *The Peloponnesian War*, 403.
34. Ayaan Hirsi Ali is a Somali-born Dutch-American writer, activist, and former politician known for her outspoken views on Islam, women's rights, and immigration.
35. "Richard Dawkins vs Ayaan Hirsi Ali: The God Debate," *UnHerd*-sponsored Dissident Dialogues Festival in New York (June 3, 2024) available at https://www.youtube.com/watch?v=DBsHdHMvucs&t=14s, starting at 22:08 (accessed November 14, 2024).

36. "Shock the middle class." The phrase refers to actions that are an afront to conventional mores.
37. "The Herd of Independent Minds: Has the Avant-Garde Its Own Mass Culture?" is the title of an article in *Commentary* magazine by Harold Rosenberg.
38. See Andrew Dalton, "Actor Gina Carano sues Lucasfilm and Disney over her firing from 'The Mandalorian,'" *Associated Press* (Feb. 7, 2024), available at https://apnews.com/article/mandalorian-gina-carano-lawsuit-lucasfilm-disney-37be85aeaa856492e3d5008add8e5100 (accessed January 21, 2025).
39. This is not to say that I agree with them. I am saying that it is in a sense noble to have the courage to defend an idea that is extremely unpopular in one's community, even if one is wrong.
40. Poole, "The Four Horsemen Review."
41. Acts 24:14.

2. Materialism 101

1. A few months after the shootings, the Columbine High School administration invited students, parents, first responders, and health care workers to participate in a "community healing" art project. Participants painted artistic designs on small ceramic tiles that were then installed on the walls of the school. My clients were invited to participate in the project, but the school rejected their tiles because they contained religious themes. We brought a First Amendment challenge to this decision, and the federal district court held that the school district violated the parents' constitutional rights. Unfortunately, that decision was later overturned on appeal. See *Fleming v. Jefferson Cnty. Sch. Dist. No. R-1*, 170 F. Supp. 2d 1094 (D. Colo. 2001), *rev'd sub nom. Fleming v. Jefferson Cnty. Sch. Dist. R-1*, 298 F.3d 918 (10th

Cir. 2002). The Tenth Circuit would almost certainly decide the case differently today because its decision conflicts with the Supreme Court's later decision in *Kennedy v. Bremerton Sch. Dist.*, 597 U.S. 507 (2022).

2. In those videos, Harris had a package of Slim Jim meat sticks that he snacked on as he and Klebold discussed their plans, and to this day, I think of him almost every time I see a package of Slim Jims at the checkout counter in the grocery store.

3. Readers familiar with litigation procedures will know that depositions are not normally taken in a courthouse. But this was not a typical case. The judge appointed a "special master" to oversee discovery in the case, and he entered an order requiring depositions to be taken in a large conference room at the federal courthouse in Denver.

4. My discussion of Columbine will focus on Eric Harris, as it is widely recognized by those who have investigated the shootings that he was the leader and Dylan Klebold was a follower. In an article published in *Slate*, Dave Cullen shared insights from law enforcement and psychological experts who examined the dynamics between the two. They unanimously concluded that Harris was the mastermind, while Klebold was a depressed, suicidal hothead who was swept up in Harris's plans. See Dave Cullen, "The Depressive and the Psychopath," *Slate* magazine, available at https://slate.com/news-and-politics/2004/04/at-last-we-know-why-the-columbine-killers-did-it.html (accessed October 22, 2024). This observation is not intended to diminish Klebold's responsibility for his actions, but Harris was clearly the *sine qua non* of the tragedy.

5. For one thing, the killers did not target *any* individuals. They did not plan for the attack to be primarily a shooting. They planned a bombing that would have indiscriminately killed hundreds. Columbine became primarily a shooting

only because the bombs they planted failed to detonate, and they improvised. See Cullen, "The Depressive and the Psychopath" (note 4).
6. They hoped their bombs would kill hundreds of students. See Cullen, "The Depressive and the Psychopath" (note 4).
7. The concepts of the two thinkers are related at a fundamental level. "Friedrich Nietzsche saw . . . an even more cosmic message in Darwin: God is dead. If Nietzsche is the father of existentialism, then perhaps Darwin deserves the title of grandfather." Dennett, *Darwin's Dangerous Idea*, 63.
8. Peter Langman, "Influences on the Ideology of Eric Harris, version 1.2," *School Shooters .Info* (Aug. 2, 2014), available at https://schoolshooters.info/sites/default/files/harris_influences_ideology_1.2.pdf (accessed November 15, 2024).
9. Id. at 4.
10. While he was a chaplain for the Sheriff's Department, Denver police officers who went to Gino's church were the first to inform him of the shootings.
11. The creed is meant to capture the materialist dogma that only the physical exists. It is not meant to be a scientific description of the universe. I am not suggesting that materialists, like the ancient Greek atomists, believe in a crude billiard-ball cosmos in which chunks of matter randomly bounce around. The four fundamental forces, dark energy, dark matter, ordinary matter, and antimatter are the stuff of the materialist universe. The point is that a materialist, by definition, insists that all of existence—the totality of reality—is subsumed within such physical stuff. Matter and energy in space/time is all there is. Consequently, all phenomena, including human consciousness, must, in principle, be reducible to that physical stuff.
12. "There is no God but Allah, and Muhammad is His Prophet."
13. Sagan, *Cosmos*, 1. Sagan also intoned this chant at the beginning of his *Cosmos* television series. See, e.g., "Carl

Sagan's 'Cosmos: A Personal Voyage' (1980), Part 1," at 3:11, available at https://www.filmsforaction.org/watch/carl-sagans-cosmos-a-personal-voyage-1980/.

14. Carroll, "Why Is There Something Rather Than Nothing?," 16–17. Available at https://philpapers.org/archive/CARWIT-11.pdf (accessed November 15, 2024).

15. Sagan wrote: "An atheist is someone who is certain that God does not exist, someone who has compelling evidence against the existence of God. I know of no such compelling evidence. Because God can be relegated to remote times and places and to ultimate causes, we would have to know a great deal more about the universe than we do now to be sure that no such God exists." Sagan, *Broca's Brain*, 396.

16. I am not disputing the standard model of cosmology, including the Big Bang. As Stephen Meyer discussed in the *Return of the God Hypothesis*, Big Bang cosmology is perfectly consistent with—indeed tends to confirm—theism. Id. at 131. The issue I am raising is that the materialist conception of the origin and development of the universe is radically incomplete. Why is there something instead of nothing? There are three possible answers to that question. (1) A necessary being (God) caused a contingent universe. (2) The universe somehow caused itself. (3) The universe is eternal. The latter two options are incoherent. The first option is not incoherent but requires accepting the concept of "necessary being" (the uncaused cause) on faith. Materialists prefer incoherence or, like Sean Carroll, simply duck the question.

17. Sagan, *The Cosmic Connection*, 190.

18. Carl Sagan's "Cosmos: A Personal Voyage" (1980), Part 1, at 6:13, available at https://www.filmsforaction.org/watch/carl-sagans-cosmos-a-personal-voyage-1980/

19. Sam Harris, "The Illusion of the Self, an Interview with Bruce Hood," available at https://www.samharris.org/blog/the-illusion-of-the-self2 (accessed October 24, 2024).

20. Dawkins, *River Out of Eden*, 133.
21. Whether Darwinian evolution accurately describes why we have an appendix (there is mounting evidence that is not vestigial after all) and strong feelings that we call morality is beside the point. As I will discuss in chapter seven, there are reasons to doubt it does. The point here is that materialists must, by definition, assume that the Darwinian account or something very much like it is true. As Phillip Johnson wrote, "if materialism is true, then some materialistic theory of evolution has to be true simply as a matter of logical deduction, [and that] theory will necessarily be at least roughly like neo-Darwinism." Johnson, "The Unraveling of Scientific Materialism." Available at https://www.firstthings.com/article/1997/11/the-unraveling-of-scientific-materialism (accessed October 10, 2024).
22. Ruse, "Evolutionary Theory and Christian Ethics," 262. (emphasis added).
23. Provine, "Scientists, Face It!," 10.
24. Shapiro, "The Most-Cited Legal Scholars," 423.
25. Posner, "The Problematics of Moral and Legal Theory."
26. Calhoun, "Grounding Normative Assertions," 39–40.
27. Posner, "Reply to Critics," 1813.
28. Singh, "Are Your Morals Too Good to Be True?"
29. Posner, "The Problematics of Moral and Legal Theory," 1645.
30. Much of what is contained in the following paragraphs first appeared in my article "Psychopath as Übermensch or Nietzsche at Columbine," available at https://uncommondescent.com/intelligent-design/psychopath-as-ubermensch-or-nietzsche-at-columbine/ (accessed November 15, 2024).
31. Is the cat cruel to the mouse? No, he is doing what cats naturally do to mice. "[Nature] does not even say that the cat is enviable or the mouse pitiable. We think the cat superior because we have (or most of us have) a particular philosophy

to the effect that life is better than death. But if the mouse were a German pessimist mouse, he might not think that the cat had beaten him at all. He might think he had beaten the cat by getting to the grave first." Chesterton, *Orthodoxy*, 190. I have always smiled at the notion of a mouse devoted to the philosophy of Schopenhauer.

32. *"Übermensch"* is from the German *"über"* meaning "over" or "beyond" or "super," and *"Mensch"* meaning "man" as in "mankind." The word has been translated into English as "superman."
33. Nietzsche, *Thus Spake Zarathustra*, 6–9.
34. Id., 321–22.
35. Langman, "Influences on the Ideology of Eric Harris," 1. (see note 8).
36. Id., 5.
37. Ibid.
38. David Brook, "The Columbine Killers," *The New York Times*, April 24, 2024.
39. See IMDb, "True Detective Quotes," available at https://www.imdb.com/title/tt2790254/quotes/?item=qt3991013 (accessed November 16, 2024).

3. Where do "Rights" Come From?

1. The video clip and a transcript of Przybyla's remarks may be viewed here: Tim Hains, "Heidi Przybyla: Extremist Conservative Christian Nationalists Believe Your Rights Come From God, Not Government," *Real Clear Politics* (Feb. 23, 2024) available at https://www.realclearpolitics.com/video/2024/02/23/heidi_przybyla_extremist_conservative_christian_nationalists_believe_your_rights_come_from_god_not_government.html (accessed December 16, 2024).
2. In response to the backlash, Przybyla took to the pages of *Politico* to clarify her remarks, which she admitted were

"clumsy." Heidi Przybyla, "The Right Way to Cover the Intersection of Religion and Politics," *Politico* (Feb. 29, 2024). She explained that she had been misunderstood. She was not suggesting there is anything wrong with invoking God-given rights as such. Instead, she was trying to make a distinction between good and bad appeals to natural law. According to Przybyla, when Martin Luther King, Jr., invoked God-given rights, he was properly celebrated as a national hero because he was liberal, but when conservatives invoke God-given rights, they are trying to impose a dictatorial theocracy and must be resisted by all right-thinking people.

3. Przybyla is hardly the only person on MSNBC who holds these views. In 2017, while covering an Alabama senate race, MSNBC host Chuck Todd said that only "fundamentalist" Christians believe our rights come from God, and anyone who believes such nonsense does not believe in the Constitution. See Alex Griswold, "Chuck Todd: Roy Moore Doesn't 'Believe in the Constitution' Because He Thinks Rights Come From God," *The Washington Free Beacon* (Sept. 27, 2017).

4. Martin Luther King, Jr., "Letter from Birmingham Jail," published as "The Negro is Your Brother" in *The Atlantic Monthly*; August 1963, Volume 212, No. 2; pages 78–88.

5. H.L.A. Hart is widely recognized as the preeminent defender of legal positivism. In his highly influential article (Hart, "Positivism and the Separation of Law and Morals."). Hart argued that law and morality have no necessary connection to one another. Id. at 594. He would have disagreed adamantly with King's assertion that an unjust law is no law at all. Hart followed up his law review article with a book —Hart, *The Concept of Law*.—which has undoubtedly been the most influential book on the philosophy of law in the last century. Positivists insist that law is a social construct.

"All modern Positivists agree that law is determined by social facts, and whether a norm is branded as a legal norm need not depend on its content or whether it has a minimum content of justice or morality." Borchers, "Legal Philosophy for Lawyers," 274.

6. *Black's Law Dictionary* (12th ed. 2024).
7. Posner, "The Problematics of Moral and Legal Theory," 1640.
8. Id., at 1642.
9. The Nazi 'Final Solution to the Jewish Question' ('*Endlösung der Judenfrage*') was the deliberate and systematic mass murder of European Jews." Holocaust Encyclopedia, available at https://encyclopedia.ushmm.org/content/en/article/final-solution-overview (accessed December 16, 2024).
10. Posner, "The Problematics of Moral and Legal Theory," 1654.
11. "Visceral" means of or relating to the viscera, i.e., the guts. David Filvaroff was my torts professor in law school. When Professor Filvaroff engaged in the back-and-forth Socratic method, woe to the student who responded to one of his questions, with "I feel . . ." Filvaroff would interrupt with "Stop right there. Your fellow students and I are not interested in the condition of your viscera! We want to know what you think, not what you feel."
12. Suttee is the immolation of a widow on her husband's bier, a practice that was accepted in Hindu society.
13. Id., at 1645.
14. See Introduction, note 33.
15. Plato, *The Republic*, Book I, 47.
16. Harari, *Sapiens*, 136.
17. Id. at 136–137.
18. Herbert, *Children of Dune*, 164. Herbert attributed the aphorism to the French author Louis Veuillot; however, there is reason to believe that it did not originate with him.

19. That said, it is no secret that materialist ideology and the extreme secularism of the left are natural bedfellows.
20. "Materialism, on the other hand, considers the unity of the universe to derive from its materiality, and that spirit (consciousness) is one of the natural characteristics of matter which emerges only when matter has developed to a certain stage," Mao Zedong, *Lecture Notes on Dialectical Materialism*.
21. Lenin declared that the philosophical basis of Marxism is "a materialism which is absolutely atheistic and positively hostile to all religion." V.I. Lenin, "The Attitude of the Workers' Party to Religion," May 13, 1909, available at https://www.marxists.org/archive/lenin/works/1909/may/13.htm (accessed November 20, 2024). Following in his footsteps, Stalin wrote that "philosophical materialism holds that matter, nature, being, is an objective reality existing outside and independent of our consciousness; that matter is primary, since it is the source of sensations, ideas, consciousness, and that consciousness is secondary, derivative, since it is a reflection of matter, a reflection of being; that thought is a product of matter which in its development has reached a high degree of perfection, namely, of the brain, and the brain is the organ of thought; and that therefore one cannot separate thought from matter without committing a grave error," J.V. Stalin, *Dialectical and Historical Materialism*, 1938, available at https://www.marxists.org/reference/archive/stalin/works/1938/09.htm (accessed November 20, 2024).
22. Some have argued that Hitler does not belong in this triumvirate, even going so far as to claim that he was a Christian. That is absolute nonsense. Hitler was a thoroughgoing materialist, especially in regard to Darwinian biology, and he had nothing but contempt for the "myths" of Christianity. He said: "Time will go by until the moment when

science can answer all the questions. . . . The dogma of Christianity gets worn away before the advances of science. Religion will have to make more and more concessions. Gradually the myths crumble. *All that's left is to prove that in nature there is no frontier between the organic and the inorganic.*" Hitler, *Table Talk*, 59. That last sentence is the very definition of materialist biology. "National Socialism, like other totalitarian dictatorships, parodied many of the eschatological and liturgical attributes of redemptive religions, while being fundamentally antagonistic towards the Churches: rivals, as the Nazis saw it, in the subtle, totalizing control of minds. However, the overwhelmingly Christian character of the German people meant that Hitler dissembled his personal views behind preachy invocations of the Almighty . . . In reality, his views were a mixture of materialist biology, a faux-Nietzschean contempt for core, as distinct from secondary, Christian values, and a visceral anti-clericalism." Burleigh, *Third Reich*, 717.

23. The kulaks were relatively prosperous farmers who understandably opposed collectivizing agriculture.

24. Joseph Stalin, "Speech on Agrarian Policy" (Dec. 27, 1929), available at https://history.hanover.edu/courses/excerpts/111stalin.html (accessed November 20, 2024).

25. There is no evidence that Stalin actually said this, but there cannot be the slightest doubt that the aphorism captures his philosophy. Indeed, the reason the quotation is so widely attributed to Stalin is that disgraced *New York Times* reporter Walter Duranty used it to describe Stalin's policies in connection with liquidating the kulaks. Duranty won the Pulitzer Prize in 1932 for his pro–Soviet Union reporting. After Stalin's atrocities became undeniable, there were calls for the revocation of the prize. In its response, the *Times* quotes a 1933 dispatch from Duranty: "'Conditions are bad, but there is no famine,' he wrote in a dispatch from Moscow

in March of 1933 describing the 'mess' of collectivization. 'But—to put it brutally—you can't make an omelet without breaking eggs.'" *"New York Times* Statement About 1932 Pulitzer Prize Awarded to Walter Duranty," *New York Times*, available at https://www.nytco.com/company/prizes-awards/new-york-times-statement-about-1932-pulitzer-prize-awarded-to-walter-duranty/ (accessed November 21, 2024). About one thing we can agree with Duranty. Stalin was brutal.
26. Dawkins, *River Out of Eden*, 96.
27. *Triggernometry* podcast (Aug. 25, 2024) 42:13, available at https://www.youtube.com/watch?v=wdfmQ2iJb6o (accessed November 20, 2024).
28. Id., beginning at 56:30.
29. Id., beginning at 101:25.
30. Dawkins, *Blind Watchmaker*, 406.
31. Lewis, *The Abolition of Man*, 27.
32. Id., at 30.
33. Id., at 33 (emphasis added).

4. Lawless Law

1. The same Gino Geraci who, 22 years earlier, had rushed to minister to the victims and first responders at Columbine High School.
2. William Shakespeare, *The Tragedy of Julius Caesar*, Act 3, Scene 1. I am not above a little melodrama.
3. As Justice Gorsuch later wryly remarked concerning similar New York regulations, "Who knew public health would so perfectly align with secular convenience?" *Roman Catholic Diocese of Brooklyn v. Cuomo*, 592 U.S. 14, 22 (2020).
4. "And let us consider one another to provoke unto love and to good works: Not forsaking the assembling of ourselves together . . ." Hebrews 10:24–25 KJV.

5. *South Bay United Pentecostal Church v. Newsom*, 140 S. Ct. 1613, and *Calvary Chapel Dayton Valley v. Sisolak*, 140 S. Ct. 2603.
6. 140 S. Ct. at 2609.
7. The change resulting from Justice Ginsburg's replacement by Justice Barrett rivals the famous 1937 "switch in time that saved nine" that marked a shift in the Court's stance regarding New Deal legislation from one of general opposition to one of general support.
8. 592 U.S. 14.
9. *High Plains Harvest Church v. Polis*, 141 S. Ct. 527.
10. Obviously, the structure of the new nation's government under the Articles of Confederation and, later, the Constitution differed from England's. However, the substrate of that law was based on English common law, and this has had ramifications to this day. According to the Supreme Court, the Constitution cannot be interpreted safely except by reference to the common law and to British institutions as they were when it was adopted. *New York State Rifle & Pistol Ass'n, Inc. v. Bruen*, 597 U.S. 1, 39 (2022). Thus, the Court frequently cites English common law principles when determining the scope of constitutional rights. For example, in 2024, the Court cited English common law in a case involving the reach of the Seventh Amendment. *Sec. & Exch. Comm'n v. Jarkesy*, 144 S. Ct. 2117, 2128 (2024).
11. Blackstone's "works constituted the preeminent authority on English law for the founding generation." *Alden v. Maine*, 527 U.S. 706, 71 (1999).
12. Alschuler, "Rediscovering Blackstone," 5.
13. Boorstin, *The Mysterious Science of the Law*, 3.
14. In 2024, the Court cited Blackstone in ten cases.
15. Modern commentators have often attributed to Blackstone the view that all legal questions, including those that implicate no moral issue, have only a single correct answer that

must be discovered by reference to natural law principles. This is a silly objection because Blackstone said exactly the opposite. Positive law often concerns the "great number of indifferent points in which both the divine law and the natural leave a man at his own liberty but which are found necessary for the benefit of society to be restrained within certain limits." Blackstone, *Commentaries on the Laws of England*, vol. 1, 43. For example, Blackstone understood that God had little interest in laws governing the export of wool to foreign countries. Id.

16. Blackstone, *Commentaries*, vol. 1, 40.
17. Like Blackstone, the founders also understood that the fundamental moral principles underlying the natural law could also be discovered by human reason through the study of nature. Thus, the Declaration also speaks of the "Laws of Nature." Thomas Jefferson was heavily influenced by Isaac Newton. He kept a portrait of Newton in his study. Conklin, "The Origins of the Pursuit of Happiness," 244. Jefferson believed that Newton's approach to physical science was adaptable to morality and social relations. Thus, the moral laws of nature are discovered through observation guided by reason in the same way physical laws are discovered. Professor Albert Alschuler has summarized this dual source approach to natural law as follows: "Natural law comes from God; it comes from the top down. A second meaning treats moral truths as truths about human nature. Natural law proceeds from the bottom up. Rather than choose between these uses, Blackstone endorsed both. He maintained that the study of God and the study of human nature led to the same understanding." Alschuler, "From Blackstone to Holmes," 493.
18. Blackstone, *Commentaries*, vol. 1, 41. Similarly, Jefferson wrote in the Declaration that man has a right to the "pursuit of Happiness."

19. Conklin, "The Origins of the Pursuit of Happiness," 203.
20. George, "Natural Law," 172.
21. Steiner, "Abraham Lincoln and the Rule of Law Books," 1302.
22. Id. at 1303. Lincoln is quoted as saying of the *Commentaries* that I "never read anything which so profoundly interested and thrilled me." Id., citing Ogden, "Lincoln's Early Impressions," 328.
23. Letter from Abraham Lincoln to John M. Brockman (Sept. 25, 1860), quoted in Lincoln, *The Collected Works of Abraham Lincoln*, vols. 4, 121.
24. Abraham Lincoln, Speech at Independence Hall, Philadelphia, Pennsylvania (Feb. 22, 1861) in Lincoln, *Abraham Lincoln: His Speeches and Writings*, 577.
25. Id.
26. Holmes, "The Path of the Law."
27. Levinson, "Strolling Down the Path of the Law," 1228.
28. Howe, *Justice Oliver Wendell Holmes*, 46, n. 41. Quoting a letter from Holmes to James Bryce dated September 17, 1919.
29. George, "Natural Law." Citing Holmes, *The Essential Holmes*, xxviii.
30. See Alschuler, *Law Without Values*. Professor Alschuler provides a book-length exploration of this topic.
31. Alschuler, *Law Without Values*, 41.
32. Holmes was invited to join the Fifty-fourth Massachusetts Regiment—the regiment depicted in the movie *Glory*—but he did not accept the invitation. *Id.* at 45.
33. See Spencer, *The Principles of Biology*, vols. 1, 444. Darwin incorporated the phrase into the sixth edition of *Origin of Species* published in 1869.
34. Letter from Oliver Wendell Holmes to Lady Pollock (July 2, 1895), in Holmes, *The Holmes-Pollock Letters*, vols. 1, 58.

35. Holmes, "The Gas-Stokers' Strike," 795–796. [Emphasis added; originally published in *American Law Review,* 7 (1873): 582].
36. Gilmore, *The Ages of American Law,* 48–49. Many people mistakenly believe that Holmes had progressive political views because of his famous dissents in favor of free speech (*Abrams v. United States,* 250 U.S. 616 (1919)) and against invalidating liberal economic regulations [*Lochner v. New York,* 198 U.S. 45 (1905)]. Nothing could be further from the truth. Indeed, as we shall see, the idea that Holmes cared about speech rights in an abstract sense or the betterment of workers for its own sake borders on the ridiculous. Holmes's famous dissenting opinions rest squarely on his Darwinian worldview and nothing else. See Heyman, "The Dark Side of the Force." Holmes opposed government censorship because he believed it interfered with the Darwinian struggle of ideas to get themselves accepted. He wrote, "the best test of truth is the power of the thought to get itself accepted in the competition of the market." *Abrams,* 250 U.S. at 630. In a later case, he stated the view even more forcefully: "If in the long run the beliefs . . . are destined to be accepted by the dominant forces of the community, the only meaning of free speech is that they should be given their chance and have their way." *Gitlow v. People of State of New York,* 268 U.S. 652, 673 (1925). See also (referring to "the struggle for existence between competing ideas."). As for *Lochner,* "Holmes understood social and political life in terms of group conflict, such as the struggle between workers and employers." Heyman, "The Dark Side of the Force," 684. He believed that "except in the most extreme cases, the courts should not interpret the Constitution to prevent the natural outcome of a dominant opinion or to interfere with the right of a majority to embody their opinions in law. Id. at 685, citing Holmes's *Lochner* dissent, 198 U.S., at 76–77.

37. Alschuler, "From Blackstone to Holmes," 498. Quoting a letter from Oliver Wendell Holmes to Sir Frederick Pollock (Aug. 30, 1929), in Holmes, *The Holmes-Pollock Letters*, Vol. 2, 252.
38. Id., quoting letter from Oliver Wendell Holmes to Lewis Einstein (Aug. 19, 1909), in Holmes, *The Holmes-Laski Letters*, vols. 2, 1125.
39. Id., n. 54, quoting letter from Oliver Wendell Holmes to Harold Laski (Jan. 11, 1929), in Holmes, *The Holmes-Laski Letters*, vols. 2, 1125.
40. Id., quoting Letter from Oliver Wendell Holmes to Lady Pollock (Sept. 6, 1902), in Holmes, *The Holmes-Pollock Letters*, vols. 1, 105.
41. Id. at 499, quoting letter from Oliver Wendell Holmes to John Chipman Gray (Sept. 3, 1905), cited in Novick, *Honorable Justice*, 283.
42. Holmes had, of course, read Nietzsche and was clearly influenced by him. See Vannatta and Mendenhall, "The American Nietzsche?," 196. Holmes did not care for Nietzsche's style and believed him to be too occupied with theological issues for which Holmes had no use. But he said Nietzsche contained "much that I have long believed, after or independently of him." Id., 194–95, quoting a 1924 letter from Holmes to Morris Cohen. Vannatta and Mendenhall examine Nietzsche's influence on Holmes and highlight parallels between their philosophies.
43. Alschuler, "From Blackstone to Holmes," 498. Quoting letter from Oliver Wendell Holmes to Harold Laski (June 1, 1927), in Holmes, *The Holmes-Laski Letters*, vols. 2, 948.
44. Id., quoting letter from Oliver Wendell Holmes to Harold Laski (Sept. 7, 1916), in Holmes, *The Holmes-Laski Letters*, vols. 1, 16.

45. Id., quoting letter from Oliver Wendell Holmes to Harold Laski (Dec. 3, 1917), in Holmes, *The Holmes-Laski Letters*, vols. 1, 116.
46. Id. at 501, quoting letter from Oliver Wendell Holmes to Lewis Einstein (May 21, 1914), in Holmes, *The Holmes–Einstein Letters*, 93.
47. Id., n. 77, quoting letter from Oliver Wendell Holmes to Harold Laski (Aug. 5, 1926), in Holmes, *The Holmes-Laski Letters*, vols. 2, 862.
48. Id. at 502, quoting Letter from Oliver Wendell Holmes to Harold Laski (Apr. 13, 1929), in Holmes, *The Holmes-Laski Letters*, vols. 2, 1146.
49. Oliver Wendell Holmes, "Ideals and Doubts," in Holmes, *Collected Legal Papers*, 306. (emphasis added)
50. Alschuler, "From Blackstone to Holmes," 503. Quoting letter from Oliver Wendell Holmes to Felix Frankfurter (Sept. 3, 1921), in Holmes, *Holmes and Frankfurter*, 125.
51. *Buck v. Bell*, 274 U.S. 200, 207 (1927). *Buck v. Bell* is far worse than you think. Professor Paul Lombardo spent decades researching the case. His findings are horrifying. In his exhaustively researched book (Lombardo, *Three Generations, No Imbeciles.*), Lombardo details how Carrie Buck was never actually diagnosed as an "imbecile" and actually made good grades while she was in school, and her supposedly feeble-minded daughter made the honor roll. Buck was railroaded at trial. Her attorney was Irving Whitehead, a passionate advocate of eugenics and a supporter of mandatory sterilization. Given that blatant conflict of interest, it is no surprise that he put up only a token defense.
52. Alschuler, "From Blackstone to Holmes," 514, n. 39. Quoting letter from Oliver Wendell Holmes to Harold Laski (May 12, 1927), in Holmes, *The Holmes-Laski Letters*, vols. 2, 942. In Holmes's defense, a passion for eugenics as the next step in the march of science was common among intellec-

tuals of his age. After all, Charles Darwin's cousin, Francis Galton, coined the term "eugenics."

53. Dowbiggin, *Keeping America Sane*, 78. *Buck v. Bell* has never been expressly overruled.

54. I struggle to resist the lawyerly temptation to get too deeply into the weeds of the philosophy of law. The vast literature on the subject defies summary, and the following is only a sketch. "Legal formalism" is the idea that relevant legal principles exist and that in each case a judge will apply those principles in a more or less mechanical way. A subset of that theory is the "law as science" formalism widely attributed to Christopher Columbus Langdell, who was dean of the Harvard Law School from 1879 to 1875. Langdell thought that by using scientific methods, lawyers could derive correct legal judgments in all cases from fundamental principles and concepts. See Grey, "Langdell's Orthodoxy," 5. "Legal realism" is the idea that law is based not on formal rules or principles but instead on how individual judges decide cases based on their personal ideas, including their ideas about social interests and public policy. The essence of the theory is encapsulated in Holmes's famous aphorism, "The life of the law has not been logic: it has been experience." Holmes, *The Common Law*, 1. The current dominant theory of law is the "legal positivism" of H.L.A. Hart, which states that all legal norms are social constructs incorporated into a "rule of recognition," and such norms have no necessary connection to morality.

Langdell believed the law is "determinate" in all cases. This means that he believed there is a pre-existing body of law (which Holmes dismissively referred to as a "brooding omnipresence in the sky") from which it is possible to resolve all cases through logical deduction. In "The Path of the Law," Holmes challenged the "notion that a given system, ours, for instance, can be worked out like mathematics from

some general axioms of conduct." Id. at 465. But Holmes added that in every system of law, the "sovereign" has announced some principles that may be applied in a formalistic way to predict the outcome of cases. Id. If it were otherwise —if judges just made up the law in each case—such predictions would be impossible. This second kind of formalism applies to this day. When I try a case to a jury, at the end of the evidence, the judge instructs the jury regarding the legal rules they are to apply to the facts they find. In most cases, those legal rules come from books containing "pattern" jury instructions that summarize the law for different kinds of cases (e.g., contract cases, negligence cases, defamation cases, etc.). Pattern jury instructions would be impossible if most cases could not be decided in a formalistic way. That said, no current school of legal philosophy believes in formalism in the Langdellian sense. Thus, it is a cliché among scholars of legal theory that "we are all realists now."
55. Holmes, "The Path of the Law," 464.
56. Id. at 457. Holmes disagreed with Augustine, Aquinas, and Martin Luther King, Jr.
57. Id. at 459.
58. Id. at 462.
59. In practice, the "needs of society" always seem to coincide with the judges' political preferences. Having watched living constitution judges hijack the Constitution this way for decades, I vacillate between disgust and amusement when the same people who advocated for *Roe v. Wade*—probably the most anti-democratic case of all time—go on about "saving democracy."
60. Carroll, *Through the Looking Glass*, 117.
61. The phrase "living constitution" has fallen into disfavor in recent years. Indeed, no judicial nominee would dare use the phrase to describe her judicial philosophy today. At her 2010 confirmation hearings, Justice Elena Kagan felt

compelled to assure the members of the Senate Judiciary Committee that "we are all originalists now." But anyone who believes that Kagan had actually abandoned the principles that animate the living constitution approach to law is hopelessly naive. If she were being honest, Justice Kagan would be the first to tell you that. In fact, she has told us that. In a 2023 appearance at Notre Dame law school, she said, "My view that *constitutional meaning evolves* is consistent with the actual, original meaning of what the document is meant to do." See Josh Gerstein, "Kagan hopes Supreme Court's ideological divide on precedent isn't permanent," *Politico* (Sept. 22, 2023), available at https://www.politico.com/news/2023/09/22/elena-kagan-supreme-court-precedent-speech-00117760 (accessed Oct. 9, 2024) (emphasis added). Leave it to Kagan to say that "originalism" means exactly the opposite of what everyone understands the word to mean. The "living constitution" lives on as ersatz originalism. At her confirmation hearings Justice Kagan was in full Humpty Dumpty mode. In this book, I use the phrase "living constitution" as shorthand for the method lawless judges actually use. I do this with the understanding that such judges (like Justice Kagan) often try to obscure what they are doing by calling it something else.

62. 539 U.S. 306 (2003). *Grutter* was overruled in 2023 in *Students for Fair Admissions, Inc. v. President & Fellows of Harvard Coll.*, 600 U.S. 181.

63. To this day, Justices Kagan, Sotomayor, and Jackson continue to say the Equal Protection clause permits racial discrimination in school admissions (in practice, primarily against Asians, but also against whites). If their dissenting opinion in *Students for Fair Admissions* had attracted two more votes, this would still be the law.

64. Nat Hentoff, "The Constitutionalist," *The New Yorker* (Mar. 12, 1990), available at https://www.newyorker.com/maga

zine/1990/03/12/the-constitutionalist (accessed September 11, 2024).
65. "Minority" in this context is broader than racial minority. It means any group that does not have enough votes to elect the legislature and/or the executive.
66. 319 U.S. 624 (1943).
67. Literally. The law required public school students to salute the flag and say the Pledge of Allegiance. Exodus 20:4–5 prohibits bowing down to "any graven image." Jehovah's Witnesses believe the flag is an "image" and they refuse to salute it. They instructed their children to disobey the law, and many of them were expelled from school and their parents prosecuted. The Supreme Court declared that forcing schoolchildren to salute the flag is unconstitutional. The Court wrote:

> If there is any fixed star in our constitutional constellation, it is that no official, high or petty, can prescribe what shall be orthodox in politics, nationalism, religion, or other matters of opinion or force citizens to confess by word or act their faith therein.

The Court responded to the criticism that its decision was anti-democratic because it overturned the will of the majority as follows:

> The very purpose of a Bill of Rights was to withdraw certain subjects from the vicissitudes of political controversy, to place them beyond the reach of majorities and officials and to establish them as legal principles to be applied by the courts. One's right to life, liberty, and property, to free speech, a free press, freedom of worship and assembly, and other fundamental rights may not be submitted to vote; they depend on the outcome of no elections.

68. Some readers might think I have a double standard for the use of judicial power. After all, I used *Grutter* to illustrate the abuse of the Supreme Court's power and *Barnett* to illustrate its proper use. Not so. Willliam F. Buckley, Jr., once countered a false claim of moral equivalence between the USSR and the U.S. with the quip, "That is like saying that the man who pushes a little old lady into the path of a bus is morally equivalent to the man who pushes her out of its path, because they both push little old ladies around." Upholding racial discrimination (*Grutter*) and striking down compelled speech (*Barnett*) are not morally equivalent uses of power.
69. Bork, *The Tempting of America*, 5.
70. Decimus Junius Juvenalis (English, Juvenal), *The Satires*, Book VI, lines 347–348.
71. Bork, *The Tempting of America*, 176. (emphasis added; emphasis in the original omitted) While Bork's message was correct, he was admittedly a flawed messenger. It was deeply ironic for him to build a moral foundation for his argument, because, as Ronald Dworkin wrote in his review of *The Tempting of America*, no one was "more firmly committed to relativism than Bork himself." Dworkin, "Bork's Jurisprudence," 659, n. 4. In this review, Dworkin cited Bork's own words, as follows: "There is no principled way to decide that one man's gratifications are more deserving of respect than another's or that one form of gratification is more worthy than another. Why is sexual gratification more worthy than moral gratification? Why is sexual gratification nobler than economic gratification? There is no way of deciding these matters other than by reference to some system of moral or ethical values that has no objective or intrinsic validity of its own and about which men can and do differ." Bork, "Neutral Principles and Some First Amendment Problems," 10. One might respond that under this view, there is no principled way to decide whether one judge's preference

for imposing his policy views on the rest of us under the guise of interpreting the Constitution is more deserving of respect than Bork's preference for actually interpreting the Constitution. As is always the case with relativism, Bork's argument collapses on itself. A moral foundation is only as firm as the morality asserted, and Bork built his foundation on sand. This is not to say that the foundation cannot be built on the rock of transcendent morality as envisioned by the founders. The point of this book is that such a foundation can be—indeed, must be—built if we hope to have a law that is distinguishable from an authoritarian despotism of willful judges.

72. See 28 U.S.C. § 453.
73. This is a simplification. It is more accurate to say that this is the only thing that protects us in the short to medium term. With consistent concerted action over many years, the people can elect presidents who will appoint judges that will vote to overturn judicial overreach and senators who will vote to confirm those judges. We have seen this happen recently. *Roe v. Wade* was forced on the nation in 1973. It was overturned 49 years (and 24 elections) later in 2022 in *Dobbs v. Jackson Women's Health Org.*, 597 U.S. 215 (2022), due to the relentless concerted effort of concerned citizens.
74. The choices made by district court judges are reviewable by circuit court judges, and circuit court judges' choices are in turn reviewable by the Supreme Court. There are two problems with this system, one practical and the other structural. The practical problem is that the circuit courts routinely handle more than 50,000 cases each year, but the Supreme Court hears oral arguments in fewer than 100 cases annually. Therefore, the vast majority of circuit court decisions are final. United States Courts, *Appellate Courts and Cases—Journalist's Guide,* available at https://www

.uscourts.gov/statistics-reports/appellate-courts-and-cases-journalists-guide (last visited September 10, 2024). This is a practical problem because lawless judges know the numbers favor them. Infamous lawless judge Stephen Reinhardt was often asked what was the point of issuing so many decisions counter to clear Supreme Court precedent. He would respond, "They can't catch them all." Linda Greenhouse, "Dissenting Against the Supreme Court's Rightward Shift," *New York Times* (Apr. 12, 2018). Reinhardt was right. They can't. The structural problem is that Juvenal's question has its most cogent application to decisions of the Supreme Court, which are final and unappealable. It may take five decades of unrelenting political effort by millions of citizens (as in *Roe v. Wade*) or a bloody civil war (as in *Dred Scott*) to reverse the harm done when they get it wrong.

75. This is not a metaphor. As we have already seen, Holmes saw no significant difference between a man and a baboon. See text at note 37. That attitude holds among materialists to this day. The late Professor Morris Goodman (formerly editor-in-chief of the journal *Molecular Phylogenetics and Evolution*) wrote: "We humans appear as only slightly remodeled chimpanzee-like apes." Wilman et al., "Implications of Natural Selection."

76. Antonin Scalia, remarks before the Senate Judiciary Committee (Oct. 5, 2011), available at https://www.govinfo.gov/content/pkg/CHRG-112shrg70991/html/CHRG-112shrg70991.htm (accessed Jan. 3, 2025).

77. Holmes, *The Essential Holmes*, ix.

78. Liptak, Adam, "An Exit Interview With Richard Posner, Judicial Provocateur," *The New York Times* (September 11, 2017), available at https://www.nytimes.com/2017/09/11/us/politics/judge-richard-posner-retirement.html (accessed December 31, 2024). In an interview some months earlier, Posner said, "I see absolutely no value to a judge of spending

decades, years, months, weeks, days, hours, minutes, or seconds studying the Constitution, the history of its enactment, its amendments, and its implementation." Richard A. Posner, "Law school professors need more practical experience," *Slate* (June 24, 2016), available at https://slate.com/news-and-politics/2016/06/law-school-professors-need-more-practical-experience.html (accessed December 31, 2024). He attempted to take it all back, but he fooled no one. See Richard A. Posner, "Richard Posner clarifies his views on the Constitution," *Slate*, (July 1, 2016), available at https://slate.com/news-and-politics/2016/07/supreme-court-breakfast-table-for-june-2016-richard-posner-clarifies-his-views-on-the-constitution.html (accessed December 31, 2024).
79. As discussed earlier (see note 74), because of the limitations of the Supreme Court's docket, the chances that Posner would be overturned in any given case were low.
80. Id., 5 U.S. at 178.
81. This phrase comes from Justice White's famous dissent in *Roe v. Wade*: "As an exercise of *raw judicial power*, the Court perhaps has authority to do what it does today; but in my view its judgment is an improvident and extravagant exercise of the power of judicial review that the Constitution extends to this Court." *Roe v. Wade*, 410 U.S. 179, 222 (1973) (White, J., dissenting) (emphasis added).

5. You're Gonna Have to Serve Somebody

1. Bob Dylan, "Gotta Serve Somebody," *Slow Train Coming*, Columbia Records, 1979.
2. This was not long after the great North Korean famine in which hundreds of thousands of people starved to death. We visited a collective farm that had no mechanized equipment,

and my church raised money to buy a small Chinese-built tractor for the farm. A few years later, American Kenneth Bae was arrested in North Korea and sentenced to 15 years of hard labor (he was released after two years). While I do not know Mr. Bae, my understanding from media reports is that he was also involved in humanitarian work. See Holly Yan, "Kenneth Bae: '735 days in North Korea was long enough,'" *CNN* (May 2, 2016). North Korea is a nightmarish place where everyone lives in constant fear. I have traveled to many countries, and it is, by far, the worst place I have ever been.

3. This was before Kim Jong Un came to power.

4. I learned this was not unusual. Every person I met in North Korea had a lapel pin with Kim Jong Il's picture on it. Every room had the leader's portrait on the wall. See Eric Lafforgue and Chris Summers, "The 'Dear Leaders' present in every home, office and school," *DailyMail.com* (Jan. 14, 2017), available at https://www.dailymail.co.uk/news/article-4117378/Big-Brothers-watching-North-Korea-Kims-wall-not-talking-Kardashian.html, (accessed March 3, 2025).

5. Associated Press, "North Korea Executes Woman for Giving Out Bibles," *New York Post* (July 24, 2009), available at https://nypost.com/2009/07/24/north-korea-executes-woman-for-giving-out-bibles/ (last accessed March 2, 2025).

6. While this is not a verbatim quote from any of his books or articles, it does capture the spirit of ideas he expressed in *Orthodoxy*.

7. "DNA neither knows nor cares. DNA just is. And we dance to its music." Dawkins, *River Out of Eden*, 134.

8. For example, Dawkins insists that teaching certain Christian doctrines to children is "child abuse." Dawkins, *The God Delusion*, 358.

9. I have had a few run-ins with the AHA myself over the years. For example, in 2013, the AHA sued a school I represented because its students were packing toys in shoeboxes and sending them to Operation Christmas Child to be distributed to poor children. Megyn Kelly interviewed Roy Speckhardt, the AHA's executive director, about his lawsuit. Kelly asked Speckhardt if the AHA had a plan for helping the poor children who were not going to get boxes of toys, and he responded that his group had helped the children by ensuring they "have a clean, neutral, free-of-church-state violation experience." I appreciated Kelly's response: "You have helped save them from the constitutional violation and that will be a warm comfort to them on Christmas morning, Roy." See "Anti-religious group defends lawsuit threat against Christmas toy drive," *Fox News* (Nov. 21, 2013), available at https://www.foxnews.com/transcript/anti-religious-group-defends-lawsuit-threat-against-christmas-toy-drive (accessed March 6, 2025). Video here: https://www.youtube.com/watch?v=yPIYn_02WyA.
10. Alison Flood, "Richard Dawkins loses 'humanist of the year' title over trans comments," *The Guardian* (April 2021).
11. Berdyaev, *The Origin of Russian Communism*, 97.
12. Ibid.
13. Davidson, *Pagan America*, 132–33.
14. Id. at 10–11
15. Ibid.
16. Id. at 61–62, discussing Holland, *Dominion*, 539–40.
17. Harari, *Sapiens*, 136–37.
18. Davidson, *Pagan America*, 64–65.
19. Feser, *Last Superstition*, 280.
20. Id.

21. Bureau of International Labor Affairs, "Against Their Will: The Situation in Xinjiang," https://www.dol.gov/agencies/ilab/against-their-will-the-situation-in-xinjiang.
22. Feser, "The Last Superstition," 277.
23. Davidson, *Pagan America*, 54.
24. As we saw earlier, after Dr. Langman conducted an exhaustive investigation of Harris and his writings and recordings, he concluded that Harris had a disturbed personality with prominent antisocial, narcissistic, and sadistic traits. Peter Langman, "Columbine, Bullying, and the Mind of Eric Harris," *Psychology Today* (May 20, 2009), available at https://www.psychologytoday.com/us/blog/keeping-kids-safe/200905/columbine-bullying-and-the-mind-of-eric-harris (accessed March 4, 2025).
25. This is especially true of the people in the "functional materialist" category.
26. *Triggernometry* podcast (Aug. 25, 2024) beginning at 101:25, available at https://www.youtube.com/watch?v=wdfmQ2iJb6o (accessed November 20, 2024).
27. Proverbs 29:18, ASV.
28. Feser, *Last Superstition*, 280.
29. What is the point of a materialist "bioethicist" like Singer anyway? He insists that there is no objective moral standard. If that is true, there is no objectively right or wrong answer to any ethical question. Therefore, everything a materialist bioethicist says can be immediately refuted by the Dude's retort: "Yeah well, that's just, ya know, like, your opinion, man." *The Big Lebowski*, directed by Joel and Ethan Coen (Working Title Films, 1998). His views are as Feser says, simply a different set of subjective moral evaluations. See text at footnote 22. He never gives us any reason why we should prefer his subjective evaluations over anyone else's.
30. Singer writes, "My view is . . . if a decision is taken, by the parents and doctors, that it is better that a baby should die,

I believe it should be possible to carry out that decision, not only by withholding or withdrawing life-support – which can lead to the baby dying slowly from dehydration or from an infection – but also by taking active steps to end the baby's life swiftly and humanely." Interestingly, Singer slinks from his own views even as he announces them. The phrase "taking active steps to end the baby's life" means the same thing as "killing the baby." Beware of euphemism. It is almost always employed in the service of evil. Singer goes on to say it is wrong to kill a healthy baby because someone other than the parents might want him, but it is still OK to kill a defective baby even if someone wants him. Singer is vague about the line between defective and healthy babies. Peter Singer's personal website FAQs, available at https://www.petersinger.info/about (last accessed March 3, 2025).

31. Davidson, *Pagan America*, 204.
32. This is why the "I'm glad we didn't abort Einstein" argument is easily misunderstood and probably misguided. A Downs baby and the world's most prolific super-genius have an equal right to life under the doctrine of *imago Dei*. I am glad Einstein's mother did not kill him in the womb because he was made in the image of God. His relative contributions to society after he was born are irrelevant to that analysis.
33. "Bill Maher Admits Abortion Is Murder," *Michael Knowles YouTube Channel* (April 15, 2024), available at https://www.youtube.com/watch?v=lMIb03DdWHA&t=17s (accessed March 3, 2025), starting at 0:44.
34. Starting at 27:10 "Full Debate: Harris vs. Trump in 2024 ABC News Presidential Debate," *The Wall Street Journal* YouTube Channel (Sept. 10, 2024), available at https://www.youtube.com/watch?v=VgsC_aBquUE (accessed March 4, 2025).
35. Id., starting at 29:02.
36. Davidson, *Pagan America*, 203.

37. Connor Mannion, "Michelle Williams Calls on Women to Protect 'Right to Choose' in Globes Speech: Vote 'In Your Own Self Interest,'" Mediaite (January 5, 2020), available at https://www.mediaite.com/entertainment/michelle-williams-calls-on-women-to-protect-right-to-choose-in-globes-speech-vote-in-your-own-self-interest/ (accessed March 4, 2025); and Davidson, *Pagan America*, 204.
38. Id., 252.
39. Ibid.
40. "Instrumentalism" is the idea that concepts should be evaluated based on their usefulness in achieving practical outcomes rather than on their correspondence to the truth.
41. Lewis, "Christian Apologetics," in Lewis, *God in the Dock*, 101.
42. Pascal, *Pensées*, 85–87.
43. Id. at 87.
44. Templeton Prize Acceptance Address (May 10, 1983), available at https://www.templetonprize.org/laureate-sub/solzhenitsyn-acceptance-speech/ (accessed February 2, 2025).

6. The Case for Christianity

1. Bacon, *The Advancement of Learning*, 9.
2. Id. at 10.
3. Id. at 9–10.
4. The arguments I present in this chapter are, due to space considerations, necessarily in summary form. I will, however, provide citations to more in-depth discussions for readers who want to dig deeper.
5. The phrase "point to God" is actually far too weak. It is more accurate to say that these features of the universe scream for all to hear: "Look, it's God!" The Psalmist wrote, "The fool has said in his heart, 'There is no God.'" Psalm 14:1. This is harsh but correct, because, as we shall

see, nature speaks with a loud voice when it says, "God exists." And only a fool stops up his ears and refuses to hear. Paul writes of those who suppress the truth (even from themselves):

> For the wrath of God is revealed from heaven against all ungodliness and unrighteousness of people who suppress the truth in unrighteousness, because that which is known about God is evident within them; for God made it evident to them. For since the creation of the world His invisible attributes, that is, His eternal power and divine nature, have been clearly perceived, being understood by what has been made, so that they are without excuse.

Romans 1:18–21.
6. In philosophy-speak, the existence of the particles in motion is "contingent" as opposed to "necessary."
7. Carroll, "Why Is There Something Rather Than Nothing?," 16–17. Available at https://philpapers.org/archive/CARWIT-11.pdf (accessed November 15, 2024).
8. Douglas Groothuis has a good summary of the cosmological argument in chapter 11 of Groothuis, *Christian Apologetics*.
9. Craig calls this the Kalam cosmological argument. See William Lane Craig, "The Existence of God and the Beginning of the Universe," *Reasonable Faith* website, available at https://www.reasonablefaith.org/writings/scholarly-writings/the-existence-of-god/the-existence-of-god-and-the-beginning-of-the-universe (accessed February 6, 2025).
10. Craig defends the premise that the universe began to exist by arguing that an actual series of past events is not possible because at infin.ite regress of moments would lead to logical absurdities.
11. Groothuis, *Christian Apologetics*, 204.

12. Meyer, *Return of the God Hypothesis*, 373. I should emphasize that while the Christian faith does not conflict with scientifically proven facts, it does not stand or fall on particular scientific theories. The standard model of cosmology, which includes the Big Bang, appears to support Christianity, but Christianity does not depend on that model being true. Thus, if the standard model were to be modified or supplanted altogether, the truth of Christianity would not be affected in the least. Moreover, the form of the cosmological argument that I present in chapter seven (see section 7.9) rests on sheer logic. It does not depend on the veracity of any scientific theory.
13. There are three kinds of logical inferences: deductive, inductive, and abductive. An abductive inference is sometimes called "inference to the best explanation."
14. Meyer, *Return of the God Hypothesis*, 378.
15. Id. at 388.
16. He wrote: "I have always thought it curious that, while most scientists claim to eschew religion, it actually dominates their thoughts more than it does the clergy. The passionate frenzy with which the big-bang cosmology is clutched to the corporate scientific bosom evidently arises from a deep-rooted attachment to the first page of Genesis, religious fundamentalism at its strongest." Hoyle, "The Universe," 23.
17. Laplace, *A Philosophical Essay on Probabilities*, 4.
18. Laplace is often quoted as telling Napoleon that he had no need for the God hypothesis, but that story is probably apocryphal. It does, however, capture the materialist attitude.
19. As quoted by Scott Bembenek, "Einstein and the Quantum," *Scientific American* blog (March 27, 2018), available at https://www.scientificamerican.com/blog/observations/einstein-and-the-quantum/ (accessed February 6, 2025).

This letter is the source of the aphorism often attributed to Einstein that God does not play dice with the universe. The letter and the aphorism can be somewhat misleading. Einstein was not a religious believer, and his veiled references to God were merely a metaphor for reality. He was not referring to a deity. The basic idea expressed in the letter is that Einstein could not wrap his head around the probabilistic nature of quantum mechanics and, at an instinctual level, felt it must be wrong.

20. Klavan, *Light of the Mind*, 155. (emphasis added).
21. Klavan, *Light of the Mind*, 158–59. To be sure, materialists posit explanations of quantum theory that do not depend on a conscious observer, such as the "many worlds" theory. But, as I explain in note 22, that interpretation is almost literally insane.
22. Materialist try to rescue their metaphysics with an almost literally insane appeal to the "many-worlds" interpretation of quantum mechanics in which every possible outcome of the probabilistic distribution generated by our measurements is actual at the same time. This is a sort of multiverse theory. We will discuss the problems with the multiverse in chapter seven, but Klavan explains how the many-worlds theory, if taken seriously, is an end to science itself: "[H]ow can 'we' say anything at all if some doppelgänger version of us is always saying the opposite in some equally valid reality—if you both wake up living each morning and die unseen of a stroke every night? A man who answers both 'yes' and 'no' to every question isn't saying everything: he's saying nothing at all. A woman whose every choice fractures her into two women isn't living in a multiverse: she's dissolving into nothing." Klavan, *Light of the Mind*, 188.
23. Id. at 178.
24. Meyer, *Return of the God Hypothesis*, 204.

25. Casey Luskin, "ID's Top Six—Fine Tuning of the Universe," *Evolution News* (November 8, 2017), available at https://evolutionnews.org/2017/11/ids-top-six-the-fine-tuning-of-the-universe/ (accessed February 6, 2025).
26. Atheists tend to invoke the "multiverse" as an explanation for the observed fine-turning. We will discuss the many problems with that explanation in chapter seven.
27. Hawking, *A Brief History of Time*, 125.
28. Hoyle, "The Universe," 16.
29. Meyer, *Return of the God Hypothesis*, 406.
30. Id. at 412.
31. Urone and Hinrichs, *College Physics*, 159. (emphasis added).
32. Granville Sewell, "Three Realities Chance Can't Explain That Intelligent Design Can," *Evolution News,* available at https://evolutionnews.org/2022/06/three-realities-chance-cant-explain-that-intelligent-design-can (accessed April 8, 2025).
33. Sagan, *The Cosmic Connection*, 190.
34. Dembski and Ewert, *The Design Inference*. Winston Ewert joined as a co-author for the second edition.
35. For example, Albert Einstein famously demonstrated relativity at a popular level using simultaneous lightning strikes observed by a person on a moving train and a person on an embankment near the track. Einstein, *Relativity*, 30.
36. Dembski and Ewert, *The Design Inference*, 244–45. Specifications are not determined subjectively. They are objectively defined mathematically in terms of low description length. Somebody can't just say, "gee, it looks recognizable to me," and therefore draw a design inference, while someone else says, "gee, it doesn't look recognizable to me," and avoid the inference. There are objective criteria for recognizability.

37. Concluding that someone is cheating is a form of design inference. In other words, if you think someone is cheating, you do not think the hand they have resulted from random cards being dealt from a thoroughly shuffled deck. Instead, you believe someone has rigged the game. You have rejected the chance hypothesis and made a design inference.
38. The first hand also had a specification (i.e., an RFS). Why couldn't you conclude design then? Because it did not meet the first criterion. While the probability of a single RFS is somewhat low, it was not nearly low enough to rule out chance using Dembski's method. Both criteria (extremely low probability and specification) must be present at the same time to detect design.
39. It is actually much worse for your friend. The probability is more like selecting a single grain of sand from all of the sand on all the beaches in the world.
40. Crick, *Life Itself*, 88.
41. Monod, *Chance and Necessity*, 180.
42. Prigogine, Nicolis, and Babloyantz, "Thermodynamics of Evolution." Prigogine firmly believed that the OOL could not have been a chance event. He was not appealing to any sort of design. In the cited article, he wrote that he believed there was a thermodynamic law that explained chemical complexification.
43. Whitesides, "Foreword," xvii. Whitesides's certainty that it is "not impossible" is driven more by his metaphysical commitment to materialism than by the evidence.
44. Dobzhansky, "Discussion of G. Schramm's Paper," 309–315.
45. As mentioned above, some thinkers, such as Prigogine, believe there is a third option, that OOL can be explained by a lawlike or quasi-lawlike force. Invoking a mysterious physical force or law to explain OOL amounts to little more than a "materialism of the gaps."

46. Whitesides, "Foreword," ix.
47. Ibid.
48. James Tour, "Much Ado About Nothing," *Inference Review*, Vol. 6, No. 4 (January 2022) (emphasis added), available at https://inference-review.com/article/much-ado-about-nothing (accessed January 7, 2025).
49. Dr. James Tour, *Origin of Life Challenge RESULTS*, available at https://www.youtube.com/watch?v=FdR-ZmdFOcg (accessed January 7, 2025).
50. Meyer, *Signature in the Cell*, 12.
51. Dawkins, *River Out of Eden*, 17. (emphasis added)
52. Gates, *The Road Ahead*, 188.
53. Meyer, *Signature in the Cell*, 364–369.
54. Yes, "nanomachines." I know. Don't get me started. By the way, "nanomachine" is not my word; that is what materialist scientists call them. See, e.g., Lane and Xavier, "To Unravel the Origin of Life," 948. The level of willful blindness it requires for materialists not to see the glaring light shining in their faces is truly astounding. There is none so blind as he who will not see. If you want to see a video of these machines at work, go to Veritasium, *Your Body's Molecular Machines* (Nov. 20, 2017), available at https://www.youtube.com/watch?v=X_tYrnv_o6A (accessed January 8, 2025).
55. Derek Muller, "What if all the world's biggest problems have the same solution?," *Veritasium* (February 10, 2025), available at https://www.youtube.com/watch?v=P_fHJIYENdI (accessed February 12, 2010).
56. Axe discusses his findings in Axe, *Undeniable*.
57. Axe, *Undeniable*, 181.
58. Dembski and Ewert, *The Design Inference*, 374.
59. Behe, *Darwin's Black Box*.
60. Psalm 139:14. NIV.

Notes

61. Reinhold Niebuhr said, "The doctrine of original sin is the only empirically verifiable doctrine of the Christian faith." Niebuhr, *Man's Nature*, 24.
62. Lewis, *Mere Christianity*, 44.
63. Rudyard Kipling's "Just So Stories" are a collection of whimsical tales written in 1902, originally for children. The phrase "just so" refers to the stories' playful, imaginative explanations of how certain things came to be. They're called "just so" because they describe events as happening in a precise, almost arbitrary way that fits the story's logic—like why the leopard got its spots or how the elephant got its trunk.
64. Groothuis, *Christian Apologetics*, 345.
65. Dawkins, *River Out of Eden*, 134. (emphasis added).
66. Id. at 245.
67. I know he would say this because he has in fact said something very similar regarding human sacrifice. Posner, "The Problematics of Moral and Legal Theory," 1652.
68. Id. at 1645.
69. As we shall see, from a materialist perspective, consciousness does not represent a "hard problem." It is an impossible problem.
70. If you would like to delve deeper into these issues, see the section "Accounting for Consciousness" in Groothuis, *Christian Apologetics*.
71. Nagel, *Mind and Cosmos*, 41.
72. Once again, Psalm 14:1 is apt. "The fool has said in his heart, 'There is no God.'"
73. Nagel, *Mind and Cosmos*, 35. Nagel uses the word "naturalism" to mean more or less the same thing as "materialism."
74. Hume, *An Enquiry Concerning Human Understanding*, Section X (emphasis in original).
75. Romans 1:20. NIV.

76. Ricky Gervais, "Why I Do Not Believe in a God," *The Wall Street Journal* (Dec. 22, 2010) available at https://www.wsj.com/articles/SB10001424052748703886904576031640102154156 (accessed March 5, 2025).
77. Hart, *The Experience of God*, 34.
78. I do not take pantheism (the universe itself is god) and similar religions and philosophies seriously. A better name for pantheism is "cosmic woo." It is an obvious attempt at "cake and eat it too" non-materialism that allows its adherents to acknowledge the explanatory deficits of materialism while remaining functional materialists.
79. A detailed polemic against Islam is beyond the scope of this book. I will just say that while Jesus proclaimed a gospel of peace and love and said that the greatest of his followers would be the one who served the most, Muhammad engaged in wars against his neighbors and owned slaves. It is difficult to credit the claim that he was the messenger of a loving God. The New Testament affirms that the God of the Torah is the same God worshiped by Christians. Christians do not assert that the God of Judaism is not the true God; instead, they maintain that those who follow Judaism have an incomplete understanding of his revelation.
80. Lewis, "Christian Apologetics," in Lewis, *God in the Dock*, 101.
81. I Cor. 15:12–17 (emphasis added).
82. Groothuis, *Christian Apologetics*, 584.
83. Ibid.
84. In this same passage, Tacitus describes Nero's persecution of Christians, which included lighting their bodies on fire to serve as illumination for his garden parties.
85. Groothuis, *Christian Apologetics*, 587–88.
86. Id. at 588.
87. Ibid.
88. Id. at 589.

89. Ibid.
90. Id. 589–90.
91. Id. at 590-91 (quoting Samples, *Without a Doubt*, 137.
92. 1 Cor. 15:3–8 NASB.
93. Groothuis, *Christian Apologetics*, 594.
94. Id. at 595.
95. Pliny the Younger, *The Letters of the Younger Pliny*, 377–779.
96. Id. at 379–80.
97. Id. at 378–79 (emphasis added).
98. Groothuis, *Christian Apologetics*, 597.
99. Id. at 598.
100. As Groothuis points out, this argument is often stated as, "No one dies for that which is false." That is not quite accurate. The 9/11 hijackers died for their faith. Unless you believe Islam is true, you are compelled to conclude that they died advancing a falsehood. The fact is that people die for false narratives all the time. The correct way to state the argument is that no one dies for something *they affirmatively know to be false*. It is one thing to be deceived and die advancing a false narrative. It is something different to suggest that someone would die defending a claim they know to be false when all they have to do is say what they know to be true.
101. Id. at 600–601.
102. Id. at 608.

7. Objection!

1. Darwin should more properly be called the co-discoverer of natural selection. He and Alfred Russel Wallace developed essentially the same idea independently, and they announced it to the world in a joint paper read on

July 1, 1858. See Darwin and Wallace, "On the Tendency of Species."

2. For example: "[T]he existence of a biological God, one who directs organic evolution and intervenes in human affairs (as envisioned by theism) is increasingly contravened by biology and the brain sciences." Wilson, *Consilience*, 241.

3. "Neo-Darwinism is the term popularly used, even today, for the synthesis between Darwin's theory of evolution by natural selection and the assumption that the variations on which selection acts are produced solely or primarily by gene mutations, though the term Modern Synthesis is more correct since George John Romanes coined the term neo-Darwinism before Gregor Mendel's work on genetics was rediscovered." Noble, "Neo-Darwinism, the Modern Synthesis," 1008. I will use the terms "neo-Darwinism" and "Modern Synthesis" interchangeably. "Modern Synthesis" is not the same thing as the "extended modern synthesis" advocated by some biologists, which I will also discuss.

4. Darwin himself never speculated in his published work about how living things made the leap from non-living matter. He admitted publicly that it was an unsolved problem, writing in 1868 that "the first origin of life on this earth . . . is at present quite beyond the scope of science." Darwin, *The Variation of Animals*, 12. Privately, in a famous 1871 letter to his friend Joseph D. Hooker, Darwin speculated about how life might have spontaneously arisen on the early earth in "some warm little pond" full of chemicals and energy. February 1, 1871, letter to J.D. Hooker, Darwin Correspondence Project, available at https://www.darwinproject.ac.uk/letter/?docId=letters/DCP-LETT-7471.xml (accessed December 5, 2024).

5. See note 4.

6. Haeckel is famous for the "biogenetic law," which asserts "ontogeny recapitulates phylogeny." This means that Haeckel believed that the growth of an organism (especially in the womb) recapitulates its evolutionary history. The theory has been discredited. Alexander Werth, "Vestiges of the natural history of development: historical holdovers reveal the dynamic interaction between ontogeny and phylogeny," *Evolution: Education and Outreach*, 7, 12 (2014), 7, available at https://doi.org/10.1186/s12052-014-0012-5 (accessed January 8, 2025).
7. Haeckel, *Last Words on Evolution*, 25. (emphasis added)
8. James Tour, "Much Ado About Nothing," *Inference Review*, Vol. 6, No. 4 (January 2022) (emphasis added), available at https://inference-review.com/article/much-ado-about-nothing (accessed January 7, 2025).
9. "Richard Dawkins vs Piers Morgan on Religion and Gender," *Piers Morgan Uncensored* (March 20, 2023), starting at 3:48, available at https://www.youtube.com/watch?v=505UazMNgLg (accessed January 7, 2025).
10. Whitesides, "Revolutions in Chemistry." (emphasis added)
11. Lane and Xavier, "To Unravel the Origin of Life."
12. Materialist biochemist Franklin Harold adds that it must be conceded "that there are presently no detailed Darwinian accounts of the evolution of any biochemical or cellular system, only a variety of wishful speculations." Harold, *Way of the Cell*, 205.
13. Meyer, *Darwin's Doubt*.
14. Joe Rogan Experience #2269 - Bret Weinstein (February 6, 2025), beginning at 2:07:08, available at https://www.youtube.com/watch?v=7ted-qUqqU4 (accessed February 11, 2025).
15. Id. beginning at 1:55:47.
16. Nagel, *The Last Word*, 130.
17. Nagel, *Mind and Cosmos*, 10–11.

18. Id., 123.
19. The Altenberg 16, all of whom were seeking a better *materialist* theory, were:
    - John Beatty (University of British Columbia)
    - Werner Callebaut (University of Hasselt)
    - Sergey Gavrilets (University of Tennessee)
    - Eva Jablonka (Tel Aviv University)
    - David Jablonski (University of Chicago)
    - Marc Kirschner (Harvard University)
    - Alan Love (University of Minnesota)
    - Gerd B. Müller (University of Vienna)
    - Stuart Newman (New York Medical College)
    - John Odling-Smee (Oxford University)
    - Massimo Pigliucci (Stony Brook University)
    - Michael Purugganan (New York University)
    - Eörs Szathmáry (Collegium Budapest)
    - Günter P. Wagner (Yale University)
    - David Sloan Wilson (Binghamton University)
    - Greg Wray (Duke University)
20. Pigliucci, "Do We Need an Extended Evolutionary Synthesis?"
21. Pigliucci and Müller, *Evolution: The Extended Synthesis*. 13
22. Id. at 14.
23. Darwin, *Origin of Species*, 146.
24. Wells, "Is Darwinism a Theory in Crisis?," 411.
25. See photograph of Professor Müller's slide at David Klinghoffer, "Doesn't the Fossil Record Prove Darwinian Theory?," *Evolution News*, (Dec. 18, 2024), available at https://evolutionnews.org/2024/12/doesnt-the-fossil-record-prove-darwinian-theory/ (accessed January 8, 2025).
26. Müller, "Why an Extended Evolutionary Synthesis Is Necessary."

27. Jablonka, "A New Vision for How Evolution Works Is Long Overdue." Reviewing Lala et al., *Evolution Evolving.*
28. Stephen Buranyi, "Do we need a new theory of evolution?" *The Guardian* (June 28, 2022), available at https://www.theguardian.com/science/2022/jun/28/do-we-need-a-new-theory-of-evolution (accessed January 30, 2025).
29. See, for example, Richard Cohen, "Scott Walker's Inartful Dodge in London," *Washington Post* (February 16, 2015). Interestingly, as David Berlinski often quips, one never hears a physicist asserting the reverse, i.e., that the theory of gravity is as firmly established as the theory of evolution. Berlinski writes: "I disagree that Darwin's theory is as 'solid as any explanation in science.' Disagree? I regard the claim as preposterous. Quantum electrodynamics is accurate to thirteen or so decimal places; so, too, general relativity. A leaf trembling in the wrong way would suffice to shatter either theory. What can Darwinian theory offer in comparison?" David Berlinski, "A Scientific Scandal, an exchange between David Berlinski and critics," *Commentary* (July/August 2003).
30. *ScienceDaily* (December 28, 2020).
31. *StudyFinds* (October 16, 2024).
32. James Tour, "Much Ado About Nothing," *Inference Review*, Vol. 6, No. 4 (January 2022) (emphasis added), available at https://inference-review.com/article/much-ado-about-nothing (accessed January 7, 2025).
33. *StudyFinds, supra.* Daniel Witt has provided a summary of several "hype" articles that misleadingly imply that some study or another has demonstrated evolution's power to construct novelty. He writes: "Yet, consistently, the observations don't show that. Instead, they fall into three categories: observations of (1) traits that were already present in the population, (2) traits that were already present in the genome, but were unexpressed, and (3) genuine

novelties which, however, did not increase the design sophistication of the organism." Daniel Witt, "'Evolution in Real Time' (Yeah, Right)," *Evolution News* (January 8, 2025), available at https://evolutionnews.org/2025/01/evolution-in-real-time-yeah-right/ (accessed January 9, 2025).

34. Richard C. Lewontin, "Billions and Billions of Demons," *The New York Review of Books* (Jan. 9, 1997), available at https://www.nybooks.com/articles/1997/01/09/billions-and-billions-of-demons/?srsltid=AfmBOorBFebkE25ENuJPVZ5bTWmWjsOnmyzOUKuTwv4wcVv1fI-qfQpV (emphasis added) (accessed March 10, 2025).

35. Phillip E. Johnson, "The Unraveling of Scientific Materialism," *First Things* (November 1997), available at https://www.firstthings.com/article/1997/11/the-unraveling-of-scientific-materialism (accessed January 9, 2025).

36. Materialist fundamentalism also blinds its adherents to the fact that the materialist account of the origin and development of biological organisms *assumes* the existence of the universe and the laws of nature in the first place. Materialism says that all of reality can be reduced to particles in motion. But it cannot explain where the particles came from and why they are in motion.

37. Wells, *Zombie Science*, 63.

38. Wells, *Zombie Science*, 64. Citing Kettlewell, "Darwin's Missing Evidence."

39. Wells, *Zombie Science*, 64.

40. Id. at 64–65, citing Kenneth Chang, "On scientific fakery and the systems to catch it," *The New York Times* (October 15, 2002).

41. Veritasium, *Your Body's Molecular Machines* (Nov. 20, 2017), available at https://www.youtube.com/watch?v=X_tYrnv_o6A (accessed January 8, 2025).

42. See, e.g., Lane and Xavier, "To Unravel the Origin of Life," 948.

Notes

43. Sagan, *Broca's Brain*, 396.
44. Dawkins, *The God Delusion*, 70. Dawkins describes his belief as follows: "I cannot know for certain but I think God is very improbable, and I live my life on the assumption that he is not there." Id. at 73.
45. Richard Dawkins, "Richard Dawkins vs John Lennox | The God Delusion Debate," *Larry Alex Taunton Youtube Channel* (Feb. 8, 2017), available at https://www.youtube.com/watch?v=zF5bPI92-5o (at 1:42:38) (accessed February 8, 2025).
46. Neil DeGrasse Tyson, *Sky News Australia*, "'Is there a God?': Piers Morgan grills astrophysicist Neil DeGrasse Tyson," (Sept. 13, 2023) at 3:19, available at https://www.youtube.com/watch?v=zoNViivs3U8 (accessed January 13, 2025).
47. Quoted in Rosten, "Bertrand Russell and God."
48. Joe Rogan Experience #2269—Bret Weinstein (February 6, 2025), beginning at 2:23:45, available at https://www.youtube.com/watch?v=7ted-qUqqU4 (accessed February 11, 2025) (emphasis added).
49. "Evidence," *Black's Law Dictionary* (12th ed. 2024).
50. This standard is the most rarely used. It applies in a few civil cases. For example, in a defamation case involving a public figure, the plaintiff must prove the defendant acted with actual malice by clear and convincing evidence.
51. This standard is most often associated with police work. For example, a police officer must establish probable cause to obtain a search warrant.
52. This standard is also associated with law enforcement. For example, a police office must establish reasonable suspicion to make what is known as a "Terry stop," which is a brief investigatory detention short of an arrest.
53. This is the kind of case that goes to trial. If a plaintiff has an overwhelmingly good case, the defendant will surely

settle. If the plaintiff has a bad case, he will settle and take what he can get. For obvious reasons, cases on the bubble that could go either way are the most likely to get to a jury.

54. And then I would give my best guess about the spectrum within a spectrum of the amount of damages each of those seven juries might award. That spectrum goes from "grand slam" where the jury gives the plaintiff everything he requests and then some, to "extremely disappointing."

55. Hoyle, "The Universe," 16. Hoyle's atheism led him to propose "panspermia" (the idea that life was seeded onto earth from space) as a solution for the obvious design of living things. However, it is obvious that panspermia is no solution at all. It just kicks the can down the road.

56. Dawkins, *The God Delusion*, 73.

57. Id. at 74.

58. Dawkins, *River Out of Eden*, 134. (emphasis added).

59. Dawkins, *The God Delusion*, 18, 23, 309.

60. Id. at 245.

61. Professor Chad Meister writes:

> If rape, racism, torture, murder, government-sanctioned genocide and so forth are objectively evil, what makes them so? What makes them truly evil, rather than simply activities we dislike? What made the atrocities of the Nazis evil, even though Hitler and his thugs maintained otherwise? One cannot consistently affirm both that there are no objective moral values, on the one hand, and that rape, torture and the like are objectively morally evil on the other.

Meister, "God, Evil, and Morality," 109.

62. Id. at 108.

63. See Plantinga, *God, Freedom, and Evil*, 54–55. In this book, Plantinga developed ideas that had been discussed earlier by Gottfried Leibniz and before him, Thomas Aquinas.

64. Ibid.
65. Draper, "The Skeptical Theist," 176–77. The full quotation is:

> Logical arguments from evil are a dying (dead?) breed. One reason for this is the following: Since even an omnipotent being's power would have logical limitations, such a being could produce goods that logically entail the existence (or possibility) of E[vil] only by allowing E[vil] (or its possibility). So, for all we know, even an omnipotent and omniscient being might be forced to allow E[vil] for the sake of obtaining some important good. Our knowledge of goods and evils and the logical relations they bear to each other is much too limited to prove that this could not be the case.

66. This version of the argument from evil, like the logical argument from evil we have already considered, seems to suffer an insurmountable problem from the outset: On materialism, the word "evil" has no objective meaning.
67. See Martha Teichner interview of Neil DeGrasse Tyson, "Neil DeGrasse Tyson on God," *CBS Sunday Morning*, (April 30, 2017), available at https://www.youtube.com/watch?v=I0nXG02tpDw (accessed January 15, 2025).
68. William Lane Craig, "The Problem of Evil," *Reasonable Faith* website, available at https://www.reasonablefaith.org/writings/popular-writings/existence-nature-of-god/the-problem-of-evil
69. Id.
70. Job 31:35.
71. See Job chapters 38–41.
72. "And without faith it is impossible to please *Him*, for he who comes to God must believe that he is and *that* he is a rewarder of those who seek Him." Hebrews 11:6.
73. In this context, "novice" means someone who is preparing to become a monk.

74. Morson, "The Greatest Christian Novel."
75. Dostoevsky, *The Brothers Karamazov*, 393.
76. Frank Turek, "Why are Atheists Angry at God?," *CrossExamined.org*, (Jan. 13, 2011), available at https://crossexamined.org/why-are-atheists-angry-at-god/ (accessed January 18, 2025). There is clinical support for the proposition that atheism is often based in anger at God or an image of God that the atheist holds. Exline et al., "Anger toward God."
77. Fyodor Dostoyevsky, written in his last notebook [1880–1881], as quoted in Martin, *Kierkegaard, the Melancholy Dane*, 86.
78. Plantinga, "Self-Profile," 35–36.
79. Job 19:25–27; 23:8–10.
80. I refer to the well-known "trolley problem," attributed to British philosopher Philippa Foot. The trolley problem presents a scenario involving a runaway trolley hurtling down a track toward several people. A bystander has the option to intervene by pulling a lever to redirect the trolley. However, by pulling the lever, the bystander will cause the death of another individual. The problem has several variations that explore the ethical implications of pulling the lever in different situations.
81. Plantinga, "Self-Profile," 36.
82. HIT has been called China's MIT.
83. "Epistemology" is the branch of philosophy that deals with knowledge—what does it mean to "know" and how do we gain knowledge?
84. "The first debate between William Lane Craig and Peter Atkins: 'What Is the Evidence for/against the Existence of God?'" (April 3, 1998) (1:09:58 to 1:11:44), available at https://subsplash.com/reasonablefaith/lb/mi/+79c1b84 (accessed January 20, 2025). A transcript of the debate is available at "William Lane Craig debates Peter Atkins, one

of Britain's most famous and outspoken scientific naturalists. Moderated by William F. Buckley," *Reasonable Faith* website, available at https://www.reasonablefaith.org/videos/debates/craig-vs.-atkins-carter-center-atlanta (accessed January 20, 2025).

85. The concept underlying *The Matrix* is not new. In 1641, Descartes wrote;

> I will suppose, then, not that Deity, who is sovereignly good and the fountain of truth, but that some malignant demon, who is at once exceedingly potent and deceitful, has employed all his artifice to deceive me; I will suppose that the sky, the air, the earth, colors, figures, sounds, and all external things, are nothing better than the illusions of dreams, by means of which this being has laid snares for my credulity; I will consider myself as without hands, eyes, flesh, blood, or any of the senses, and as falsely believing that I am possessed of these; I will continue resolutely fixed in this belief . . .

Descartes, *Meditations*, 224. Substitute "computer simulation" for "malignant demon," and one realizes that Descartes was talking about the same thing.

86. Neil DeGrasse Tyson's Fascinating Interview With Piers Morgan, *Piers Morgan Uncensored* (Sept. 30, 2022), beginning at 39:40, available at https://www.youtube.com/watch?v=dYV5glYwCH8 (accessed January 20, 2025).

87. "*Ex nihilo*" means "from nothing." Theists believe that matter and energy and space/time are not eternal and God called the universe into being from nothing.

88. Feser, *Five Proofs*, 158.

89. See Feser, *Five Proofs*, chapter 5.

90. Hawking and Mlodinow, *The Grand Design*, 180.

91. Hawking, *A Brief History of Time*, 190.

92. I am not suggesting that Hawking intentionally mislead his readers. Equivocation is often (perhaps usually) the result of sloppy thinking and can be quite unintentional.
93. Feser, *Five Proofs of the Existence of God*, 161–163.
94. Philosophers use the word "being" instead of "thing." In the metaphysics of ontology (the branch of philosophy that deals with the nature of being and existence) a "being" is something that exists. In all of reality, the categories "contingent being" and "necessary being" exhaust the possibilities.
95. For a more in-depth technical takedown of the multiverse, see Gordon, "Does the Multiverse Refute Cosmic Design?"
96. See Neil DeGrasse Tyson's Fascinating Interview at Note 86.
97. Elie Feder and Aaron Zimmer, "Naive Multiverse," *Physics to God, A Guided Journey*, available at https://www.physicstogod.com/post/naive-multiverse (accessed January 25, 2025).
98. Guth, "Inflation," 49.
99. Feder and Zimmer, note 97.
100. Elie Feder and Aaron Zimmer, "The Typical Universe in the Multiverse," *Physics to God, A Guided Journey*, available at https://www.physicstogod.com/post/the-typical-universe-premise (accessed January 25, 2025). Feder and Zimmer explain the typical universe premise and how it operates in their essay.
101. Aaron Zimmer, "Why The Multiverse Fails: More With Elie Feder and Aaron Zimmer," *ID the Future*, available at https://idthefuture.com/2002/ (accessed January 25, 2025).
102. Id.
103. Elie Feder, "Why The Multiverse Fails: More With Elie Feder and Aaron Zimmer," *ID the Future*, available at https://idthefuture.com/2002/ (accessed January 25, 2025).

104. Id. Feder and Zimmer continue by explaining the multiverse theorists' failure to solve the so-called "measure" problem, which is beyond the scope of this discussion. The thrust of the problem is that there is no known scientific fact justifying the existence of a way to measure the typicality of universes. The idea is obviously an ad hoc way to try to rescue the theory.
105. Ockham's razor, also known as the principle of parsimony, is attributed to Willian of Ockham. While Ockham wrote similar things, such as *Numquam ponenda est pluralitas sine necessitate* ("Never posit pluralities without necessity"), the classic formulation *"Entia non sunt multiplicanda praeter necessitatem"* has been attributed to John Punch. Schaffer, "What Not to Multiply Without Necessity," 644–645.
106. Meyer, *Return of the God Hypothesis*, 625–26.
107. Id. at 626.
108. Popper, *The Logic of Scientific Discovery*, 137–38.
109. Dr. James Tour, *Origin of Life Challenge RESULTS*, available at https://www.youtube.com/watch?v=FdR-ZmdFOcg (accessed January 7, 2025).
110. James Tour, "Much Ado About Nothing," *Inference Review*, Vol. 6, No. 4 (January 2022) (emphasis added), available at https://inference-review.com/article/much-ado-about-nothing (accessed January 7, 2025).
111. Meyer, *Signature in the Cell*, 347.
112. Feynman, *Surely, You're Joking*, 343.
113. Specifically, he wrote ". . . blind Fate could never make all the Planets move one and the same way in Orbs concentrick, some inconsiderable Irregularities excepted, which may have risen from the mutual Actions of Comets and Planets upon one another, and which will be apt to increase, till this System wants a Reformation." Newton, *Opticks*, 402.

114. Leibniz wrote: "Mr. Newton and his followers also have a very strange view concerning the work of God. According to them God needs to wind up his watch from time to time, otherwise it would cease to operate. . . . This machine of God is even so imperfect that he is forced to clean it from time to time by an extraordinary concourse, and even to repair it like a watchmaker . . ." Letter from Gottfried Wilhelm Leibniz to Caroline of Brandenburg (November 1715), in Brown, *The Leibniz–Caroline–Clarke Correspondence*, 313.
115. I say "perhaps" because in context, it is not at all clear that this was Newton's considered view. This is demonstrated by the fact that the passage quoted above comes from an offhand comment near the end of *Opticks*, not a book about cosmology or planetary motion.
116. For an encyclopedic resource exploring this issue in great detail, see Haines, "Comprehensive Guide."
117. Dutka, "Eratosthenes' Measurement," 55.
118. Gould, *Rock of Ages*, 114.
119. Irving, *Life and Voyages*, 62.
120. Russell, *Inventing the Flat Earth*, 37.
121. Draper, *History of the Conflict Between Religion and Science*, 160.
122. Russell, *Inventing the Flat Earth*, 42. White was more of a scholar than Draper and attempted to defend the flat-earth myth more systematically. Russell utterly destroys White's arguments. See *id.* at 44–47.
123. White, *Warfare of Science with Religion*, vols. 1, 97.
124. In Haines, "Comprehensive Guide."
125. Id. at 512.
126. Id. at 511.
127. The following discussion is based on id. at 512–518.
128. Id. at 515, quoting Maxwell, as quoted in Stanley, "By Design."

129. Id. at 519–23.
130. Id. at 523.
131. Id. at 6543, citing Richard Seltzer, "Poll draws portrait of U.S. scientists' views," *Chemical & Engineering News* 66 (November 7, 1988), 6.
132. Materialists sometimes say Giordano Bruno and/or Michael Servetus were burned at the stake because of their scientific views. This is not correct. It is true that they were burned at the stake, and that is inexcusable. But they were declared heretics because of their theological views, not their scientific views. David Haines discusses these cases at great length in Haines, "Comprehensive Guide," 68–69.
133. Quoted in Sobel, *Galileo's Daughter*, 6.
134. This quip is often attributed to atheist Victor J. Stenger. Argument by slogan is almost always a bad idea because it only invites counter-slogans such as "Scientists build bioweapons and Christians build hospitals to treat their victims." Exchanging evidence and logic is always better than exchanging slogans.
135. Do you know where there is a true war between a belief system and science? When materialists insist that science conform to the precepts of materialism. In the early cold war Soviet Union, several areas of physics were suppressed for ideological reasons. Piergiorgio Pescali describes this suppression as follows:

> Objective scientific laws had to toe the party line. This included disciplining the Big Bang, quantum mechanics, and Einstein's theory of relativity. On June 24, 1947, Andrei Zhdanov extended his policy to astronomy and cosmology, claiming that these fields should be cleansed from bourgeois lies and illusions. Quantum theory was rejected as it does not describe the matter as a unique and real structure, apparently negating materialism. In the essays *Against idealism in modern physics*, released

in 1948, the theory of relativity was labelled as "idealistic" and "Einsteinianism" denounced. The relativistic theory of a closed, expanding universe was defined a "cancerous tumour that corrodes modern astronomical theory and is the main ideological enemy of materialist science."

The most controversial and discussed theory was the Big Bang, still rejected at the time by many scientists, including Western ones. However, if the Western scientific community was still skeptical because of the lack of clear evidence, in the Soviet Union the opposition was purely ideological. According to Stalinian cosmology, the universe was infinite (no space limit, no matter limit) and eternal (never began, never will end). Matter was only a material manifestation of motion and energy (no wave-particle duality contemplated). Galactic redshifts, discovered by Vesto Slipher in 1912, did not indicate that the space is expanding and all the theories had to fit in materialism and dialectical philosophy. The Big Bang was deemed to resemble the Bible's Genesis and branded as a pseudo-scientific, idealistic theory.

Piergiorgio Pescali, "Stalin, the big bang and quantum physics," *Osservatorio Balcani e Caucaso Transeuropa* (Feb. 2, 2017). Mao's China experienced similar repression of quantum theory because it conflicted with materialism. See "Quantum Study Simplified in Pei-Ching University—Another Victory for the Mao Tse-Tung Ideology" (Sept.14, 1960), available at https://apps.dtic.mil/sti/tr/pdf/ADA379963.pdf (accessed January 29, 2025).

136. It is easy to lose sight of the fact that Edwin Hubble proved the existence of galaxies other than the Milky Way only a little over 100 years ago in 1923.
137. The pale blue dot image is reproduced at Gonzalez and Richards, *Privileged Planet*, 238.

138. Sagan, *Pale Blue Dot*, 12–13.
139. For the sake of simplicity, I assume that Copernicus immediately displaced Ptolemy. That is not the case.
140. Ptolemy, *Almagest*, Book I, Chapter 4, page 40.
141. Ptolemy, *Almagest*, Book I, Chapter 6, page 43.
142. Ibid.
143. Psalm 8:3–5.
144. Sagan, *Demon-Haunted World*, 305.
145. Lewis, "Religion and Science," in Lewis, *God in the Dock*, 74–75.
146. Gonzalez and Richards, *Privileged Planet*, 226. The immutable celestial regions beyond the orbit of the moon were considered far superior to the sublunar region. Id.
147. These bullets are drawn from Appendix A to *The Privileged Planet*.
148. Lewis, "Christian Apologetics," in Lewis, *God in the Dock*, 100.
149. Gonzalez, "Do We Live on a Privileged Planet?," 239.
150. Romans 2:14–15.
151. Some materialists play word games by asserting they have an objective moral code in the sense that it is an objective fact that evolution caused them to hold certain moral values. That is just silly. It is the same as saying that strawberry ice cream is objectively good because it is an objective fact that you prefer it.
152. William Lane Craig, "Can We Be Good without God?" *Reasonable Faith* website, available at https://www.reasonablefaith.org/writings/popular-writings/existence-nature-ofgod/can-we-be-good-without-god (accessed January 31, 2025).
153. Feser, *Last Superstition*, 280.
154. I won the case.
155. Atheists often argue that this is not a valid comparison because the Wars of Religion were fought in the name of

Christianity, while the atheist regimes did not go to war in the name of atheism. However, as we have seen, those regimes' materialist outlook shaped systems that justified the slaughter of millions of innocent victims. Stalin's purges and Mao's Cultural Revolution, to cite two of many examples, demonstrate that atheist regimes are far from inherently peaceful. Indeed, all officially atheist regimes have been brutal totalitarian hellholes.

156. This statement is traditionally attributed to Rabbi Eliezer ben Hyrcanus. It is found in the Mishnah, specifically in Shevi'it 8:10.
157. Luke 10:25–37.
158. Luke 6:27.
159. Holland, *Dominion*, 542.
160. Dawkins, *The God Delusion*, 259. Quoting Michael Shermer in Shermer, *Science of Good and Evil*.
161. John 14:15
162. Hebrews 12:5–11.
163. "DNA neither knows nor cares. DNA just is. And we dance to its music." Dawkins, *River Out of Eden*, 134.
164. Bielenberg, *When I Was a German*, 249–50.
165. Dennis Prager, "How Do You Act if No One Is Watching?" PragerU, (Jan. 23, 2024), available at https://www.prageru.com/video/how-do-you-act-if-no-one-is-watching (accessed February 3, 2025).
166. Finger et al., "Caught in the Act."
167. David Sanderson, "Ending religion is a bad idea, says Richard Dawkins," *The Times* (October 5, 2019), available at https://www.thetimes.com/article/ending-religion-is-a-bad-idea-says-richard-dawkins-sqqdbmcpq (accessed February 26, 2025).
168. See Marks, "Will Intelligent Machines Rise Up?," 443. Citing Gilder, "The Materialist Superstition."

169. This does not mean that AI in the wrong hands employed for evil purposes is not dangerous. It certainly is. It is just not—and never will be—conscious.
170. Marks, *Non-Computable You*, 18.
171. Ibid.
172. The Turing test is named after Alan Turing, who proposed it in his 1950 paper "Computing Machinery and Intelligence." The test is conceptually simple. A computer interacts with an evaluator in a text-based conversation. It passes the test if the evaluator cannot reliably distinguish the computer's responses from a human's.
173. Dembski and Ewert, *The Design Inference*, 170.
174. Hoyle, "The Universe: Past and Present Reflections," 4–6. There are at least two problems with Hoyle's argument. Even if the universe itself were infinite, scientists currently estimate the age of the Earth to be only 4.7 billion years. Hoyle tried to solve this problem by appealing to "panspermia," the idea that life emerged somewhere else and was seeded onto Earth from space. However, panspermia offers no real solution to how life might have emerged; it just kicks the can down the road. The second problem is that Big Bang cosmology is almost universally accepted. The universe had a beginning. Hoyle was one of the last holdouts.
175. John 14:6. NIV.
176. The English word "scandal" has its roots in the Greek word *skándalon*. That word did not necessarily mean a disgraceful action or circumstance. It could, and in the Bible often did, mean something that causes someone to fall—a trap, a stumbling block, an offense.
177. 1 Peter 2:7–8.
178. William Lane Craig, "No Other Name": A Middle Knowledge Perspective on the Exclusivity of Salvation Through Christ," *Reasonable Faith* website, (emphasis

added), available at https://www.reasonablefaith.org/writings/scholarly-writings/christian-particularism/no-other-name-a-middle-knowledge-perspective-on-the-exclusivity-of-salvatio (accessed February 11, 2025).

179. Ibid.
180. Lewis, *Mere Christianity*, 67–68.
181. Strobel, *Case for Miracles*, 146–47.
182. See, e.g., Palestinians CONVERTING After Encountering Jesus In Dreams & Visions, *The Rosenberg Report* (Dec. 23, 2023), available https://www.youtube.com/watch?v=6PWvAbbBqGk (accessed February 11, 2025).
183. "Hiddenness of God," *Stanford Encyclopedia of Philosophy* (July 8, 2022), available at https://plato.stanford.edu/entries/divine-hiddenness/ (accessed February 11, 2025).
184. Groothuis, *Christian Apologetics*, 433.
185. Rosten, "Bertrand Russell and God."
186. Luke 16:29–31. NIV.
187. Pascal, *Pensées*, 198.
188. Pascal, *Pensées*, 207.
189. Groothuis, *Christian Apologetics*, 436.

8. Can We Fake it Till We Make it?

1. Plato, *The Republic*, Book III, 414–415.
2. Defining terms is important. Here, I use "God" to mean the creator of the universe, the transcendent ground of all being.
3. "As Hume so famously pointed out, there is a huge gap between is and ought." Jordon Peterson Interview with Douglas Murray and Jonathan Pageau (September 22, 2022), available at https://www.youtube.com/watch?v=4Modzh94MVw (at 13:10) (accessed November 26, 2024).
4. The title of the book is ironic, because, as mentioned, Peterson does not actually believe in God in any meaningful sense. When it comes to the word "God," Peterson has gone

full Humpty Dumpty. For him, that word "means just what I choose it to mean—neither more nor less." Christians believe that the word "God" refers to the eternally existing necessary ground of all being who created the universe and sustains it in existence. For Peterson, "God" is a fictional Jungian archetype or a metaphor for that which a person values most.

5. I made the same observation in chapter three in connection with an exchange between Konstantin Kisin and Richard Dawkins. *Triggernometry* podcast (Aug. 25, 2024) 42:13, available at https://www.youtube.com/watch?v=wdfmQ2iJb6o (accessed November 20, 2024).
6. Peterson, *We Who Wrestle with God*, 6–7.
7. Alex O'Connor, "Interesting Ideas From Philosophy For A Better Life—Alex O'Connor," *Chris Williamson Podcast* (January 8, 2024), available at https://www.youtube.com/watch?v=bSJhaTWZxQs&t=0s starting at 1:31:20 (accessed February 4, 2025).
8. The materialist explanation for widespread belief in a truth claim they say is false (the claims of religion) has always fascinated me. Doesn't that explanation eat materialism itself? If the overwhelming majority of people who have ever existed believed a false idea (religion) because it is evolutionarily adaptive, it demonstrates that natural selection selects for survival, not truth. If that is true, does it not also hold for materialism itself? Materialists insist that free will does not exist. Material forces determine our thoughts and beliefs, and sometimes those material forces cause us to believe things (like religion) that are false. Who is to say those material forces did not cause materialists to believe materialism even though it is false? That sword cuts both ways.
9. Harari, *Sapiens*, 27.
10. Id. at 28 (emphasis added).

11. *Triggernometry* podcast, "Richard Dawkins: God, Truth & Death," July 5, 2023, available at https://www.youtube.com/watch?v=MVq4GLepUwI&t=1833s (accessed November 22, 2023). Beginning at 40:25.
12. *Peterson Podcast*, "Dawkins vs Peterson: Memes & Archetypes," available at https://www.youtube.com/watch?v=8wBtFNj_o5k (accessed November 27, 2024).
13. Schopenhauer, *Religion: A Dialogue and Other Essays*, 106.
14. Ibid.
15. Lewis, "Christian Apologetics," in Lewis, *God in the Dock*, 101.
16. Metaxas, *Religionless Christianity*, 9.
17. I Cor. 15:12-16.
18. I Cor. 1:23; Gal. 5:11.
19. In this context, the word "frame," means state of mind, as in "frame of mind." "So you see, brethren, you and I live for God according to a holy, high spiritual logic and not according to shifting and changing frames of mind or moods." Tozer, *I Call It Heresy*, 48–50.
20. Some of my readers may respond that when O'Connor asked Peterson if someone went back in time with a video camera, would they record Jesus coming out of the tomb, and Peterson said "yes." Navigating Belief, Skepticism, and the Afterlife, (May 23, 2024), available at https://www.youtube.com/watch?v=T0KgLWQn5Ts, beginning at 25:11 (accessed February 5, 2025). That is true. But O'Connor then asked Peterson why he does not then affirm the historical fact that Jesus rose from the dead. As he typically does, Peterson dissembled. He said, "Because I have no idea what that means, and neither did the people who saw it." That is hogwash. I call the game Peterson was playing "Definition Derby." You can avoid being pinned down on any matter by pretending you don't know what normal English words

mean. Bill Clinton famously played Definition Derby when he said, "It depends on what the meaning of the word 'is' is."
21. Metaxas, *Religionless Christianity*, 137.
22. West, *Stockholm Syndrome Christianity*, 199.

9. Give Love a Chance

1. 1 John 4:7-8. NKJV.
2. John 3:16. NASB.
3. Stuart Townend, "How Deep the Father's Love." 1995.
4. Dostoevsky, *The Brothers Karamazov*, 394.
5. Romans 8:22-23.
6. David Bentley Hart, "Tsunami and Theodicy," *First Things* (March 1, 2005), available at https://firstthings.com/tsunami-and-theodicy/ (accessed March 6, 2025).
7. Ibid.

Bibliography

Alschuler, Albert W. "From Blackstone to Holmes: The Revolt against Natural Law Historic Proponents and the Critics of Higher Law." *Pepperdine Law Review* 36 (2009): 491–505.
———. *Law Without Values: The Life, Work and Legacy of Justice Holmes*. Chicago: University of Chicago Press, 2000.
———. "Rediscovering Blackstone." *University of Pennsylvania Law Review* 145, no. 1 (1996): 1–55.
Axe, Douglas. *Undeniable: How Biology Confirms Our Intuition That Life Is Designed*. New York: HarperCollins, 2016.
Bacon, Francis. *Of the Proficience and Advancement of Learning Divine and Human*. 5th ed. Oxford, UK: Clarendon Press, 1926.
Behe, Michael. *Darwin's Black Box: The Biochemical Challenge to Evolution*. 2nd ed. New York: Free Press, 2006.
Berdyaev, Nikolai. *The Origin of Russian Communism*. Glasgow: Robert MacLehose and Company Ltd., 1948.
Bielenberg, Christabel. *When I Was a German, 1934–1945: An Englishwoman in Nazi Germany*. Lincoln, NE: University of Nebraska Press, 1998.
Boorstin, Daniel J. *The Mysterious Science of the Law*. Cambridge, MA: Harvard University Press, 1941.
Borchers, Patrick J. "Legal Philosophy for Lawyers in the Age of A Political Supreme Court." *Tennessee Law Review* 90, no. 2 (2023): 223–97.
Bork, Robert H. "Neutral Principles and Some First Amendment Problems." *Indiana Law Journal* 47, no. 1 (1971): 1–35.

———. *The Tempting of America: The Political Seduction of the Law*. New York: The Free Press, 1990.

Brown, Gregory, ed. *The Leibniz–Caroline–Clarke Correspondence*. Oxford: Oxford University Press, 2023.

Burleigh, Michael. *The Third Reich: A New History*. New York: Hill and Wang, 2001.

Calhoun, Samuel W. "Grounding Normative Assertions: Arthur Leff's Still Irrefutable, but Incomplete, 'Sez Who?' Critique." *Journal of Law and Religion* 20, no. 1 (2005): 31–96.

Camus, Albert. *The Myth of Sisyphus*. New York: Vintage International, 1942.

Carroll, Lewis. *Through the Looking Glass and What Alice Found There*. New York: Harper & Bros., 1902.

Carroll, Sean M. "Why Is There Something Rather Than Nothing?" In *The Routledge Companion to Philosophy of Physics*, edited by Eleanor Knox and Alastair Wilson. London: Routledge, 2022.

Chesterton, G.K. *Orthodoxy*. London: John Lane Co., 1908.

Cicero, Marcus Tullius. *De Natura Deorum (On the Nature of the Gods)*. Translated by Charles Duke Yonge. London: Henry G. Bohn, 1852.

Conklin, Carli N. "The Origins of the Pursuit of Happiness." *Washington University Jurisprudence Review* 7, no. 2 (2015): 195–262.

Crick, Francis. *Life Itself, Its Origin and Nature*. New York: Simon and Schuster, 1981.

Darwin, Charles. *The Origin of Species by Means of Natural Selection or the Preservation of Favoured Races in the Struggle for Life*. 6th ed. London: John Murray, 1873.

———. *The Variation of Animals and Plants Under Domestication*. London: John Murray, 1868.

Darwin, Charles, and Alfred Russel Wallace. "On the Tendency of Species to Form Varieties; and on the Perpetuation of Varieties and Species by Natural Means of Selection." *Zoological Journal of the Linnean Society* 3, no. 9 (1858): 45–62.

Davidson, John Daniel. *Pagan America: The Decline of Christianity and the Dark Age to Come*. Washington, DC: Regnery Publishing, 2024.

Dawkins, Richard. *River Out of Eden: A Darwinian View of Life*. New York: Basic Books, 1995.

———. *The Blind Watchmaker: Why the Evidence of Evolution Reveals a Universe without Design*. New York: W.W. Norton & Company, 1996.

———. *The God Delusion*. HarperCollins, 2006.

Dembski, William A., and Winston Ewert. *The Design Inference*. 2nd ed. Seattle: Discovery Institute Press, 2023.

Dennett, Daniel C. *Darwin's Dangerous Idea: Evolution and the Meaning of Life*. New York: Simon and Schuster, 1996.

Descartes, René. *Meditations on First Philosophy, in Which the Existence of God and the Immortality of the Soul Are Demonstrated*. New York: M. Walter Dunne, 1901.

Dobzhansky, Theodosius G. "Discussion of G. Schramm's Paper." In *The Origins of Prebiological Systems and of Their Molecular Matrices*, edited by Sidney A. Fox. New York: Academic Press, 1965.

Dostoevsky, Fyodor. *The Brothers Karamazov*. Translated by Richard Pevear and Larissa Volokhonsky. New York: Farrar, Straus and Giroux, 1990.

Dowbiggin, Ian. *Keeping America Sane: Psychiatry and Eugenics in the United States and Canada, 1880–1940*. Ithaca, NY: Cornell University Press, 1997.

Draper, John William. *History of the Conflict Between Religion and Science*. New York: D. Appleton and Co., 1875.

———. "The Skeptical Theist." In *The Evidential Argument from Evil*, edited by Daniel Howard-Snyder. Bloomington, IN: Indiana University Press, 1996.

Dutka, Jacques. "Eratosthenes' Measurement of the Earth Reconsidered." *Archive for History of Exact Sciences* 46, no. 1 (1993): 55–66.

Dworkin, Ronald. "Bork's Jurisprudence." *University of Chicago Law Review* 57 (1990): 657–77.

Einstein, Albert. *Relativity: The Special and General Theory*. New York: Henry Holt and Company, 1921.

Exline, Julie J., Crystal L. Park, Joshua M. Smyth, and Michael P. Carey. "Anger toward God: Social-Cognitive Predictors, Prevalence, and Links with Adjustment to Bereavement and Cancer." *Journal of Personality and Social Psychology* 100, no. 1 (2011): 129–48.

Feser, Edward. *Five Proofs of the Existence of God*. San Francisco: Ignatius Press, 2017.

———. *The Last Superstition: A Refutation of the New Atheism*. South Bend, IN: St. Augustine's Press, 2010.

Feynman, Richard P. *Surely You're Joking, Mr. Feynman! Adventures of a Curious Character*. New York: W.W. Norton & Co., 1985.

Finger, Elizabeth C., Abigail A. Marsh, Niveen Kamel, Derek G.V. Mitchell, and James R. Blair. "Caught in the Act: The Impact of Audience on the Neural Response to Morally and Socially Inappropriate Behavior." *Neuroimage* 33, no. 1 (2006): 414–21.

Gates, Bill. *The Road Ahead*. New York: Viking Press, 1995.

George, Robert P. "Natural Law." *Harvard Journal of Law and Public Policy* 31, no. 1 (2008): 171–96.

Gilder, George. "The Materialist Superstition." *The Intercollegiate Review* 31, no. 2 (Spring) (1996): 6–14.

Gilmore, Grant. *The Ages of American Law*. New Haven, CT: Yale University Press, 1977.

Gonzalez, Guillermo. "Do We Live on a Privileged Planet?" In *The Comprehensive Guide to Science and Faith*, edited by William A. Dembski, Casey Luskin, and Joseph M. Holden. Eugene, OR: Harvest House Publishers, 2021.

Gonzalez, Guillermo, and Jay W. Richards. *The Privileged Planet: How Our Place in the Cosmos Is Designed for Discovery*. New York: Skyhorse Publishing, 2024.

Gordon, Bruce L. "Does the Multiverse Refute Cosmic Design?" In *The Comprehensive Guide to Science and Faith*, edited by William A. Dembski, Casey Luskin, and Joseph M. Holden, 457–69. Eugene, OR: Harvest House Publishers, 2021.

Gould, Stephen Jay. *Rock of Ages: Science and Religion in the Fullness of Life*. New York: Random House, 1999.

Grey, Thomas C. "Langdell's Orthodoxy." *University of Pittsburgh Law Review* 45 (1983): 1–53.

Groothuis, Douglas. *Christian Apologetics: A Comprehensive Case for Biblical Faith*. 2nd ed. Downers Grove, IL: IVP Academic, 2022.

Guth, Alan H. "Inflation." In *Measuring and Modeling the Universe*, edited by Wendy L. Freeman. Cambridge: Cambridge University Press, 2004.

Haeckel, Ernst. *Last Words on Evolution: A Popular Retrospect and Summary*. Dansville, NY: A. Owen & Co., 1906.

Haines, David. "Does Science Conflict with Biblical Faith?" In *The Comprehensive Guide to Science and Faith: Exploring the Ultimate Questions About Life and the Cosmos*, edited by William A. Dembski, Casey Luskin, and Joseph M. Holden. Eugene, OR: Harvest House Publishers, 2021.

Harari, Yuval Noah. *Sapiens: A Brief History of Humankind*. New York: HarperCollins, 2011.

Harold, Franklin. *The Way of the Cell: Molecules, Organisms and the Order of Life*. Oxford: Oxford University Press, 2001.

Hart, David Bentley. *The Experience of God: Being, Consciousness, Bliss*. New Haven, CT: Yale University Press, 2013.

Hart, H.L.A. "Positivism and the Separation of Law and Morals." *Harvard Law Review* 71, no. 4 (1958): 593–629.

———. *The Concept of Law*. Oxford: Oxford University Press, 1961.

Hawking, Stephen. *A Brief History of Time*. Expanded, Tenth anniversary edition. New York: Bantam Books, 1998.

Hawking, Stephen, and Leonard Mlodinow. *The Grand Design*. New York: Bantam Books, 2010.

Hemingway, Ernest. *The Sun Also Rises*. New York: Charles Scribner's Sons, 1926.

Herberg, Will. *Judaism and Modern Man. An Interpretation of Jewish Religion*. New York: Farrar, Straus and Young, 1951.

Herbert, Frank. *Children of Dune*. New York: Berkley Publishing Corp., 1976.

Heyman, Steven J. "The Dark Side of the Force: The Legacy of Justice Holmes for First Amendment Jurisprudence." *William & Mary Bill of Rights Journal* 19, no. 3 (2011): 661–723.

Hitler, Adolf. *Table Talk, 1941–1944*. Translated by Norman Cameron and R.H. Stevens. Philadelphia: Enigma Books, 2000.

Holland, Tom. *Dominion: How the Christian Revolution Remade the World*. New York: Basic Books, 2019.

Holmes, Oliver Wendell. *Collected Legal Papers*. New York: Harcourt, Brace and Co., 1920.

———. *Holmes and Frankfurter: Their Correspondence, 1912–1934*. Edited by Robert M. Mennel and Christine L. Compston. Lebanon, NH: University Press of New England, 1996.

———. *The Common Law*. New York: Macmillan and Co., 1882.

———. *The Essential Holmes: Selections from the Letters, Speeches, Judicial Opinions, and Other Writings of Oliver Wendell Holmes, Jr.* Edited by Richard A. Posner. Chicago: University of Chicago Press, 1992.

———. "The Gas-Stokers' Strike." *Harvard Law Review* 44 (1931): 795.

———. *The Holmes–Einstein Letters*. Edited by James Bishop Peabody. New York: St. Martin's Press, 1964.

———. *The Holmes-Laski Letters: The Correspondence of Mr. Justice Holmes and Harold J. Laski, 1916–1935*. Edited by Mark DeWolfe Howe. Cambridge, MA: Harvard University Press, 1953.

———. *The Holmes-Pollock Letters: The Correspondence of Mr. Justice Holmes and Sir Frederick Pollock, 1874–1932*. Edited by Mark DeWolfe Howe. Cambridge, MA: Harvard University Press, 1941.

———. "The Path of the Law." *Harvard Law Review* 10 (1897): 457–78.

Howe, Mark DeWolfe. *Justice Oliver Wendell Holmes, Vol. 2: The Proving Years 1870–1882*. Cambridge, MA: Harvard University Press, 1963.

Hoyle, Fred. "The Universe: Past and Present Reflections." *Annual Review of Astronomy and Astrophysics* 20 (1982): 1–35.

Irving, Washington. *The Life and Voyages of Christopher Columbus*. Chicago: Belford Co., 1890.

Jablonka, Eva. "A New Vision for How Evolution Works Is Long Overdue." *Nature* 637 (2025): 539–41.

Johnson, Phillip. "The Unraveling of Scientific Materialism." *First Things*, November 1997.

Judd, John W. *The Coming of Evolution: The Story of a Great Revolution in Science*. Cambridge: Cambridge University Press, 1912.

Kettlewell, H.B.D. "Darwin's Missing Evidence." *Scientific American* 200, no. 3 (1959): 48–53.

Klavan, Spencer. *Light of the Mind, Light of the World: Illuminating Science Through Faith*. New York: Skyhorse Publishing, 2024.

Lala, Kevin N., Tobias Uller, Nathalie Feiner, Marcus Feldman, and Scott F. Gilbert, eds. *Evolution Evolving: The Developmental Origins of Adaptation and Biodiversity*. Princeton, NJ: Princeton University Press, 2024.

Lane, Nick, and Joana C. Xavier. "To Unravel the Origin of Life, Treat Findings as Pieces of a Bigger Puzzle ." *Nature* 628 (2024): 948–51.

Laplace, Pierre-Simon. *A Philosophical Essay on Probabilities*. Translated by Frederic W. Truscott and Frederick L. Emory. New York: John Wiley & Sons, 1902.

Leff, A. A. "Unspeakable Ethics, Unnatural Law." *Duke Law Journal* 28 (1979): 1229–49.

Levinson, Sanford. "Strolling Down the Path of the Law (and Toward Critical Legal Studies)." *Columbia Law Review* 91 (1991): 1221–52.

Lewis, C.S. *God in the Dock*. New York: HarperCollins, 1970.

———. *Mere Christianity*. London: Geoffrey Bles, 1952.

———. *The Abolition of Man*. New York: HarperCollins, 1943.

Lincoln, Abraham. *Abraham Lincoln: His Speeches and Writings*. Edited by Roy P. Basler. Cleveland: The World Publishing Co., 1946.

———. *The Collected Works of Abraham Lincoln*. Edited by Roy P. Basler. New Brunswick, NJ: Rutgers University Press, 1953.

Lombardo, Paul A. *Three Generations, No Imbeciles: Eugenics, the Supreme Court, and Buck v. Bell*. Baltimore: Johns Hopkins University Press, 2008.

Marks, Robert J., II. *Non-Computable You: What You Do That Artificial Intelligence Never Will*. Seattle: Discovery Institute Press, 2022.

———. "Will Intelligent Machines Rise Up and Overtake Humanity?" In *The Comprehensive Guide to Science and Faith*, edited by William A. Dembski, Casey Luskin, and Joseph M. Holden. Eugene, OR: Harvest House Publishers, 1998.

Martin, Harold Victor. *Kierkegaard, the Melancholy Dane*. Peterborough, Cambridgeshire, UK: Epworth Press, 1950.

Meister, Chad. "God, Evil, and Morality." In *God Is Great, God Is Good: Why Believing in God Is Reasonable and Responsible*, edited by William Lane Craig and Chad Meister. Westmont, IL: InterVarsity Press, 2009.

Metaxas, Eric. *Religionless Christianity*. Washington, DC: Regnery Faith, 2024.

Meyer, Stephen C. *Darwin's Doubt, The Explosive Origin of Animal Life and the Case for Intelligent Design*. San Francisco: HarperOne, 2013.

———. *Return of the God Hypothesis: Three Scientific Discoveries That Reveal the Mind Behind the Universe*. New York: HarperCollins, 2021.

———. *Signature in the Cell: DNA and the Evidence for Intelligent Design*. San Francisco: HarperOne, 2009.

Monod, Jacques. *Chance and Necessity: An Essay on the Natural Philosophy of Modern Biology*. New York: Alfred Knopf, 1971.

Morson, Gary Saul. "The Greatest Christian Novel." *First Things*, May 2021.

Müller, Gerd B. "Why an Extended Evolutionary Synthesis Is Necessary." *Interface Focus* 7, no. 5 (2017): 20170015.

Nagel, Thomas. *Mind and Cosmos: Why the Materialist Neo-Darwinian Conception of Nature Is Almost Certainly False*. Oxford: Oxford University Press, 2012.

———. *The Last Word*. Oxford: Oxford University Press, 1997.

Newton, Isaac. *Opticks, a Treatise on the Reflections, Refractions, Inflections & Colours of Light*. Garden City, NY: Dover Publications, 1952.

Niebuhr, Reinhold. *Man's Nature and His Communities: Essays on the Dynamics and Enigmas of Man's Personal and Social Existence*. New York: Charles Scribner's Sons, 1965.

Nietzsche, Friedrich. *Beyond Good and Evil*. New York: The Modern Library, 1925.

———. *The Gay Science*. New York: Vintage Books, 1974.

———. *Thus Spake Zarathustra*. New York: Random House, 1917.

Noble, Denis. "Neo-Darwinism, the Modern Synthesis and Selfish Genes: Are They of Use in Physiology? ." *Journal of Physiology* 589, no. 5 (2011): 1007–15.

Novick, Sheldon M. *Honorable Justice: The Life of Oliver Wendell Holmes*. Boston: Little Brown and & Co., 1989.

Ogden, James M. "Lincoln's Early Impressions of the Law in Indiana." *Notre Dame Law Review* 7, no. 3 (1932): 325–29.

Pascal, Blaise. *Pensées*. Translated by W.S. Trotter. London: J.M. Dent & Sons, 1931.

Peterson, Jordan B. *We Who Wrestle with God: Perceptions of the Divine*. London: Penguin Publishing Group, 2024.

Pigliucci, Massimo. "Do We Need an Extended Evolutionary Synthesis?" *Evolution* 61 (2007): 2743–49.

Pigliucci, Massimo, and Gerd B. Müller, eds. *Evolution: The Extended Synthesis*. Cambridge, MA: MIT Press, 2010.

Plantinga, Alvin. *God, Freedom, and Evil*. Grand Rapids, MI: William B. Eerdmans Publishing Co., 1977.

———. "Self-Profile." In *Alvin Plantinga*, edited by James E. Tomberlin and Peter van Inwagen, 3–97. Dordrecht, Netherlands: D. Reidel Publishing Co., 1985.

Plato. *The Republic*. Translated by Paul Shorey. Cambridge, MA: Harvard University Press, 1937.

Pliny the Younger. *The Letters of the Younger Pliny*. London: Trübner & Co., 1879.

Poole, Steven . "The Four Horsemen Review—Whatever Happened to 'New Atheism'?" *The Atlantic*, January 31, 2019.

Popper, Karl. *The Logic of Scientific Discovery*. Abingdon, Oxfordshire, UK: Taylor & Francis, 1959.

Posner, Richard A. "Reply to Critics of the Problematics of Moral and Legal Theory." *Harvard LW Review* 111, no. 7 (1998): 1796–1823.

———. "The Problematics of Moral and Legal Theory." *Harvard Law Review* 111, no. 7 (1998): 1637–1717.

Prigogine, Ilya, Grégoire Nicolis, and Agnessa Babloyantz. "Thermodynamics of Evolution." *Physics Today* 25, no. 11 (1972): 23–28.

Provine, William. "Scientists, Face It! Science and Religion Are Incompatible." *The Scientist* 2, no. 16 (September 5, 1988).

Ptolemy. *Almagest*. Translated by G.J. Toomer. London: Gerald Duckworth and Co., 1984.

Rosten, Leo. "Bertrand Russell and God: A Memoir." *The Saturday Review*, February 23, 1974, 25–26.

Ruse, Michael. "Evolutionary Theory and Christian Ethics." In *The Darwinian Paradigm*, edited by Michael Ruse. Abingdon, Oxfordshire, UK: Routledge, 1989.

Russell, Jeffrey Burton. *Inventing the Flat Earth: Columbus and Modern Historians*. Westport, CT: Praeger Publishers, 1991.

Sagan, Carl. *Broca's Brain: Reflections on the Romance of Science*. New York: Random House, 1979.

———. *Cosmos*. New York: Random House, 1980.

———. *Pale Blue Dot: A Vision of the Human Future in Space*. New York: Ballantine Books, 1997.

———. *The Cosmic Connection*. New York: Doubleday, 1973.

———. *The Demon-Haunted World: Science as a Candle in the Dark*. London: Headline Book Publishing, 1997.

Samples, Kenneth. *Without a Doubt*. Grand Rapids, MI: Baker Books, 2004.

Schaffer, Jonathan. "What Not to Multiply Without Necessity." *Australasian Journal of Philosophy* 93, no. 4 (2015): 644–64.

Schopenhauer, Arthur. *Religion: A Dialogue and Other Essays*. Translated by T. Bailey Saunders. London: George Allen & Unwin, Ltd., 1915.

Shapiro, Fred R. "The Most-Cited Legal Scholars." *Journal of Legal Studies* 29, no. S1 (2000): 409–26.

Shermer, Michael. *The Science of Good and Evil: Why People Cheat, Gossip, Care, Share, and Follow the Golden Rule*. New York: Henry Holt and Co., 2004.

Singh, Manvir. "Are Your Morals Too Good to Be True?" *The New Yorker*, September 9, 2024.

Sobel, Dava. *Galileo's Daughter: A Historical Memoir of Science, Faith, and Love*. Dava. New York: Viking Press, 1999.

Spencer, Herbert. *The Principles of Biology*. London: Williams and Norgate, 1864.

Stanley, Matthew. "By Design: James Clerk Maxwell and the Evangelical Unification of Science." *British Journal for the History of Science* 45 (2012): 57–73.

Steiner, Mark E. "Abraham Lincoln and the Rule of Law Books." *Marquette Law Review* 93, no. 4 (2010): 1283–1324.

Strobel, Lee. *The Case for Miracles: A Journalist Investigates Evidence for the Supernatural*. Grand Rapids, MI: Zondervan, 2018.

Thucydides. *The History of the Peloponnesian War*. Translated by Richard Crawley. New York: E.P. Dutton and Co., 1950.

Tozer, A. W. *I Call It Heresy!: And Other Timely Topics From First Peter*. Edited by Gerald B. Smith. Camp Hill, PA: WingSpread Publishers, 1991.

Urone, Peter Paul, and Roger Hinrichs. *College Physics*. Houston, TX: OpenStax, 2017.

Vannatta, Seth, and Allen Mendenhall. "The American Nietzsche? Fate and Power in the Pragmatism of Justice Holmes." *UMKC Law Review* 85, no. 1 (2016): 187–205.

Wells, Jonathan. "Is Darwinism a Theory in Crisis?" In *The Comprehensive Guide to Science and Faith*, edited by William A. Dembski, Casey Luskin, and Joseph M. Holden. Eugene, OR: Harvest House Publishers, 2021.

———. *Zombie Science: More Icons of Evolution*. Seattle: Discovery Institute Press, 2017.

West, John. *Stockholm Syndrome Christianity: Why America's Christian Leaders Are Failing—and What We Can Do About It*. Seattle: Discovery Institute Press, 2025.

White, Andrew Dickson. *A History of the Warfare of Science with Theology in Christendom*. New York: D. Appleton and Co., 1897.

Whitesides, George M. "Foreword: The Improbability of Life." In *Fitness of the Cosmos for Life: Biochemistry and Fine-Tuning*, edited by John D. Barrow, Simon Conway Morris, Stephen J. Freeland, and Charles L. Harper, Jr., xi–xx. Cambridge: Cambridge University Press, 2008.

———. "Revolutions in Chemistry." *Chemical and Engineering News* 85, no. 13 (2007): 12–25.

Wilman, Dereck E., Monica Uddin, Guozhen Liu, Lawrence Grossman, and Morris Goodman. "Implications of Natural Selection in

Shaping 99.4% Nonsynonymous DNA Identity between Humans and Chimpanzees: Enlarging Genus Homo." *Proceedings of the National Academy of Sciences* 100 (2003): 7181–88.

Wilson, Edward O. *Consilience: The Unity of Knowledge.* New York: Alfred Knopf, 1998.

Index

acid, 1, 7, 33, 78
Ali, Ayaan Hirsi, 7
Altenberg 16, 102
American Humanist
    Association, 52
Aquinas, Thomas, 26
Atkins, Peter, 120
atom, 2, 66
Augustine, St., 26

Bacon, Francis, 63, 136
Barnett, West Virginia Board of
    Education v., 47
Beloved, 61, 173
Berdyaev, Nicolas, 52
Bielenberg, Christabel, 151
Big Bang, 17, 65–66, 68, 70–72,
    123, 127, 137, 155
Big Tech, 60
Blackstone, William, 38
Book of God's Word, 51, 56,
    134, 136–137, 145, 157–
    158, 166–167, 169–171, 173
Bork, Robert, 47
Brennan, William J., 47

Brooks, David, 23
Brothers Karamazov, The, 116
Brownshirts, 30
Buck v. Bell, 43
Byzantine monk, 51

Calvary Chapel of South
    Denver, 15, 35
Cambrian explosion, 100
Camus, Albert, 6
Carano, Gina, 9
Carroll, Sean M., 16
Chemistry, 1, 15, 69, 74, 76, 84,
    102, 112, 135
Chesterton, G.K., 51
China, 54, 119
Christianity, 8, 10, 28, 53, 55,
    59–60, 62–63, 80, 89, 92,
    95, 97, 132, 134, 138, 142,
    144, 147, 149, 157–158,
    166–167, 169–172
civil disobedience to
    segregation laws, 25
classical Newtonian physics,
    66–67

Clinton, Bill, 57
Colorado health order, 36
Columbine High School, 15
Columbine shootings, 13
Columbus, Christopher, 133
complex specified information, 130–131
Conditioners, 32–33
Copernican principle, 142
COVID-19 pandemic, 35
Craig, William Lane, 64, 86, 90, 115–117, 120–121, 146, 158
creation, 28, 38, 86, 105, 116–118, 123, 136, 174
creatures, 80, 88, 118, 140–141, 173
cross, 91, 119, 146, 148, 150, 168, 171–172, 174

Darwin, Charles, 1–4, 6, 14, 40–41, 79, 97–100, 102, 107–108, 133–134
Davidson, John Daniel, 52
Dawkins, Richard, 2, 7, 18, 31, 51, 56, 76, 81, 97, 99, 109, 112, 150, 168
death, 4, 20, 30, 43, 63, 67, 90–91, 94–95, 111, 119, 133, 147, 151, 158, 171, 174–175
Declaration of Independence, 25, 38–39
DeGrasse Tyson, Neil, 109, 115, 122, 126
Dennett, Darwin's Dangerous Idea, 1–3
Dennett's Universal Acid, 28
design, 2–3, 18, 70, 72, 74–81, 97, 99–100, 113, 123, 128–130, 156–157
Design argument, 129, 156
DNA, 52, 74, 76–77, 99, 105, 108, 151
Dobzhansky, Theodosius, 75, 98
Dostoevsky, 116–118, 169, 174
Dostoevsky, Fyodor, 116
Dylan, Bob, 51, 62

Einstein, Albert, 67
ethical system, 53–54
evidentiary argument, 118
evolution, 2–3, 23, 28–29, 75, 78–79, 97–98, 100–107, 145
evolutionary biology, 20, 103–104
explanation for design, 66–67, 132

Father's love, 174
Feser, Edward, 53, 86, 146
Feynman, Richard, 131
fiction, 128, 133, 166–170
flat earth myth, 134
fossil record, 44, 100
free will, 17–19, 31, 55, 115, 145, 173–174
Free Will Defense, 115

Geraci, Gino, 15, 35

Gervais, Ricky, 87–89
Ginsburg, Ruth Bader, 37
God, 1–8, 10–11, 16, 20–21, 23, 25–29, 33, 36, 38, 40, 51–52, 55–56, 58–72, 79–82, 84–90, 93–95, 97, 101, 107–119, 122, 124–126, 128–131, 136–140, 144–146, 149–152, 158–163, 165–171, 173–174
Gorsuch, Neil, 37
Gould, Stephen J., 133
grace, 55, 158, 162, 174
Grand Universe problem, 127–128
Groothuis, Douglas, 86, 89, 94–95
Grutter v. Bollinger, 46

Harari, Yuval Noah, 28, 30, 53, 168
Harris, Eric, 14–15, 23–24, 55
Harris, Kamala, 57
Hart, David Bentley, 87
Hawking, Stephen, 69, 123
Herberg, Will, 6
High Plains Harvest Church, 36
Hitchens, Christopher, 117
Holmes, Oliver Wendell Jr., The Path of the Law, 40, 44
Hood, Bruce, 17
Hoyle, Fred, 66, 69, 112, 155–156
human consciousness, 153

Hume, David, 84, 166

imago Dei, 28, 55–56
infinite monkeys, 155–156
irreducible complexity, 79

Jefferson, Thomas, 38
Jesus of Nazareth, 2, 10, 60, 62–63, 87, 89–95, 118–119, 136–137, 147–150, 157–161, 169, 171–172, 174–175
jury, 110–112

Karamazov, Alyosha, 116
Karamazov, Ivan, 162, 174
Kennedy assassination, 13
Kepler, Johannes, 136
Kettlewell, Bernard, 106
Kim Il Sung, 51
Kim Jong Il, 51
Kingdom, 175
Kisin, Konstantin, 31, 56, 168
kulaks, 30–31

Langman, Peter, 15
Leff, Arthur, 4, 20, 114, 146
Lewis, C. S., 32–33, 60, 81, 86, 89, 141–142, 144, 159, 170
Lewis, C.S., 32, 159
Lewontin, Richard, 106
Lincoln, Abraham, 39
Lucretius, 3, 107

Maher, Bill, 57

Marbury v. Madison, 49
Marshall, John, 38, 49
Marxism, 52
materialism, 1–11, 13, 15–20, 22–24, 26–34, 40–41, 44, 48, 53, 55–56, 64–68, 70–72, 74–77, 79, 81–84, 97–109, 113–114, 119–120, 122–123, 126–127, 129–132, 139, 141, 145–146, 153, 155–157, 165–166, 168, 175
Metaxas, Eric, 170
Meyer, Stephen, 65, 69, 77, 86, 100–101, 129–131
Mill, John Stuart, 55, 59
miracles, 74, 84–86, 169
Morson, Gary Saul, 117
Multiverse, 122, 126–128, 138–139
Murray, Douglas, 166, 169

Nagel, Thomas, 84, 101–102
natural law theory, 26, 39
natural selection, 2, 21, 23, 75, 97, 100–102, 107
Neo-Darwinism, 102, 106
Newton, Isaac, 102, 131, 136
Nietzsche, Friedrich, 3–4, 7, 14, 20, 22–23, 40, 42
noble lie, 165, 167
North Korea, 51

objective moral values, 81–82

Occam's razor, 128
origin of life, 74–76, 98–99, 105, 107–108, 130–132
Origin of Species, 1–2, 5, 97, 100, 102

Pageau, Jonathan, 166
Pascal, Blaise, 136
Pascal's Wager, 61–62
Paul (Apostle), 70, 86, 89, 91–92, 94, 115, 171
Peterson, Jordan, 165
Peterson, Jordon, 60, 171
Plato, 165, 167
Plato, The Republic, 165
Polis, Jared, 35
Popper, Karl, 129
Posner, Richard, 19, 22, 27, 29, 49–50, 82
Prager, Dennis, 152
Provine, William, 19, 59
Przybyla, Heidi, 25, 33

quantum mechanics, 66–67, 87

Religionless Christianity, 170
resurrection, 10, 63, 89–95, 169–172
River Out of Eden, 3
Roman Catholic Diocese of Brooklyn v. Cuomo, 37
Romans (Bible), 2, 37, 91, 93, 95
Ruse, Michael, 18

Russell, Bertrand, 109, 161

Sagan, Carl, 16, 106, 108, 140
Sapiens, 28, 168
Sapiens: A Brief History of Humankind, 28
Scalia, Antonin, 48
Schaefer, Henry F., 135
Schopenhauer, Arthur, 169–170
science, 10, 16, 28–29, 63–64, 70–71, 97–99, 103–109, 119–121, 124–125, 127–129, 131–132, 134–138, 141–142, 152
science and religion, 132–134
Sean Carroll, 16, 64
sin, 23, 42, 52, 80, 89, 92, 119, 148, 150, 158, 169, 174
Singer, Peter, 56
Singh, Manvir, 20
Solzhenitsyn, Alexander, 61
Spencer, Herbert, 40
Stockholm Syndrome Christianity, 172
suffering, 31, 52, 115–119, 149, 161–162, 174–175
suicide rates, 6

Tacitus, Cornelius, 90
The Guardian, 47–48, 103
Thrasymachus, 7
Thrasymachus' dictum, 27
Tour, James, 75–76, 99, 105, 130–132, 135

Triggernometry podcast, 31

universal acid, 1, 3, 33, 40, 45, 48, 107, 175
universe, 3, 6–7, 16–19, 23, 28–29, 38, 40, 52, 59, 63–70, 74, 77, 81–82, 99, 101, 108–109, 112–113, 119, 122–128, 136, 138–144, 155–156, 173–174
Uyghurs, 54

Voltaire, 8–9

We Who Wrestle With God, 60, 166
Weinstein, Bret, 101, 109
West, John, 172
Whitesides, George, 99, 132
Whitesides, George M., 74–76
Wilberforce, Samuel, 134
Williams, Michelle, 59
Williamson, Chris, 167
ἀγάπη, 10, 55, 58, 116–117, 119, 140, 147–150, 159, 173, 175

Made in the USA
Monee, IL
13 May 2025